Nathaniel Russell House,
Charleston, South Carolina

NATIONAL GEOGRAPHIC
GUIDE TO

America's Great Houses

More than 150
Outstanding Mansions
Open to the Public

by Henry Wiencek and Donna M. Lucey

Opposite: Marble House, Rhode Island
Cover: Old Westbury Gardens, New York

ontents

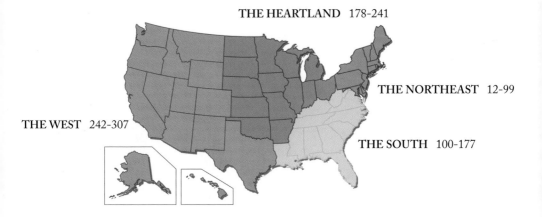

The Northeast

Olana, New York

The South

Stanton Hall, Mississippi

The Heartland

Terrace Hill, Iowa

The West

Hearst Castle, California

S helter as a Fine Art

Almost two centuries ago a French nobleman, the Marquis de Chastellux, visited Thomas Jefferson at his mansion in Virginia. Charmed by Monticello, the marquis wrote a glowing description of it, remarking that Jefferson was the first American "who has consulted the fine arts to know how he should shelter himself from the weather." Perhaps without realizing it, the marquis had penned a useful definition of what architects do. This book gathers some of the best efforts of Americans to merge fine art with the practical business of putting a roof over one's head. The combinations have been virtually infinite, producing houses in a range from classic simplicity to overpowering grandeur.

At the height of the Gilded Age, for example, one of the country's richest men, George Vanderbilt, erected the immense Biltmore estate in North Carolina—the largest private residence in America—in the style of a French château. His guests dined in a baronial banquet hall under a barrel-vaulted ceiling that rose 70 feet from the floor. In California, the mining and newspaper tycoon William Randolph Hearst lavished more than 30 million dollars in the construction and furnishings of his castle, part of a mini-kingdom of luxurious guest mansions, swimming pools, and cultivated landscapes overlooking the Pacific Ocean. In the nation's Heartland, Lanier Mansion shows how an Indiana financier used Greek Revival architecture as a sign of his region's prosperity and stability. Nearby in Ohio, travelers will find the magnificent Tudor mansion called Stan Hywet, built in this century by a tire magnate fascinated by the trappings of medieval England.

Natchez and Newport retain clusters of houses built to proclaim fabulous wealth and lofty status, while Naumkeag, in the Berkshire Hills of Massachusetts, reveals a powerful man's yearning for a place of peace. Delightful eccentricity reigns over Scotty's Castle in Death Valley, a house that made its owner so happy that he put up a Spanish inscription saying, "Ah, what joy." In these houses, "simplicity" comes in many forms—from the gracious brick facade of Wilton, a colonial plantation in Virginia, to the austere geometry of Gropius House, a modernist landmark in Massachusetts.

Opposite: D'Evereux, Mississippi

Great architecture and lavish interiors represent only part of the appeal of these houses. Many contain fascinating stories as well—stories of family dynasties, of wealth gained and lost, of romance, and war. In Virginia, Kenmore tells the story of George Washington's sister and her husband, who sacrificed all for the Revolutionary cause. Nearby Stratford Hall, the grand colonial mansion where Robert E. Lee was born, fell upon such difficult times when Lee was a child that his father had to chain the front doors shut to keep his creditors out. During the Civil War, invading Union officers took Shadows-on-the-Teche as their headquarters, but the Louisiana plantation mistress refused to leave, defiantly occupying the second floor, where she died rebellious to the end. Ashton Villa, built by a slave, survived the great Galveston hurricane of 1900. The builder of Nevada's Bowers Mansion boasted that he was so wealthy he had "money to throw at the birds"; he died just three years after finishing his dream house, and his wife ended her days as a penniless fortune-teller. The stories of these houses reveal the deep attachment we have to the notion of "home." As Samuel L. Clemens said of his home in Hartford, "to us our house was not unsentient matter—it has a heart & a soul & eyes to see us."

History is here, too, in the homes of Presidents, magnates, writers, and one king (of Hawaii). These places contain what the novelist Henry James called "the mystery of antiquity." On a visit to Charleston early in this century, James sought "some small inkling" of the South as it had been before the Civil War. He got the briefest glimpse of his goal when he knocked at what he thought was the home of a friend. A servant answered his knock and "just barely held open for me a door through which I felt I might have looked straight and far back into the past. The past, that of the vanished order, was hanging on there behind her." Alas, James was at the wrong address, and the door was quickly shut in his face. Today, in contrast, the doors of America's venerable houses swing wide open for the curious visitor seeking to explore the mystery of antiquity or to savor the manifold beauties of American architecture.

We invite you to begin.

*H*ow to Use This Guide

*T*he National Geographic Guide to America's Great Houses showcases the country's grandest, most opulent residences in the 50 states and the District of Columbia. Selected from the thousands of outstanding buildings that grace the American landscape, the houses meet the following criteria: They are open to the public, preserved and furnished as residences, and evoke and illustrate the history and culture of the United States. Through pictures and text we show how the houses' furnishings, gardens, and structural lines lend insight into the lives and tastes of their architects, interior designers, and owners. Most sites are listed on the National Register of Historic Places, and many are National Historic Landmarks as well.

The guide is divided into four regional chapters, with the states of each region arranged geographically. Every house includes an information block with a number cross-referenced to the regional map found at the beginning of the chapter, and provides practical information (see below for key). Phone ahead for specific hours. Unless stated otherwise, most houses close on Thanksgiving and Christmas, and may be shut on other holidays. Note that opening times apply to houses only; gardens, gift shops, restaurants, and libraries may have different schedules. Information about every house has been carefully checked and to our knowledge is accurate as of press time. However, call ahead when possible, since visitor information can change. While planning a visit, keep in mind that special events take place throughout the year—themed house tours, springtime garden shows, tree-lighting ceremonies, crafts fairs, ghost walks, period decorating, and the like; call ahead for information.

We also recommend other houses of interest within a roughly 20-mile radius of the featured houses. These sites are briefly noted as "Nearby" at the end of many entries.

Finally, we thank the families, preservationists, historians, architects, public and private agencies, and numerous volunteers who have had the foresight and resources to preserve these architectural gems for the public, so we all can share in their special heritage, enjoy their splendor, and relive a bit of the past. We feel confident that, with this book in hand, you will enjoy many hours exploring America's Great Houses.

The information block at the end of each featured entry includes the official name of the site, its physical address, telephone number, opening days, and website (if applicable), as well as symbols indicating the following:

Ⓢ **Entrance fee**, shown when there is a fee for entry or parking. Special programs and tours may charge an additional fee, which is not noted.

🧍 **Guided tours available**, varying from guides posted in individual rooms to formal tours. Phone ahead for tour reservations. Houses will often make special arrangements for groups.

♿ **Wheelchair access.** Accommodations for people with disabilities are often limited; phone ahead for specifics.

🍴 **Food available on site**, from a full menu restaurant (often quite elegant), to a café, snack bar, or tearoom.

🅿 **Parking available in on-site lot.** Street parking is often available but not noted.

 Gift shop on-site.

The Northeast

MAINE • NEW HAMPSHIRE

VERMONT • MASSACHUSETTS

RHODE ISLAND • CONNECTICUT

NEW YORK • NEW JERSEY

PENNSYLVANIA • DELAWARE

MARYLAND • DISTRICT OF COLUMBIA

❧

From colonial mansions to modernist masterpieces, the Northeast offers a splendid sampling of American houses. Residences of shipping magnates stud the coastline, along with the awesome "cottages" of the Gilded Age. Inland, grand estates of industrialists lie near the imaginative houses of inventors and authors—and everywhere the traveler will sense the presence of history.

View of the Hudson River as seen from Olana, New York

The Northeast

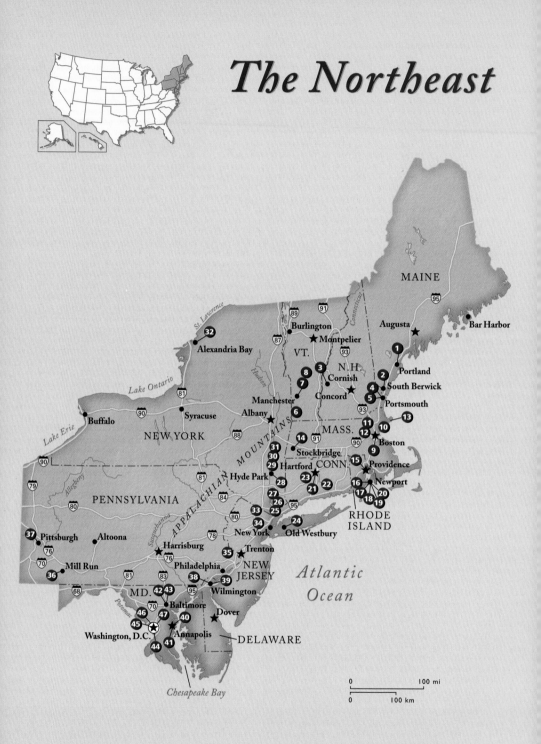

MAINE

95

89   91

Burlington

32

Alexandria Bay   Montpelier   Augusta   Bar Harbor

87   VT.   1

Lake Ontario   8   3   N.H.   2   Portland
                                          7   Cornish   South Berwick
81   Manchester   Concord   4   Portsmouth
90   Albany   6   5   13
Buffalo   Syracuse   93

Lake Erie   NEW YORK   11   10
90   88   14   91   12   Boston
                                          MASS.   9
79   31   Stockbridge   15   Providence
                          30   Hartford   CONN.
PENNSYLVANIA   81   29   23   16   Newport
80   84   Hyde Park   28   17   RHODE
                    27   21   22   18   19   ISLAND
37   Pittsburgh   Altoona   26   25   20
76   33   95
70   Mill Run   78   34
36   New York   24   Old Westbury
68   Harrisburg   35   Trenton
        Susquehanna   76   Atlantic
        MD.   Philadelphia   NEW   Ocean
        42   43   38   JERSEY
46   47   Baltimore   39   Wilmington
45   Washington, D.C.   40   Dover
        44   41   Annapolis   DELAWARE

Chesapeake Bay

NEW YORK

PENNSYLVANIA

APPALACHIAN MOUNTAINS

0   100 mi

0   100 km

Victoria Mansion

PORTLAND, MAINE

*A Home
for a Hotelier
With Grandiose
Taste*

Rising above the tidy white clapboard and redbrick houses of Portland, a four-story tower proclaims the presence of the imposing Italianate villa built for Ruggles Sylvester Morse, now called Victoria Mansion. Having made a fortune as a hotelier in New Orleans, Morse spared no expense in building a palatial summer mansion for himself and his wife, Olive. Morse hired the well-known Connecticut architect Henry Austin, who completed the house in 1860 to effusive praise: "A perfect architectural gem," the local newspaper raved.

The dignified brownstone exterior gives little hint of the exuberant and eclectic interior design and decoration. Inspired by French, Italian, classical, and even Gothic influences, the rooms are filled with colorful frescoes painted in the trompe l'oeil style, splendid wood paneling, sculptures, beautifully carved marble fireplaces, stained glass, and enormous mirrors with gold-leaf frames. Even the knobs and hinges of the 10.5-foot doors are silver plated. Gustave Herter, a German immigrant who was one of the first interior designers in the country—and who became a favorite of New York society—coordinated everything from the intricate plasterwork to the window hangings and furniture, much of which he designed himself. In addition, Giuseppe Guidicini, an Italian-American artist who specialized in decorating opera houses, brought in a team of painters to create the frescoes seen throughout the house. The result is theatrical, on a scale so large and design so grand that the mansion feels more like a public space than a private home. This is exactly what Morse had in mind—having lived his life in grand hotels, he wanted to create that same aura of luxury and ostentatious display in his own summer home.

The dramatic three-story entry hall hosts a flying staircase carved out of San Domingo mahogany. Elaborate plaster brackets, frescoes, and paintings of Italian peasant scenes embellish the hall's walls and ceiling while images portraying the cardinal virtues of Fortitude, Prudence, and Justice are painted above the doorways. The fourth cardinal virtue—Temperance—is noticeably absent, as much of Morse's wealth was generated from his hotels' barrooms, and he kept a well-stocked wine cellar in his own house.

The theme of the arts figures prominently in the formal reception room, where carved dancers adorn the marble fireplace and the lunettes are painted with female figures personifying Music, Architecture, Literature, and Painting. An adjacent room is dominated by a beautifully carved and decorated bird's-eye maple-and-rosewood cabinet and desk. Next, enter the French Second Empire-style drawing room, done in cool shades of cream, gray, and gold. Its decor centers around the theme of romance; note the cupids aiming arrows from the gilded bronze gasolier. Look closer and you will see cherubs and garlands of roses, Victorian symbols of love painted on the walls, sculpted in the marble fireplace, carved in the rosewood furniture, and even woven into the design of the rug. In contrast, the dining room features rich wood tones—from the faux wood ceiling to the chestnut-paneled walls and built-in oak furniture. Careful inspection reveals plaster reliefs of fruits, vegetables, game—and even a Maine lobster—decorating the walls. Carved ears of corn and artichokes surround the mantle clock.

The arched doorway in Victoria Mansion's ornate reception room frames one of Gustave Herter's most impressive pieces—a carved, incised, and inlaid cabinet and desk.

Ruggles Morse died in 1893, and within a year his widow sold the house and furnishings to J.R. Libby, who had made his fortune in the retail business. The family left the mansion in 1929, and by 1940 it was scheduled for demolition. Luckily, this spectacular example of Italianate design and lavish Victorian decoration was saved by local preservationists, who carefully restored the house and opened it to the public in 1941.

❶ *Victoria Mansion* 109 Danforth Street, Portland, Me. 04101. (207) 772-4841. Open May through Oct. Tues.-Sun. www.portlandarts.com/victoriamansion 🔳🔳🔳

> NEARBY: **McLellan House** *(103 Spring Street, Portland, Me. 207-775-6148)* The first home of the Portland Museum of Art, this elegant federal-style mansion is slated for restoration.

ℋamilton House

SOUTH BERWICK, MAINE

A Landmark of Colonial Times, Rescued by an Author

Hamilton House—like Carter's Grove mansion on the James River in Virginia (see p. 117)—represents both the colonial era of the 18th century and the colonial revival of the late 19th and early 20th centuries. Built circa 1787 on the Salmon Falls River, the wood-frame residence exhibits the formal symmetry characteristic of Georgian architecture. Its simple yet elegant exterior is marked principally by pediments over the dormer windows and four enormous chimneys. The builder, Col. Jonathan Hamilton, prospered as a shipping merchant and enjoyed a prominent place in local society. After his death in 1802, however, the family suffered a decline that forced his heirs to sell the property in 1815. Subsequent owners could not afford the upkeep on the large estate, and it deteriorated over the 19th century. Then the author Sarah Orne Jewett, a South Berwick resident who admired the downtrodden house, persuaded Emily Tyson and her stepdaughter Elise to purchase the property in 1898. The women thoroughly dedicated themselves to restoring the house and grounds following the colonial revival movement popular at the time. Assisted by Boston architect Herbert Browne, the Tysons created a romantic vision of a colonial New England home, decorated with a mix of antiques, murals, and country furniture. Jewett reaped a literary dividend from their work, using Hamilton House as the primary setting for her last book, a Revolutionary War novel entitled *The Tory Lover,* completed in 1901.

The interior remains a distinctive blend of the Hamilton and Tyson periods, with Georgian, Palladian, and colonial revival motifs evident in the room arrangements, window moldings, patterned wallpaper, and eclectic furnishings, including Elise Tyson's collection of 19th-century dolls and toys. The property features a formal garden created by the Tysons and embellished with hedges and statuary.

❷ *Hamilton House* 40 Vaughan's Lane, South Berwick, Me. 03908. (207) 384-5269. Open daily. www.spnea.org 🔳🔳🔳

> NEARBY: **Sarah Orne Jewett House** *(5 Portland Street, South Berwick, Me. 207-384-2454)* This stately Georgian residence was home to writer Sarah Orne Jewett, who was largely responsible for its eclectic blend of 18th-century furnishings.

The beautifully proportioned Hamilton House is reflected in the placid waters of the Salmon Falls River.
Sarah Orne Jewett, who helped rescue the estate from ruin, described it as having a "certain grand air."

Aspet

CORNISH, NEW HAMPSHIRE

Center of the Cornish Colony of Artists

In the 1880s the renowned sculptor Augustus Saint-Gaudens, one of the great American artists of the Gilded Age, redesigned a small, historical inn to become his country retreat and studio. Fleeing the hot and humid summers of New York City, he purchased Huggin's Folly, a federal-style structure built in 1805, and converted it into a residence for himself and his family. He remade a barn into a studio, where he could work on his large numbers of commissions. Aspet, named after his father's French birthplace, formed a social center for the "Cornish colony," a group of artists and friends that included Maxfield Parrish and Isadora Duncan.

Although Saint-Gaudens intended to live at Aspet only part-time, he made several significant changes to the house and landscape immediately after his arrival. For the house,

Early summer hollyhocks bloom outside of Saint-Gaudens' studio. While working, the artist could admire some of his own additions to Aspet—the columned porch and the handsome stepped roof.

he added dormers and several rooms in the attic area, and divided the second-floor dance hall into bedrooms. Outside, he added a columned porch overlooking the pastoral landscape, a place to enjoy the natural breezes.

A formal garden, which echoed the aesthetic principles of Italian Renaissance formal gardens, linked the artist's studio with the main house. Nearby, Saint-Gaudens constructed a bowling green and a nine-hole golf course, both of which he used to keep fit. Despite Saint-Gaudens' healthy, outdoor lifestyle, he died of cancer at 59 while in the prime of his life and his career. Today the house and studio preserve many of the artist's personal items and examples of his evocative work.

3 *Aspet: Saint-Gaudens National Historic Site* Off N.H. 12A on Rural Route 3, Cornish, N.H. 03745. (603) 675-2175. Open daily late May through Oct. www.sgnhs.org ⑨ 🚶 🅿 🏛

*P*ortsmouth Houses
Macphaedris-Warner House,
Moffatt-Ladd House

Built along one of the finest harbors on the Atlantic coast, formed by the mouth of the Piscataqua River, Portsmouth gained prosperity in colonial times as a center of international trade. With its waterway to the interior, the town became the loading point for the immense pine trees of New Hampshire's virgin forests, 200-foot-long timbers eagerly sought by Britain's Royal Navy for masts. By the early 1700s, Portsmouth's shipwrights were successfully competing with England's. Trade in fish, furs, and unfortunately, slaves, brought even more wealth to the city's merchants in the decades before the American Revolution. The houses built by Portsmouth's merchants reflect these soaring fortunes and the elegant society that flourished here. Though a fire in 1813 swept away some of the town's oldest structures, many survived, including some of the finest examples of New England colonial and 19th-century architecture.

Macphaedris-Warner House

PORTSMOUTH, NEW HAMPSHIRE

A Colonial Home's Enduring Artistic Mystery   Built between 1716 and 1718 for Capt. Archibald Macphaedris, perhaps in honor of his marriage to Sarah Wentworth, the Georgian Macphaedris-Warner House is an outstanding example of the use of brick in early American architecture. Its fine points are worth a close look, as they tell a subtle but interesting architectural tale. The builder, an English joiner named John Drew, departed from the long-standing New England tradition of timber framing, choosing instead to use bricks laid in a pattern of alternating headers and stretchers (a short side alternating with a long side), a sequence known as Flemish bond. Though unusual for New England, his choice of brick brought the house closer in spirit to the masonry houses of aristocratic England. Other architectural elements of the house further signified a grand lifestyle and wealthy, upper-class ownership. For example, the heavy pediment, supported by Corinthian pilasters, harkens back to the work of the Italian Renaissance architect Andrea Palladio, whose designs were popular among English aristocrats.

The house contains many original family furnishings, from the 18th century to the 1930s, including the parlor furniture purchased after the marriage of the Macphaedrises' daughter, Mary, to Jonathan Warner, a Portsmouth merchant for whom the house is also named. Be sure to see the fascinating set of murals in the stair hall, believed to be the earliest colonial wall paintings still in their original setting. Probably painted just after the construction of the house, they depict allegories of nature and religion, some perhaps relating to Archibald Macphaedris' birthplace in Ireland. One scene of note depicts the biblical episode of Abraham's intended sacrifice of his son Isaac, halted by the arrival of an angel. Overall, however, the murals present such a variety of scenes and situations as to defy interpretation. Also note the paintings of two Iroquois chiefs that flank the stairwell window, reproduced by a local artist from mezzotints, which were popular in the Colonies at that time.

④ *Macphaedris-Warner House* 150 DANIEL STREET, PORTSMOUTH, N.H. 03801. (603) 436-5909. OPEN DAILY JUNE THROUGH OCT. 🟦 🚶 ♿ 🏛

Moffatt-Ladd House

PORTSMOUTH, NEW HAMPSHIRE

*Five
Generations
of American
History*

This imposing three-story Georgian residence is remarkable both for its architecture and for its history—five generations of the same family occupied the house continuously from prerevolutionary times to the early 20th century. A clapboard structure with corner quoining, the house is topped with a captain's walk enclosed by a handsome balustrade ornamented with urn finials. From that vantage point the master of the house, Capt. John Moffatt, a British sea captain turned wealthy merchant and shipbuilder, could see his wharves and warehouses a short distance away in the protected, deepwater Portsmouth harbor.

When the house was finished in 1763, Captain Moffatt turned it over to his newlywed son Samuel and his daughter-in-law, Sarah. Five years later, however, Samuel was bankrupted after the loss of a ship and fled to the West Indies to avoid imprisonment. The elderly Captain Moffatt moved back into the house along with his daughter Katharine and her husband, William Whipple, a future signer of the Declaration of Independence and Revolutionary War brigadier general.

The unusually spacious front hall, one of the finest in 18th-century New England, takes up more than a quarter of the first floor. Upon entering the house, the visitor is greeted by a richly detailed staircase carved by the craftsman Ebenezer Deering, as well as scenic 1820s wallpaper made in Paris by Joseph Dufour. Furnishings in the dramatic stair hall include a carved mahogany sofa and a side chair made in Portsmouth. Nearby, the parlor features Chinese Chippendale furniture probably imported from England, as well as a Portsmouth teakettle stand. The upstairs bedroom, known as the yellow chamber for its yellow worsted damask window-seat cushions and curtains, is one of the best documented 18th-century American rooms. The wallpaper is unique—copperplate hunting prints framed by a

*Benches flanking a sundial create a restful nook in the gardens behind Moffatt-Ladd House.
The four-level garden was begun in the 18th century and has retained its basic structure.*

geometric design to simulate plaster moldings. Family portraits fill the home, including one by Gilbert Stuart beneath which hangs the original bill submitted by the artist—for $101.50. Four 18th-century Moffatt portraits still occupy their original frames.

Another family heirloom grows in the side yard. After signing the Declaration of Independence, William Whipple brought chestnuts back from Philadelphia and planted them. One of the resulting trees still stands, the largest ornamental of that species in New England and an apt symbol for this venerable house, a survivor of more than 200 years.

5 *Moffatt-Ladd House* 154 MARKET STREET, PORTSMOUTH, N.H. 03801. (603) 436-8221. OPEN DAILY MID-JUNE TO MID-OCT. AND BY APPOINTMENT.

NEARBY IN PORTSMOUTH: **Governor John Langdon House** *(143 Pleasant Street. 603-436-3205)* Once home to Portsmouth's leading citizen, this ornate 18th-century house features a McKim, Mead & White addition. **Rundlet-May House** *(364 Middle Street. 603-436-3205)* This home testifies to the wealth of merchant James Rundlet and still contains many of his furnishings, as well as original formal gardens, orchards, and outbuildings. **Wentworth-Coolidge Mansion** *(375 Little Harbor Road. 603-436-6607)* This 42-room mansion represents three periods of New England architecture and was the official residence of Benning Wentworth, the first royal governor of New Hampshire.

Park-McCullough House

NORTH BENNINGTON, VERMONT

A House Built
from Gold
Rush Fortune

Designed as a lavish monument to a local man's ambition and success, the Park-McCullough House was built for Trenor Park, who rose from poverty to become a successful land-grant lawyer and speculator during the California gold rush. Returning to North Bennington from San Francisco in 1863, Trenor and his wife, Laura, began construction of this opulent French and Italianate Victorian house on property owned by Laura's father, Hiland Hall, a former congressman and governor of Vermont. Architect Henry Dudley, a founding member of the American Institute of Architects, designed the 35-room, clapboard-over-brick mansion using the latest in technological advances and machine production.

One of the oldest surviving Victorian residences of the Second Empire style, the house is remarkable for its avant-garde design, picturesque massing, and for its central observatory tower, which projects a story and a half above the bell-cast mansard slate roof. Be sure to linger on the graceful veranda that wraps around three sides of the house. Today proffering period wicker furniture, the porch is adorned with slender columns, openwork brackets, and

The morning room of the Park-McCullough House retains such original items as Laura Park's 1860s desk and an album displaying foliage that Laura collected in Yosemite Valley in the 1850s.

a turned balustrade. Inside, a theatrical central hall extends 75 feet in length, accented by polished woodwork and patterned wall coverings. Arched doorways lead visitors from the hall to large rooms intended for entertaining. The family's more private quarters, on the second and third floors, are reached via a monumental wooden staircase topped by a stained glass skylight and arched Italianate loggia. The grounds also host a playhouse in the style of the main residence and a stable that displays a collection of period carriages.

The house remained in the Park family for more than a hundred years, until the death of the Parks' granddaughter, Mrs. Elmer Johnson, in 1965. Today the house hosts permanent and rotating exhibitions highlighting a costume and period clothing collection.

6 *Park-McCullough House* Park and West Streets, North Bennington, Vt. 05257. (802) 442-5441. Open daily late May through late Oct. 🏷️ 🚶 ♿ 🅿️ 🏛️

*H*ildene

MANCHESTER, VERMONT

Summer Home of Lincoln's Son

Set on a scenic promontory overlooking the Battenkill Valley, Hildene was built in 1904 as a summer home for Robert Todd Lincoln, the eldest and sole surviving son of President Abraham Lincoln. Robert and his mother, Mary Todd Lincoln, stayed at a resort hotel in the area (Equinox House, which still stands) during the Civil War, and planned to bring the President there for a vacation in the summer of 1865. He was assassinated that April.

A millionaire lawyer, statesman (he served variously as secretary of war and as minister to the Court of St. James), and businessman (he became chairman of the Pullman Company), Robert Todd Lincoln returned to the Green Mountains, purchased a 500-acre farm for his country retreat, and hired the noted Boston architects Shepley, Rutan and Coolidge to design this 24-room Georgian Revival mansion. Every spring when the family traveled to Hildene by private railroad car, Lincoln brought with him eight trunks filled with his father's papers, transporting them back to Chicago or Washington at the end of the season. He finally donated the papers to the Library of Congress in 1919, but not before reportedly burning sensitive documents in Hildene's library fireplace. Also known as the red room, the library's furniture is upholstered in fabric similar to that used in Pullman cars.

The last Lincoln descendant to live in Hildene died in 1975, leaving behind a time capsule of the family—a grand house filled with original furnishings and personal effects. These include the front hallway's working tall case clock with a mercury pendulum, purchased by the Lincolns at Tiffany's in the 1890s. Note the Aeolian pipe-organ installed in 1908 at the rear of the entry hall, with its nearly one thousand organ pipes cleverly concealed behind spindled cabinets on the stair landing. The instrument was restored in the 1980s and is now in working order, offering 242 original music rolls.

7 *Hildene* Vt. 7A, Manchester, Vt. 05254. (802) 362-1788. Open daily mid-May through Oct. www.hildene.org
🏷️ 🚶 ♿ 🍴 🅿️ 🏛️

Following pages: The back of Hildene looks out onto a formal garden designed by Robert Todd Lincoln's daughter, Jesse, with privet hedges clipped to look like the panes in Gothic cathedral windows.

Wilson Castle

PROCTOR, VERMONT

A Hypnotist's Castle in the Mountains

At the heart of 115 acres in Vermont's Green Mountains stands the realization of an Englishman's dream—a castle in the Americas. John Johnson, a "magnetic healer" who treated his patients with hypnotism, began building his elaborate residence around 1885. With few exceptions, Johnson imported all the building materials from outside the United States, hiring British and European workers to complete construction of the house. The resulting three-story, brick Victorian mansion is a picturesque amalgamation of architectural elements, including turrets, parapets, and a heavy veranda with outstanding views of Killington Peak. After viewing the house's exterior, you are in for a visual treat in the rich decorative abundance inside. At one time referred to as Johnson's Folly, the house exhibits an unusual opulence, bedecked with 13 fireplaces, 84 stained-glass windows, European, American, and Chinese antiques, and illusionary three-dimensional trompe l'oeil ceilings.

A fountain and a bronze eagle with its wings outstretched stand before the entrance to Wilson Castle. The original owners built an aviary on the grounds and imported birds from Europe.

In the drawing room, two round stained-glass windows flanking the fireplace depict allegorical figures of Thought and Music; the central window above the mantel portrays a glass view of the Thames River.

Expensive woodwork abounds throughout. Note the Honduras mahogany paneling in the grand reception hall, accented by hand-carved Ionic columns and pilasters. The furniture collection includes a Louis XVI table with Sienna onyx top and Louis XVI crown-jewel case, both housed in the sumptuous drawing room. The impressive grand stairway, illuminated by cathedral stained-glass windows, is paneled in mahogany with a ceiling fresco by Chiapine. The splendor of the mansion continues in the octagonal music room and the soaring spaces of the art gallery with its 34-foot-high ceiling and skylight.

Following Mrs. Johnson's death in 1900, the mansion was sold to a succession of 17 owners, ending with Col. Herbert Wilson and his wife, who purchased the house in the 1930s. They restored the residence as a summer home and opened it to the public in 1962. Today administered by the Wilson Foundation, the estate includes barns, stables, a carriage house, and an aviary for peacocks.

8 *Wilson Castle* WEST PROCTOR ROAD, PROCTOR, VT. 05736. (802) 773-3284. OPEN DAILY LATE MAY THROUGH LATE OCT.

$\mathcal{H}$arrison Gray Otis House

BOSTON, MASSACHUSETTS

*Adamesque
Style in
Full, Colorful
Flower*

One of the most important examples of federal domestic architecture in New England, this stately, beautifully proportioned house built in 1795-96 was the first of three homes designed by Charles Bulfinch for his lifelong friend Harrison Gray Otis. America's first native-born professional architect, Bulfinch introduced the British Adamesque style of neo-classicism to the United States. The Otis House facade stands as a textbook example of the style. The three-story redbrick mansion's bands of white marble, or "stringcourses," divide the exterior into horizontal segments. You can get a sense of the restrained elegance of the Adamesque style at the entrance, with its elliptical fanlight above the door and narrow sidelights on either side. Note, too, how the Palladian window draws your eye upward to the second floor.

Inside, the house is laid out in traditional colonial fashion—two rooms on either side of a central hall with a separate kitchen ell. On the first floor, walk into the dining room and note the elaborate mantel relief ornament depicting the "Triumph of Mars." As in the rest of the house, furnishings combine period and Otis family pieces. The oval Boston mahogany dining table dates from around 1818, while the 12 mahogany side chairs belonged to Otis' half-sister, as did the dessert service of French porcelain. Harrison Gray Otis, as painted by Gilbert Stuart in 1809, presides over the room.

As this imposing house took shape, Harrison Gray Otis was a prominent young lawyer, entrepreneur, and rising politician. A member of Congress, Otis would eventually become a U.S. senator and mayor of Boston. He also prospered as a land speculator, amassing a fortune by developing a hillside covered with prickly shrubs, wild berries, cow paths, and small cedar trees into a grand residential district, Beacon Hill. Otis was a convivial host, renowned for his sumptuous dinner parties, about which John Quincy Adams wrote to his father, "It has not fallen to my lot to meet a man more skilled in the useful art of entertaining his friends than Otis." A portrait of Otis' wife, Sally—attributed by some to Chester Harding—hangs in the second-floor central hallway above the family's blue-and-white Lowestoft punch bowl. Every afternoon, this was filled with punch and set in a niche halfway up the stairs to refresh guests on their way to the second floor withdrawing room, the most elegant room in the house. Be sure to visit this room yourself, where family and guests would "withdraw" after dinner to drink tea or brandy, play board games, or enjoy musical entertainments, as Otis was an amateur composer of some skill. Note the doors of mirrored mahogany, and the English japanned chairs and Chinese settee that belonged to the Otises.

In 1801 the Otis family sold the house to John Osborn, a wealthy paint merchant, who lived here until his death in 1824. As the neighborhood became more commercial, the house passed through a number of hands. Careful scholarship and scientific analysis of walls and floors helped a 1970s restoration of the house overturn the erroneous but long-held belief that federal houses were decorated in rather bland, pastel colors. In fact, early 19th-century taste called for bright, vibrant paints, wallpapers, and carpets. Restored by the Society for the Preservation of New England Antiquities, the house now serves as their headquarters.

9 *Harrison Gray Otis House* 141 Cambridge Street, Boston, Mass. 02114. (617) 227-3956. Open Wed.-Sun. WWW.SPNEA.ORG

A table set for tea is surrounded by a trio of shield-back side chairs, two of which belonged to Boston patriot John Hancock. The original mantel, also from the 18th century, shows intricate neoclassic details.

NEARBY: **William Hickling Prescott House** *(55 Beacon Street, Boston, Mass. 617-742-3190)* Designed in the federal style by Asher Benjamin in 1808, the house contains Prescott's fully restored private study and relics from the 18th century. **Isabella Stewart Gardner Museum** *(280 The Fenway, Boston, Mass. 617-566-1401)* A Venetian-style palace housing 2,500 art objects, one of the greatest private art collections in the world, it features a spectacular four-story courtyard garden. **Henry Wadsworth Longfellow House** *(105 Brattle Street, Cambridge, Mass. 617-876-4491)* Now housing a museum collection, Longfellow's colonial mansion was used by George Washington as his headquarters during the siege of Boston.

Jeremiah Lee Mansion

MARBLEHEAD, MASSACHUSETTS

Sumptuous Home of a Revolutionary Patriot

Widely acclaimed as one of the best surviving examples of late colonial Georgian architecture, the Jeremiah Lee Mansion reflects the prosperity brought to the seaport of Marblehead, and to merchant and shipowner Jeremiah Lee, by the burgeoning Atlantic trade in the 1750s and '60s. In the midst of town, Colonel Lee purchased and cleared three older buildings to make space for his impressive residence. Lee's 15-room mansion retained the proportions of earlier New England houses but on a grander scale—standing seven bays wide (its doorway flanked by six windows) and a full three stories—in contrast to the typical New England house which stood only two stories high with five bays. The wooden boards on all four facades are scored and beveled to simulate English stone-block construction. The corners lack the decorative raised blocks, or quoins, so popular in the Colonies, lending the mansion greater monumentality and the grandeur of an aristocratic British home. Lee relied heavily on English pattern books such as Abraham Swan's *British Architect,* published in London in 1745. But where other builders altered Swan's patterns to suit their own tastes, Lee's interior carvings are copied directly from Swan.

Along with other Marblehead merchants, Lee's fortune came from the Atlantic trade, in which New England salt fish was sold on exchange to coastal Atlantic Colonies, the West Indies, Spain, and Portugal. Profits were invested in the purchase of English manufactured goods, which were in turn sold in the Colonies. On the strength of this trade Marblehead grew to be the sixth largest city in the Colonies. At the outbreak of the Revolution, Lee chose the patriot cause and served as head of the Massachusetts Committee for Safety and Supplies. His patriotism cost him his life. He died in 1775 from a fever contracted on a cold, wet morning while fleeing a British search for traitors to the Crown. After Lee's death, title to the house passed among mortgage holders until 1804, when the newly established Marblehead Bank, the town's first, purchased it for office space. A conservative institution, the bank's only significant change was to paint a faux wood grain on the original yellow paneling in the formal parlor on the first floor; floor plan, carvings, and moldings were left untouched. Thus, although the house holds only a few Lee furnishings, the decorations of his era remain intact.

Upon entering, the visitor will sense the spaciousness of the house immediately, since the central entrance hall is twice as wide as that of the typical New England home of that era. Be sure to examine the English hand-painted wallpapers in the main hall, upstairs hall, and two front upstairs bedrooms. As only one other hand-painted English scenic wallpaper survives from this period, and that in a museum, these examples are extremely rare. Their designs, copied from 18th-century prints of landscapes and ruins, were painted on small sheets, pasted together into strips, and then hung. Reflecting Marblehead's nautical heritage, one room depicts sailors, seaports, and Neptune, the Roman god of the sea.

In 1909 the Lee Mansion was purchased by the Marblehead Historical Society and served as its headquarters until 1998. The society kept the building as it was and attempted to return important historical furnishings to the mansion.

10 *1768 Jeremiah Lee Mansion* 161 WASHINGTON STREET, MARBLEHEAD, MASS. 01945. (781) 631-1768. OPEN DAILY MID-MAY THROUGH OCT.

*G*ropius House

LINCOLN, MASSACHUSETTS

A Modernist Masterpiece in a New England Setting

A landmark of modern architecture rose up in tradition-bound New England when the noted architect Walter Gropius fled Nazi Germany in the mid-1930s and accepted an appointment at Harvard University. An artistically minded philanthropist, Mrs. James Storrow, commissioned the architect, provided the property, and financed construction of what became known as Gropius House, one of the earliest international style residences in New England. Constructed in 1938, the house showcases the modernist aesthetic and utilitarian principles championed by its architect and occupant.

In this revolutionary house, Gropius' first U.S. residential commission, he employed modern European design principles while incorporating regional influences through use of traditional New England building materials. The clean lines of the house's "white box" exterior are distinctly New England, with vertical wooden clapboards laid over a natural fieldstone foundation, punctuated by a painted brick chimney. Gropius' modernism can also be seen in the delicate, iron, spiral stair leading to the second story, and in the diagonal entryway, partially enclosed by a luminescent glass-block wall. Industrial materials decorate the elegant interior as well— polished stainless steel tubes accentuate the main stair, equipped with a sinuously curved metal handrail. Enormous windows, a sunbathed second-story roof deck, and a steel-framed screened porch blur the boundaries between the house and the landscape.

Gropius House's simple unornamented walls and flat roof are hallmarks of the international style. An interior drainpipe leading to a dry well eliminates the need for gutters and downspouts.

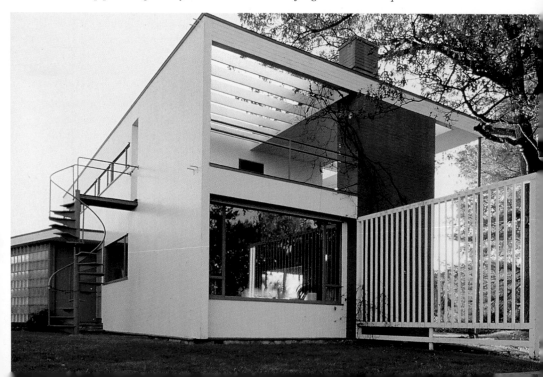

The building has been restored to its 1960s appearance, the latest period of the Gropius family's occupancy. Unique modernist furnishings owned by Gropius remain in the house, including a collection of pieces designed for him by Marcel Breuer and made in the Bauhaus workshops in Germany. Paintings by significant artists such as Josef Albers, Henry Moore, Joan Miró, and László Moholy-Nagy adorn the interior. Gropius, his wife, Ise, and their daughter leased the house until his death, and it is one of the area's four modernist residences sponsored by Mrs. Storrow, collectively referred to as the Woods End Colony.

11 *Gropius House* 68 Baker Ridge Road, Lincoln, Mass. 01773. (781) 259-8098. Open June to mid-Oct. Wed.-Sun.; mid-Oct. through May Sat.-Sun. www.spnea.org

Codman House
LINCOLN, MASSACHUSETTS

A Showcase for Four Generations of Exquisite Taste

Owned by four generations of the Codman family, this country house on 16 acres of landscaped grounds reveals the taste and cultivation of a family that ranked among Boston's most successful merchants, traders, and financiers. In the 19th century, the family also produced one of the nation's most influential designers, Ogden Codman, Jr., who once remarked that "Houses and furniture and genealogy are my three hobbies." Codman House—also known as the Grange—combines the three "hobbies" this family of Boston Brahmins avidly pursued.

Originally a two-story Georgian mansion built around 1740, the house was acquired by the merchant John Codman in the 1790s and turned into a summer retreat for his family. He made extensive renovations in 1797-98, adding a third story and nearly doubling the size of the house. In the 1860s, his grandson Ogden Codman, Sr., hired John Hubbard Sturgis, an English architect and designer who was also Codman's brother-in-law, to redecorate the residence. Sturgis transformed a rear parlor into an Elizabethan Revival dining room, with a strapwork ceiling, paneling, and a fireplace all made of butternut wood.

The final evolution of the house began in the 1890s when Ogden Codman, Jr., coauthor with Edith Wharton of the influential *The Decoration of Houses*, sought to return the house to its 18th-century spirit while conveying the evolution of the family's taste. He replaced the Victorian wallpapers of the 1860s with painted surfaces, and decorated with imported chintzes and toiles. He is also thought to have added the Italianate garden with fountains, statuary, and a reflecting pool with water lilies. Be sure to enter the southeast parlor, then called the morning room, which most fully reveals Codman's approach. Retaining the handsome paneling dating from the construction of the house in the 1740s, he furnished the room with items the family had subsequently acquired, such as early 19th-century English armchairs, and a caned Chinese sofa, French armchairs, and a chest of drawers purchased by his father in Brittany. The room neatly symbolizes how each generation of Codmans left its mark on the house, creating a chronicle of patrician American taste.

12 *Codman House* Codman Road, Lincoln, Mass. 01773. (781) 259-8843. Open June to mid-Oct. Wed.-Sun. www.spnea.org

The Codman House sits proudly atop a knoll, exuding an air of solidity and refinement. The corner quoining and columned open porch on the east side of the house were added in the 1860s.

NEARBY: **Historic Gore Estate** *(52 Gore Street, Waltham, Mass. 781-894-2798)* A 22-room federal brick mansion situated amid 45 acres of lawns, gardens, and fields and decorated with early American, European, and Oriental furnishings.

*B*eauport

GLOUCESTER, MASSACHUSETTS

An Eclectic
Labyrinth
by the Sea

Sited at the entrance to Gloucester Harbor, Beauport rises prominently from the granite rocks of the New England shore. A fascinating residence planned by Henry Davis Sleeper from the inside out, the house represents his visionary interpretation of American and European history. Beauport began in 1907 as a simple, summer retreat of about a dozen rooms, designed by Sleeper in consultation with local architect Halfdan M. Hanson. The two continually modified, expanded, and elaborated on the original modest plan for the next 27 years, resulting in an eclectic creation characterized by Tudor, Gothic, Norman, and shingle-style architectural features. At Beauport the visitor encounters a pleasing and picturesque

fusion of towers, gables, chimneys, and dormers, supported by heavy stone and brick walls. As you stroll around the mansion's exterior you will notice architectural elements the builders salvaged from other New England houses, merging them in appealing compositions.

But the real splendor is the interior, an enormous labyrinth of more than 40 rooms decorated in a dramatic style based on historical and literary themes. The names of the rooms—Benjamin Franklin Room, Shelley Room, Indian Room, Byron Room, and Mariner's Room, among others—indicate Sleeper's flair for imaginative motifs. Colonial period architecture and objects fascinated Sleeper, who collected paneling from the 1728 Cogswell House in Essex, Connecticut, a pedimented doorway from Newport, Rhode Island, and wood paneling from a 17th-century house in Ipswich, and reinstalled them at Beauport. The Pine Kitchen, thought to be his favorite room, consists almost entirely of salvaged materials, including doors (used as paneling), ceiling beams, floorboards, and the chimney itself.

Look carefully—every nook, niche, and corner of the house is filled with curiosities, folk art, china, memorabilia, redware, silhouettes, and other items, all part of Sleeper's continually growing collection of American and European pieces, arranged to create dramatic compositions. His extensive collection of colored glass fills shelves framed by antique window moldings, expressively lit from behind. Sleeper's conception for each room sometimes hinged on his acquisition of unusual and extraordinary items. In 1923, for example, the purchase of unused, pristine, delicately hand-painted scenic wallpaper—originally ordered from China by Robert Morris, a signer of the Declaration of Independence—resulted in the China Trade Room, which supplanted a previous, Gothic-style medieval hall theme.

Beauport's eclectic grandeur brought Sleeper renown, and the house received widespread recognition in popular magazines during the colonial revival period of the 1920s and 1930s. Prominent citizens and Hollywood celebrities commissioned him to design their residential interiors. Joan Crawford, Frederick March, and Henry Francis du Pont all utilized his talents. Guests entertained at the mansion include John D. Rockefeller, Henry Frick, and the painters Childe Hassam and John Singer Sargent. Sleeper's work at Beauport, protecting and preserving important architectural artifacts, antiques, and other articles of daily life, influenced the later establishment of the Winterthur Museum in Delaware (see p. 81) and the American Wing of the Metropolitan Museum of Art in New York.

After Sleeper's death in 1934, Charles and Helena McCann, heirs to the Woolworth fortune, became Beauport's owners. They left most of the decor intact, recognizing the significance of the collection. McCann heirs donated Beauport to the Society for the Preservation of New England Antiquities, and it is now maintained as a museum property.

13 *Beauport: The Sleeper-McCann House* 75 EASTERN POINT BOULEVARD, GLOUCESTER, MASS. 01930. (978) 283-0800. OPEN MID-MAY TO MID-SEPT. MON.-FRI.; MID-SEPT. TO MID-OCT. MON.-SAT.

⑤ 🚶 🅿 🏛

NEARBY: **Hammond Castle Museum** *(80 Hesperus Avenue, Gloucester, Mass. 978-283-7673)* The stone castle oceanside home of the American inventor Dr. John Hays Hammond, Jr., now houses his collection of early Roman, medieval, and Renaissance artifacts.

A vivid, hand-painted, 18th-century, Cantonese wallpaper depicting Chinese people cultivating rice and making porcelain enlivens the aptly named China Trade Room at Beauport.

Naumkeag

STOCKBRIDGE, MASSACHUSETTS

Stanford White's
Shingle-style
Masterpiece

One of the finest works by renowned architect Stanford White, Naumkeag was the Berkshire retreat of the prominent New York attorney Joseph Hodges Choate and his family. Choate acquired the site—a hilltop with a commanding view of mountains to the west—in 1884 and hired White to design the house on the advice of an acquaintance, Charles McKim, a partner in McKim, Mead & White. According to family archives, the lawyer also sought the services of Frederick Law Olmsted to design the grounds, but when Olmsted proposed cutting down the family's favorite tree to site the house at the middle of the hill, the Choates let him go.

For Naumkeag, White conceived an artful melding of two contrasting styles. The roadside facade imparts a sense of aristocratic status, recalling a Norman French château with

A 16th-century Flemish tapestry and an English tall case clock grace the wood-paneled stair hall at Naumkeag.

salmon-colored brick walls, an arched entryway, turrets, and dormer windows that seem to emerge organically from the shingled roof like a set of hooded eyes. In contrast to these smoothed and rounded surfaces, White's masterful, shingle-style rear facade—all angles and broken lines—manages to be both restful and energetic. The design successfully captured the personality of the Choate family—worldly and successful, yet artistically inclined and sensitive to their lovely surroundings.

Caroline Choate and her daughter Mabel furnished the 26-room house with antiques purchased largely in New York shops. Although one of Choate's law partners teased him, "your women-folk will be the ruin of you yet," they had fine, but not extravagant, taste. Mrs. Choate christened the house with the Native American name for her husband's birthplace, Salem, Massachusetts. They translated Naumkeag to mean "haven of rest."

Naumkeag did indeed provide a peaceful haven for Choate, who had one of the most demanding law practices in New York in the second half of the 19th century. A native of Massachusetts and a Harvard graduate, his clients included Standard Oil, Native American tribes, the Turkish government, and many prominent socialites. This mix allowed him such situations as arguing a case on behalf of a consortium of milk farmers against New York railroads, then turning around and representing those same railroads, before the same tribunal, in a case involving government regulation. Choate gained legal fame when he argued the 1894 income tax case before the Supreme

The rear facade of Naumkeag, a dramatic shingle-style design punctuated with gables and chimneys, looks out onto terraced gardens created by Mabel Choate and landscape architect Fletcher Steele.

Court, persuading the justices that a graduated tax based on an individual's income was unconstitutional. It would be another two decades before an income tax that passed constitutional muster was finally approved. In Stockbridge he was a generous philanthropist, donating $10,000 to the local library, for example. When approached for a donation to build a fence around a cemetery, however, he declined, explaining that the fence was unnecessary: "Nobody inside can get out, and no one on the outside wants to get in."

In 1926 Mabel Choate, who inherited the property after the deaths of her parents, embarked on a remarkable 30-year landscaping project in partnership with the landscape architect Fletcher Steele. Their legacy includes an afternoon garden, a Chinese garden, a rose garden, and the elegant, French deco-style Blue Steps—four flights of stairs framing a series of fountains. At her death in 1958, Mabel bequeathed Naumkeag to The Trustees of Reservations, with funds to preserve its architecture, furnishings, and "aura of good times and gracious living."

14 *Naumkeag House and Gardens* 5 PROSPECT HILL ROAD, STOCKBRIDGE, MASS. 01262. (413) 298-3239. OPEN DAILY MEMORIAL DAY WEEKEND THROUGH COLUMBUS DAY.

NEARBY: **Chesterwood** *(4 Williamsville Road, Stockbridge, Mass. 413-298-3579)* Chesterwood was the summer estate of Daniel Chester French, sculptor of the Lincoln Memorial. Models, studies, and full-size sculptures of French's works are displayed in the studio, museum gallery, summer home, and gardens. **The Mount** *(2 Plunkett Street, Lenox, Mass. 413-637-1899)* Built by Edith Wharton at the turn of the century, The Mount expresses her influential views on design. The house and its formal gardens are currently undergoing an extensive long-term restoration.

John Brown House
PROVIDENCE, RHODE ISLAND

A Trader's Georgian Mansion

Built soon after the Revolutionary War, the majestic John Brown House, a restored late-Georgian manor, reflects the prosperity of the Providence merchant class in the late 18th century, when the city was a busy ship-building and trading port. The house was completed in 1788 for John Brown, a wealthy trader in the triangle route between Africa, the West Indies, and the eastern United States. His brother, Joseph, designed the brick three-story mansion, incorporating such Georgian elements as the second-floor Palladian window and projecting portico.

The interior of the house is furnished with antiques and decorative arts dating from the 18th and 19th centuries. A number of pieces on display were owned by John Brown and his wife, Sarah, including a collection of silver and china, and two parlor sofas. Be sure to note the exceptional "nine-shell" bookcase-desk, once the property of Joseph Brown, in the study. While the seashell motif was a common one in furniture of the period, Rhode Island examples are prized for their intricate detail.

The mansion was owned by Brown's descendants until the beginning of the 20th century and remained little changed. In 1901, Marsden Perry, a local businessman, purchased the house, updating the building while maintaining most of its original features. Particularly captivating is his lavishly decorated second-floor bathroom, ornamented with colorful stained glass surrounded by hand-painted and glazed tiles. A scene above the tub depicts a frolicking group of nymphs and satyrs. Perry's changes were preserved when a descendant of the Brown family repurchased the home in the 1930s and entrusted it to the stewardship of the Rhode Island Historical Society.

15 *John Brown House* 52 POWER STREET, PROVIDENCE, R.I. 02906. (401) 331-8575. OPEN TUES.-SUN.

Newport Mansions
Château-sur-Mer, Kingscote, Marble House, The Breakers, Rosecliff

Newport, virtually synonymous with the Gilded Age, hosts the finest collection of high-style mansions in the country. Designed by such architectural luminaries as Stanford White and Richard Morris Hunt, Newport's palatial residences offered seaside relief—and lavish entertainments—to the very wealthy. Vanderbilts and Wetmores spent several million dollars to build and furnish retreats, airily referred to as "cottages." More than a hundred mansions stood along the preferred addresses of Bellevue Avenue, Ocean Drive, and Harrison Avenue. Many of the most opulent are administered by the Preservation Society of Newport County and open to the public with both single admission and combination tickets sold at the mansions themselves. Even those that remain in private hands can be glimpsed by strolling along Cliff Walk, a 3-mile path by the shore with free ocean views.

The Duchess of Marlboro, née Consuelo Vanderbilt, enjoys the scene at the polo grounds in Newport, the playground for high society and the ultrarich at the turn of the century.

Château-sur-Mer

NEWPORT, RHODE ISLAND

One Mansion Within Another

Originally built in 1852 and enlarged in the 1870s, this house signaled the beginning of a new and grand lifestyle in Newport, becoming the first of the massive "cottages" along Bellevue Avenue. In its earliest version, built for William Shepard Wetmore, Château-sur-Mer was a modestly scaled but solid Italianate villa, made of rough-cut granite with a grand lawn and a view of the ocean. Then in 1862 Wetmore's son George Peabody Wetmore inherited the property. He proceeded to commission the first of several additions that would transform the house into a colossal home of epic proportions. His architect, Paris-trained Richard Morris Hunt, so dramatically changed the building's appearance that many visitors assumed that the old residence had been demolished and this built in its place. In fact, the earlier house stands within the added mansard roofs, tower forms, and porte cochere. Hunt replaced the servants' quarters with a billiard room in the northwest part of the mansion, building new servants' quarters to the northeast. A dramatic three-story hall, taller roofs, and additional stories enhanced the height of the structure. In its architecture and decoration, Château-sur-Mer remains one of Newport's finest and most impressive illustrations of Victorian style. Inside you can see superb samples of Hunt's powerful woodwork, designs inspired by Charles Eastlake. Although the overall decor of the rooms built by Hunt, exemplified by the billiard room, could be termed masculine, feminine influences appeared later in interiors created by the noted designer Ogden Codman, Jr., whose principles of lighter and less-ornate decoration make themselves felt in the French Salon.

16 *Château-sur-Mer* BELLEVUE AVENUE, NEWPORT, R.I. 02840. (401) 847-1000. OPEN DAILY MARCH THROUGH SEPT., CALL FOR WINTER HOURS. WWW.NEWPORTMANSIONS.ORG

Kingscote

NEWPORT, RHODE ISLAND

A Southerner's Northern Retreat One of the first summer cottages to rise on fashionable Bellevue Avenue, but decidedly more modest than those that followed, Kingscote was built for George Noble Jones of Savannah in 1841. Jones hired the architect Richard Upjohn to design a house of some eight rooms, including servants' quarters and water closets, a new convenience. Upjohn created a charming, asymmetrical, Gothic Revival house, with projecting gables and Victorian woodwork. Although the Gothic style is typically associated with a dark and gloomy atmosphere, Jones' house was light, airy, and open, taking advantage of the view of the landscape and the healthful breezes that blew in off the ocean.

With the outbreak of the Civil War, Jones moved his family back to the South, leaving the house in the care of his friend William Henry King. A merchant in the China trade, King bought the house outright in 1863, naming it Kingscote. In 1881 the family hired the

A removable spool-and-spindle screen of mahogany opens onto Kingscote's elaborate dining room.

firm of McKim, Mead & White to add a dining room and bedrooms. To retain the house's pleasing asymmetry, the service wing was moved about 30 feet to the northwest with an addition placed between it and the main house. The result preserved the purity of Upjohn's lines and gables. Be sure to visit the dining room, one of Stanford White's most appealing creations, where Tiffany glass bricks and opalescent brick tiles complement a Sienna marble fireplace. The upper panels of glass bricks contain lovely stained-glass dahlias. Note the pattern of the parquet floors, which echoes that of the cork acoustic tiles on the walls and ceiling, while also matching the delicate spindle screen that partitions the space. The Kings' library, originally the Joneses' dining room, displays paintings of the China trade hung on William Morris wallpaper.

17 *Kingscote* BELLEVUE AVENUE, NEWPORT, R.I. 02840. (401) 847-1000. OPEN DAILY MARCH THROUGH SEPT., CALL FOR WINTER HOURS. WWW.NEWPORTMANSIONS.ORG

Marble House

NEWPORT, RHODE ISLAND

Newport's own Petit Trianon, Built in Secrecy

Designed by Richard Morris Hunt in 1888 for William K. Vanderbilt's wife, Alva, Marble House epitomizes the Vanderbilts' energy, drive, and architectural ambitions. Wishing to awe Newport with this house, the family imposed no limit on what Hunt could spend. In order to heighten the drama of the project, the Vanderbilts insisted on total secrecy throughout the four years of construction, erecting large fences around the property and sequestering the artisans to prevent them from gossiping about the design.

Modeled after the Petit Trianon, Marie Antoinette's Versailles retreat, the estate utilizes 500,000 cubic feet of marble, including a fountain at the base of the circular drive and the facade's four massive Corinthian columns. The interiors illustrate the lengths that Hunt, with Vanderbilt's open checkbook, was able to exploit his talent for splendor. Expanses of yellow Sienna and pink Numidian marble are surrounded by richly gilded ornament and sculpture, most of which was created by the Paris firm of Jules Allard & Sons. In the ballroom, allegorical paintings and sculpture recall the elaborate French palace of Versailles. Following the classical tradition, Hunt left his mark, placing a portrait of himself in the great hall, next to his idol, Jules Hardouin Mansart.

When completed, Marble House clearly rivaled, if not surpassed, the other Bellevue Avenue mansions, securing Alva Vanderbilt's position as a leading society hostess. Having reportedly spent some 11 million dollars on the house to enhance his wife's social status, William was divorced from Alva only three seasons after the house was completed. Alva kept the estate, and later contracted Hunt to design a Chinese-style teahouse near the water for more informal events, a charming complement to the awesome mansion.

18 *Marble House* BELLEVUE AVENUE, NEWPORT, R.I. 02840. (401) 847-1000. OPEN DAILY MARCH THROUGH SEPT., CALL FOR WINTER HOURS. WWW.NEWPORTMANSIONS.ORG

The stately classical exterior of Marble House (opposite) pales next to the stunning opulence of the mansion's Gold Ballroom (right), which epitomizes Gilded Age extravagance.

The Breakers

NEWPORT, RHODE ISLAND

One Vanderbilt Outbuilds Another

The second of two Vanderbilt mansions built by Richard Morris Hunt in Newport, The Breakers surpassed Marble House in grandeur and scale. Cornelius Vanderbilt purchased the property in 1885 along with a two-story villa, which burned in 1892. Vanderbilt and his wife, Alice, rebuilt in a larger and more grandiose fashion, working directly with Hunt, pacing out rooms and giving thoughts on size, scale, and decoration. The resulting 70-room extravaganza is an imitation of a Renaissance palazzo, with loggias and porches integrating interior rooms with exterior views. The rear facade, a great critical success at the time, opens toward the ocean view and the crashing waves that gave The Breakers its name. As the first house here had been lost by fire, the architect constructed the mansion out of stone and brick, with some structural steel beams for support. As added precautions, Hunt placed the kitchen in a separate wing, and located the heating plant and fuel a hundred yards away from the house.

The interior decor is equal in size and grandeur to the exterior, with a great hall rising three stories, offering views of the lawn and the ocean. Wander through the rooms opening off the great hall, where Renaissance architectural motifs may be seen in the blue morning room. Here large Ionic columns frame paintings of the muses of classical mythology. Throughout, color enlivens the massive house—gray-green Cippolino marble in the billiard room, contrasting with the ornate rose alabaster and gilded bronze capitals of the two-story dining room. Upstairs, lighter decorations designed by Ogden Codman, Jr., grace family and guest bedrooms in gentle shades of green and pink.

19 *The Breakers* OCHRE POINT AVENUE, NEWPORT, R.I. 02840. (401) 847-1000. OPEN DAILY MARCH THROUGH SEPT., CALL FOR WINTER HOURS. WWW.NEWPORTMANSIONS.ORG

The rear facade of The Breakers (opposite) includes an arched double loggia facing out to the ocean. Inside, the elaborate vaulted dining room ceiling rises above two 12-foot-tall Baccarat crystal chandeliers.

Rosecliff

NEWPORT, RHODE ISLAND

A Court of Love by the Sea

Between 1899 and 1902, Theresa Fair Oelrichs, heir to a Nevada silver fortune, built one of Newport's most elegant mansions with lavish entertainments in mind. She retained Stanford White of the firm McKim, Mead & White to design the mansion, which she would name Rosecliff, in honor of the cottage and rose garden of the site's previous owner, the historian and diplomat George Bancroft. White created a massive residence, reminiscent of the Grand Trianon at Versailles, though on a smaller scale. Built in the shape of an H, its two wings are connected in the center by an enormous ballroom. Dazzling white-glazed terra-cotta tiles give the building a light and airy feeling typical of Gilded Age architecture. From the outside the visitor will see only two stories, but there is a third, containing servants' quarters, hidden from view behind a balustrade.

The design of the house centers on the ballroom, the largest in Newport. Measuring 40 feet by 80 feet, this room hosted many sensational events, and was later used as a set for several films, including *The Great Gatsby*. Elaborate plaster moldings surround a sky blue ceiling, which gives the illusion of an open roof or an outdoor space. The doors along the ocean side open to veranda and lawn, allowing parties to spill out into the surrounding nature. White designed another striking feature of the house, a heart-shaped staircase.

Tessie Oelrichs, one of the most flamboyant figures to grace Newport's Gilded Age, was the daughter of an Irish immigrant who reaped an immense fortune from Nevada's Comstock Lode. Her mother staged San Francisco's most elaborate wedding ever when Tessie married the socialite sportsman Hermann Oelrichs in 1890. Despite Tessie's vast wealth and social prominence, her roots in the mining camps of the West emerged in her predilection for bursting into "up-to-the-minute profanity," and among her servants she earned a reputation as "a dragon of a mistress." When displeased with the quality of the housekeeping, she would fire everyone in sight, grab a mop herself, and buff the floors to the desired sheen.

After Tessie's death in 1926, her son occupied Rosecliff until 1941. A subsequent owner, having spent a small fortune refurbishing the house, died on the way to his first stay at Rosecliff in an auto accident. The Monroe family of New Orleans purchased the house in 1947, and donated it to The Preservation Society of Newport County in 1971.

20 *Rosecliff*   BELLEVUE AVENUE, NEWPORT, R.I. 02840. (401) 847-1000. OPEN DAILY MARCH THROUGH SEPT., CALL FOR WINTER HOURS. WWW.NEWPORTMANSIONS.ORG

NEARBY IN NEWPORT: **Belcourt Castle** *(Bellevue Avenue. 401-846-0669)* Three hundred craftsmen were brought over from Europe to construct this 60-room castle designed by architect Richard Morris Hunt. **The Elms** *(Bellevue Avenue. 401-847-1000)* Costing nearly 1.5 million dollars when it was completed in 1901, The Elms was modeled after the 18th-century French château d'Asnières. **Hunter House** *(54 Washington Street. 401-847-1000)* Built for Jonathan Nicholas, Jr., Hunter House is furnished with examples from Newport's great colonial furniture makers, the Townsend-Goddard family. **Isaac Bell House** *(Bellevue Avenue. 401-847-1000)* A classic example of shingle-style architecture, the Isaac Bell House was designed by McKim, Mead & White in 1883 for a wealthy cotton broker.

Elaborate wrought-iron grillwork embellishes the main entrance to Rosecliff and sets it apart from the enormous arched windows and doors that line the first floor of this elegant "cottage."

Mark Twain House

HARTFORD, CONNECTICUT

A House as Imaginative as Its Owner

Few American authors have housed themselves as extravagantly as Samuel L. Clemens, better known as Mark Twain. Matching the owner's oversize personality, his Hartford residence is a festive, exuberant, American home. Clemens and his wife, Livy, commissioned the noted New York architect Edward Tuckerman Potter to design the house in 1873 and spared no expense, spending more than a million dollars in today's money on its construction and interior decoration. The resulting asymmetrical brick structure supports three turrets, one a 50-foot-high octagon. Bricks laid at angles and painted variously black and vermillion create dramatic stripes and unusual exterior designs. In addition, hexagonal-shaped slate in different hues forms patterns in the steeply pitched roof. The colorful facade continues with sweeping wooden cornices, gables, and balconies. A rambling one-story wooden veranda, which Clemens referred to as an *ombra* (Italian for "shadow"), adds to the rustic charm. Twain's biographer, Justin Kaplan, later described the house as "permanent polychrome and gingerbread Gothic…part steamboat, part medieval stronghold and part cuckoo clock."

The interior design is even more flamboyant. Louis Comfort Tiffany and his interior design firm, Associated Artists of New York, oversaw the decoration of the first-floor rooms, using rich colors and decorative elements drawn from India, the Middle East, Africa, and Asia. In

A study in contrasting shapes, colors, and materials, the eccentric Mark Twain House, like the author himself, inspired strong opinions—people either loved it or hated it.

the large and gracious entry hall, restored to Tiffany's original design, you will see how the elaborate silver-toned stenciling on the wood-paneled walls creates an illusion of inlaid ivory. Above, walls and ceiling are painted a rich red and stenciled with a black geometric border. A large fireplace embellished with wooden panels and brass decorations from India further welcomes guests.

In the dining room the visitor immediately notices an unusually placed window directly over the fireplace, which in winter allowed Clemens to watch snowflakes and flames at

Mark Twain's library features geometric patterns stenciled onto the walls and ceiling, and richly carved bookcases and mantel.

the same time. In the book-lined library, the author read his manuscripts aloud to family and friends and his children performed dramas. Here, the fireplace mantel, elaborately carved with a knight's helmet and shield, is one salvaged by the Clemenses from a Scottish castle in the 1870s. A brass plate above the firebox expresses the owner's philosophy, "The ornament of a house is the friends that frequent it."

Indeed, a constant round of guests and dinner parties enlivened the house with some of the most important personages of the day—Civil War generals William T. Sherman and Philip Sheridan, journalists Thomas Nast and William Dean Howells, explorer Henry Stanley, and writer Bret Harte. Though he was producing a steady stream of important books in the 1880s—*The Prince and the Pauper, Adventures of Huckleberry Finn,* and *A Connecticut Yankee in King Arthur's Court*—Clemens' lavish entertaining and unwise investments left him unable to maintain the house. To raise funds, he moved his family to Europe and embarked on a worldwide lecture tour. Then, in 1896 the Clemens' 24-year-old daughter contracted spinal meningitis while visiting friends in Hartford and died. The only solace for her heartbroken father was that, "Susy died at *home.* She had that privilege. . . . To us our house was not unsentient matter—it has a heart & a soul & eyes to see us." The Clemens family never lived in the house again; it would have been too painful.

Sold in 1903 for a mere $28,000, the residence saw use as a school, an apartment house, and a public library. Restoration began in 1955 to return it to its original grandeur—a unique fusing of personality, architecture, and interior design.

21 *Mark Twain House* 351 FARMINGTON AVENUE, HARTFORD, CONN. 06105. (860) 493-6411. OPEN DAILY MEMORIAL DAY TO MID-OCT.; WED.-MON. REST OF YEAR. 🛈 🚶 ♿ 🅿 🏛

NEARBY: **Harriet Beecher Stowe House** *(71 Forest Street, across from the Mark Twain House, Hartford, Conn. 860-525-9317)* One of the first Victorian houses in the country to undergo restoration, this author's residence features some of her paintings, her writing table, family and professional memorabilia, period furnishings, and historical gardens.

Local fieldstone and hand-hewn southern white oak lend a rustic charm to Gillette Castle's great hall, which holds a 6-foot-wide fireplace.

*G*illette Castle
EAST HADDAM, CONNECTICUT

A Stage Talent's Home on the Connecticut River

In the early 1900s, the world-famous actor, director, and playwright William Gillette created a whimsical castle for his retirement home. A crew of fifteen masons and five carpenters labored five years, between 1914 and 1919, to complete it at a cost of approximately one million dollars. Evoking the medieval castles on Germany's Rhine River, Gillette Castle looms over the Connecticut River, offering a panoramic view from its rough-hewn, battlemented walls. Constructed on a steel framework, the walls are of fieldstone purchased from local farmers delighted to find a buyer for the nuisance rock they had to dredge up from their fields. The 24 rooms also used exposed stone for walls and pillars, imparting an old-fashioned baronial effect enhanced by heavy oak that covered the steel beams.

Gillette, who had gained fame and a substantial fortune for his stage portrayals of the detective Sherlock Holmes, was also an inveterate tinkerer and a lover of gadgets. This combination of showman and inventor is apparent in the house through many amusing features: Second-floor mirrors were placed so Gillette could see who was arriving while remaining hidden himself (in case he wished to be unavailable); the bar—defiantly installed during Prohibition—sported a clever locking mechanism that baffled guests. And no visit to the castle was complete without a whirlwind ride on Gillette's private railroad. From his own railroad station, called "grand central," Gillette would take the controls of one of his two locomotives and drive guests over bridges and through tunnels along a 3-mile track at 20 miles an hour.

The actor occupied his congenial castle until his death in 1937 at the age of 83. His will held the stipulation that the house not fall into the hands of "any blithering saphead or person who does not know who he is or with what surrounded." Today the state of Connecticut owns and maintains the castle, which displays original furnishings and personal items, including stage props Gillette used in his performances as Sherlock Holmes.

22 *Gillette Castle* 67 River Road, East Haddam, Conn. 06423. (860) 526-2336. Site is undergoing renovation in 1999, call for hours. ⑤ ♿ 🍴 🅿 🏛

Hill-Stead Museum

FARMINGTON, CONNECTICUT

Landmark House by a Pioneering Architect
A milestone in American architectural history, Hill-Stead was built between 1898 and 1901 to designs by Theodate Pope Riddle, one of the first women in the country to become a licensed professional architect. (Riddle also completed other private homes and schools in Connecticut and worked on the restoration of Theodore Roosevelt's boyhood home in New York.) Riddle designed Hill-Stead for her parents, Ada and Alfred A. Pope, who desired a gracious retirement home in which to display their accumulated artworks and entertain society friends.

The picturesque residence, planned in consultation with the architecture firm McKim, Mead & White, represents an early example of colonial revival architecture. Such is the charm of the house that for many years it was believed to be the work of the eminent Stanford White himself. Riddle's handsome, white-clapboard exterior presents a two-story columned porch across the front facade, a feature inspired by the similarly broad and welcoming piazza George Washington designed for his home, Mount Vernon (see p. 105).

A splendid collection of Impressionist paintings, one of the earliest private assemblages of its type, distinguishes Hill-Stead as a significant New England residential museum. Alfred Pope, a wealthy industrialist, purchased French and American Impressionist masterpieces by such artists as Monet, Degas, Whistler, and Cassatt. The paintings themselves inspired the multihued interior decorating schemes. The Popes' many trips to Europe also yielded a significant assortment of furniture, sculpture, ceramics, and silver. For her part, Theodate acquired early American pieces consistent with her vision for the home.

Located in the historic town of Farmington, Hill-Stead's flourishing 152 acres functioned as a working farm for many years. Recent research uncovered plans, dated circa 1916, by the noted landscape architect Beatrix Farrand for a formal garden at Hill-Stead. Restored in 1986 with historical and modern foliage, the profusely planted sunken garden blooms from April through September. The house was opened to the public in 1947, preserved in its entirety with all its contents as instructed by Theodate Riddle at her death.

23 *Hill-Stead Museum* 35 Mountain Road, Farmington, Conn. 06032. (860) 677-9064. Open Tues.-Sun. ⑤ 🚶 ♿ 🅿 🏛

Old Westbury Gardens

OLD WESTBURY, NEW YORK

*A Long
Island Manor
in Old English
Style*

Built in 1904, the opulent estate known as Old Westbury Gardens resurrected on Long Island the essence of the great 17th-century English country manors. Englishman George Abraham Crawley designed the lavishly appointed mansion and gardens for financier and sportsman John Shaffer Phipps, and his wife, Margarita Grace, shortly after their marriage. John was the son of Henry Phipps, a longtime partner of the industrialist Andrew Carnegie. The Phippses selected an area north of the Hempstead Plain on Long Island for their house, acquiring 200 acres in what had been an 18th-century Quaker community. Crawley was assisted by the American architect Grosvenor Atterbury, who was responsible for the engineering aspects of the plan, and by John Phipps himself, each man contributing ideas as the design materialized. Mrs. Phipps applied her talents and refined tastes to the landscape plans, developing a sophisticated traditional English garden surrounding the residence.

The estate is filled with unexpected surprises: architectural follies in the gardens, contrasting north and south facades at the house, and hidden doorways and closets inside. Note how the three-story, Charles II-style mansion built of red brick and stone offers a relatively simple north front, with the central entryway dramatically emphasized by a columned, one-story, projecting portico. Above, an oversized, arched brick dormer inset with a Palladian window dominates the roofline. In comparison, the more complex south facade is distinguished by matching end pavilions that frame the Red Ballroom inside.

Guests ascended to the ballroom from the south lawn by an enormous ceremonial stairway, adorned at the sides by large topiary plantings. Climbing wisteria leading up the stairway formed a colorful, fragrant transition between garden and house. The family enjoyed entertaining in luxury, with afternoon tea in the White Drawing Room, banquets in the mahogany-paneled dining room, and formal parties in the Red Ballroom.

As you enter each room, look up and see the trompe l'oeil, three-dimensional painted ceilings framed by a rich variety of delicate plaster-cast moldings in the Adamesque style. Each space is marked by a striking diversity in color and arrangement and appointed with fine furniture and art. Georgian period pieces are displayed in the front hall, also notable for its immense marble mantel and an elaborately carved wood screen at the main stairs. In Margarita's study, a hidden closet, disguised by facsimiles of bookbindings, held costly violins—a Stradivarius and a Guarnerius. The Phippses' decorative arts collection emphasizes 18th-century pieces, including a pair of English lead sphinxes on the south terrace, paintings by Sir Joshua Reynolds, hand-painted Chinese wallpaper, and oriental porcelains. Additional objects dating from the 17th century include a number of William & Mary furnishings.

The gardens of Old Westbury were planned and executed with the same attention to detail. Wrought-iron gates, ornamental pools, fountains, and statuary decorate the themed areas, including a lilac walk, a rose garden, and a boxwood garden noted for its 200-year-old boxwood specimens. Hybridized roses, not yet released to the public, are displayed in the All-American Rose Selection trial garden, judged annually for awards. When visiting the

A wrought-iron gate decorated with hunting symbols frames the southern facade of Westbury House.

Enormous walls of glass in the west porch at Westbury House seem to bring the landscape within.

estate, be sure to stroll along the fancifully named Primrose Path to the playful Cottage Garden, where you can enjoy such miniatures as log cabins and a thatched cottage presented to the Phippses' only daughter, Peggie, for her tenth birthday. Later in life, Peggie Phipps Boegner initiated the establishment of Old Westbury Gardens as a nonprofit property open to the public.

24 *Old Westbury Gardens* 71 Old Westbury Road, Old Westbury, N.Y. 11568. (516) 333-0048. Open late April through Dec. www.plantamerica.org/oldwestbury

---

NEARBY: **Falaise** *(Sands Point Preserve, 95 Middleneck Road, Sands Point, N.Y. 516-571-7900)* Built for a member of the Guggenheim family in 1924, Falaise was designed to resemble a French manor house and still displays original furnishings. **Sagamore Hill** *(20 Sagamore Hill Road, Oyster Bay, N.Y. 516-922-4447)* Theodore Roosevelt's home and "summer White House," noted for its Queen Anne-style design and wide porches, remains furnished as it was during his lifetime.

Hudson River Mansions

Lyndhurst, Kykuit, Boscobel, Vanderbilt Mansion, Mills Mansion, Montgomery Place, Olana

Few American landscapes east of the Rockies rival the grandeur of New York's Hudson River Valley. The broad river and the mountains that loom over it inspired painters and writers, including Henry James who declared the valley part of the "geography of the ideal." Steeped in history since the days of the Dutch colonists, the Hudson took on a new role in the 19th century as the retreat of New York's wealthy families. Livingstons, Vanderbilts, and Rockefellers put up mansions with restful views of a rolling landscape and a soothing river which, at an appropriate distance, also bustled with the commerce that augmented their wealth. Linked with the nation's interior by the Erie Canal in 1825, the Hudson became a commercial highway that vastly enriched New York City, creating crowds, confusion, and the need to escape to the riverside. Many of the great houses remain today in splendid isolation, with views much as they were in the early 19th century, when Washington Irving described the sight Rip Van Winkle saw: "the lordly Hudson ... moving on its silent but majestic course." Conveniently for the modern traveler, the Hudson Valley's architectural treasures lie mainly along the eastern shore, within a reasonable driving distance of each other.

Lyndhurst

TARRYTOWN, NEW YORK

A Robber Baron's Gothic Revival Palace on the Hudson

Lyndhurst stands as a supreme image of picturesque Gothic Revival residential architecture in the United States, while its size and grandeur illustrate the rising fortunes of three New York families. The estate is along the Hudson bluffs only 30 miles from Manhattan, a convenient location for prosperous urbanites seeking a quiet retreat from the rapidly expanding population of New York City. In 1838, Gen. William Paulding, a former mayor of New York, commissioned Alexander Jackson Davis to create a Tudor Gothic villa on the banks of the Hudson River for his retirement years. Lyndhurst is unique in the extent of its Gothic Revival theme, with windows, stained glass, doors, mantels, and decor following a similar motif. Davis, a prolific and talented architect, designed the interiors and furnishings as well, completing bookcases, chairs, tables, and bedposts.

In 1864 a new owner, George Merritt, worked with Davis to expand the mansion to more than twice its original size, literally raising the roof to increase the scale of the house. Merritt, a merchant who held the patent for a railroad car spring, desired a majestic residence to convey his newly monied status. Under his direction, Davis added the lofty square tower rising to the north, a dining room and library wing, and an open veranda around three sides of the building. The interiors were also remodeled, with Gothic-style plasterwork ribs applied to the ceilings, arched spandrels installed to define the wall spaces, and ornamental hoods placed over windows and doors.

The stone exterior of Lyndhurst offers a "picturesque outline of towers, turrets, gables, and pinnacles," according to Alexander Jackson Davis, the house's original architect.

In 1880, financier Jay Gould purchased the property, commuting to his office on Wall Street aboard his 150-foot yacht. Gould and his heirs retained the property for the next 80 years, expanding the estate and elaborating on the fine details of the home. Additions included an indoor swimming pool modeled on classical Roman baths and a shingle-style building housing a two-lane bowling alley. The last private owner, Anna, Duchess of Tallyrand-Perigord, youngest daughter of Jay Gould, bequeathed the property to the National Trust for Historic Preservation in the early 1960s. The residence now accommodates the cumulative collections of the three families, representing a remarkable portrait of great wealth and high-style taste.

㉕ *Lyndhurst: A National Trust Historic Site* 635 SOUTH BROADWAY, TARRYTOWN, N.Y. 10591. (914) 631-4481. OPEN MID-APRIL THROUGH OCT. TUES.-SUN.; NOV. TO MID-APRIL SAT.-SUN. WWW.NTHP.ORG

NEARBY: **Sunnyside** *(150 White Plains Road, Tarrytown, N.Y. 914-591-8763)* Built before the Civil War, the home of author Washington Irving still contains many of his furnishings, books, and memorabilia.

Kykuit

POCANTICO HILLS, NEW YORK

A Restful Country Retreat for the Rockefellers

Atop a hill that early Dutch settlers had named Kykuit (pronounced kie-kit), meaning "lookout" for its sweeping view of the Hudson River and its palisades, John D. Rockefeller built a country retreat that later became one of the Rockefeller family's main residences. The first version of Kykuit had hardly been completed in 1908 when Rockefeller declared his dissatisfaction with the house—the fireplaces smoked, noise from the delivery entrance disrupted his sleep, and many rooms felt cramped. Although the Standard Oil magnate, famed for his personal frugality, did not want a palatial house, he did want a comfortable one. The family decided to remodel the residence, using the services of architects Chester Holmes Aldrich and William Adams Delano, interior designer Ogden Codman, Jr., and landscape architect William Welles Bosworth. In 1909 the team set to work, raising the old roof to create ample bedrooms on the third and fourth floors, removing colonial revival porches, and adorning the facade with a sculpted pediment. Although the completed house exuded a more extravagant feel than Rockefeller had originally desired, the graciousness of its classical facade and English country house interior won him over.

Codman's interiors reflect beaux arts planning, moving away from lavish Victorianism to a more restrained classicism. Pilasters, columns, moldings, and sculpture recall the English houses of William Kent, with light colors softening and enriching the interior. Note, for example, how Codman's placement of Sheridan-style chairs upholstered in a soft cream and blue in the drawing room was a leap back in time over the dark, cluttered interiors of the Victorian era into the atmosphere of 18th-century Adamesque designs. His work caught the attention of other tastemakers, with *House Beautiful* magazine praising in 1909 how Kykuit's drawing room was "entirely removed from the elaborate and overdone schemes often found in the homes of American millionaires."

Walk into the music room, which also serves as a staircase hall, and look up at the oculus, or oval opening in the ceiling. This feature is reminiscent of one in a 17th-century London residence, Ashburnham House. Still in place is the family's 1908 Steinway piano, but unlike many grand country houses built in the early part of this century, Kykuit contains no ballroom—being strict Baptists, John D. and his wife, Laura, permitted no dancing or drinking in their home. The dining room, however, was the scene of many dinner parties that feted leaders from around the world, including Presidents Lyndon Johnson and Richard Nixon, King Hussein of Jordan, President Anwar Sadat of Egypt, and British Prime Minister Edward Heath. They dined under the gaze of John D. Rockefeller, whose 1917 portrait by John Singer Sargent hangs in the room. The library combines the architectural formality of pilasters and pediments with comfortable furniture for the entire family grouped near the fireplace, revealing their emphasis on reading and education.

The gardens remain faithful to Bosworth's plan and are generally considered his finest work. They borrow from European sources, combining the formal Italian style with the informal English landscape. Near the house, for example, you will see how hedges and trees in geometrical alignments frame views of the surrounding natural landscape. A series of courtyards and garden spaces emanate from the house, while symmetry and order integrate building and landscape harmoniously. Farther from the mansion, an informal landscape creates a peaceful setting in a picturesque English style.

Kykuit's classical facade (above) complements the house's elegant interior. A portrait of Senator Nelson Aldrich, John D. Rockefeller, Jr.'s father-in-law, hangs in the music room (opposite).

The builder's grandson Nelson Rockefeller, Governor of New York and Vice President of the United States, lived at Kykuit from 1960 until his death in 1979. He converted several downstairs rooms into galleries for his noted collection of modern American art, and placed 120 pieces from his renowned collection of outdoor sculpture on the grounds, including works by Pablo Picasso, Constantin Brancusi, Alberto Giacometti, Alexander Calder, Henry Moore, and Louise Nevelson.

26 *Kykuit* POCANTICO HILLS, TARRYTOWN, N.Y. 10591. (914) 631-9491. OPEN DAILY. TOURS DEPART FROM PHILIPSBURG MANOR, SLEEPY HOLLOW, N.Y., CALL AHEAD FOR TICKETS AND DIRECTIONS.

Boscobel

GARRISON, NEW YORK

An Adamesque Dream House Rescued and Restored

Elegant Boscobel was built in the early 1800s for States Morris Dyckman, who had lived in England and was familiar with the Adamesque British homes that gave inspiration to the federal period on these shores. Though its architecture is superb, Boscobel has also become widely known for its outstanding collection of a federal-period decorative arts. Of Dutch ancestry, States Morris Dyckman remained a loyal British subject during the Revolution, living in England from 1778 to 1789, and returning there again a decade later. Having secured a fortune for his services to British quartermasters during the Revolution, Dyckman purchased many items while abroad, including china, jewelry, and books—items he hoped projected an image of wealth to those around him.

In 1804 Dyckman began constructing a two-story country house with a recessed portico and porch on the front facade. Most of the materials had been purchased, but only the foundation was complete when Dyckman succumbed to a chronic illness. His wife, Elizabeth, 18 years his junior, took over and finished the project, adding furniture and decorative arts to the great number of expensive items inherited from her husband. Following her death in 1823, Boscobel remained in the family until 1888, when it passed into the hands of the final owner's creditors.

A long period of uncertainty ensued. The house was threatened with demolition in 1924, but purchased by the Veterans Administration with the intention of making it into a hospital. In 1955, unoccupied, it was sold for $35 to a demolition company. In a final effort to save the house, Harvey Stevenson, then the head of a concerned organization called Boscobel, Inc., purchased the facade and moved most of the woodwork to Long Island. Meanwhile Boscobel Restoration, Inc., a new group under the leadership of Benjamin West Frazier, managed to raise enough money to disassemble the remaining structure and have it moved to a new, but as yet undetermined location. Friends and neighbors stored pieces of the house while Frazier worked on finding a new spot. An anonymous donation of $50,000 finally allowed the purchase of the present 15-acre lot approximately 15 miles north of its original location. Boscobel's woodwork was retrieved from Long Island and a full-scale restoration began. The anonymous donor revealed herself as Lila Acheson Wallace, cofounder of *Reader's Digest*, who continued to work with Boscobel Restoration, Inc. to restore the house.

Unexpectedly, inventories of the Dyckman furnishings and receipts for later purchases made by Elizabeth were found in the 1970s, allowing for a historically accurate restoration to the federal period. Thus today you can see reproduction and federal-period furniture mingled with such original Dyckman pieces as a dessert service purchased by States Dyckman while abroad. Of particular note are a pair of rare yellow upholstered cabriole chairs, made between 1795 and 1805 in England or America and believed to have been owned by the Livingston family. Sideboards represented a new fashion in America in the early 1800s—and Boscobel's dining room features a handsome mahogany example, over 6 feet wide, of a Sheraton "pedestal end" sideboard made in New York in 1810. Don't miss the unusual, mahogany stand from the New York shop of Duncan Phyfe, used at teatime for holding a hot-water or tea urn. Throughout the house hang portraits, by unknown artists, of both States and Elizabeth Dyckman, the latter depicted as a lovely, redheaded woman with a thoughtful expression.

27 *Boscobel* 1601 N.Y. 9D, GARRISON, N.Y. 10524. (914) 265-3638. OPEN DAILY APRIL THROUGH DEC. WWW.BOSCOBEL.ORG

Vanderbilt Mansion

HYDE PARK, NEW YORK

A Renaissance Palazzo for a Shy Vanderbilt

Completed in 1898 at a cost of three million dollars, this Hyde Park estate was the spectacular setting for the spring and fall recreations of a branch of the Vanderbilt family. Frederick William Vanderbilt purchased the site and existing house in 1895, at the suggestion of his friend and subsequent Hudson Valley neighbor Ogden Mills. Like his siblings, Frederick had inherited ten million dollars from his father, but he was the only Vanderbilt of his generation to enlarge his fortune to the grand sum of eighty million by the time of his death. Although Frederick enjoyed many sports, especially boating and yachting, his true passion was landscape gardening. He loved all forms of nature, especially trees. While his residence would rival the other lavish estates of the era, it also included a historical natural landscape.

Long before Frederick Vanderbilt arrived on the scene, the Hyde Park estate had a reputation for outstanding romantic landscape design, widely recognized and praised by designers like Andrew Jackson Downing. The original landscape plan was executed by André Parmentier, a Belgian immigrant, for the then owner David Hosack, a physician and amateur horticulturist. One of the first landscape architects in America, Parmentier's sophisticated

The Vanderbilt Mansion's classical portico overlooks the "noble Hudson for sixty miles in its course," in the words of one 19th-century visitor to the site.

Stanford White decorated the sumptuous dining room, purchasing the 16th-century Isphahan rug and the pair of Renaissance mantels while on a European shopping spree for Vanderbilt.

design created elaborate vistas of trees, roads, bridges, garden follies, and temples while incorporating Hosack's ornamental garden and collection of specimen trees. Parmentier's original plan remained intact until Vanderbilt purchased the property.

The original house had been built for the Langdon family, who bought the property from Hosack. By the time of Vanderbilt's tenure, the mansion was structurally unstable and Charles McKim of the firm McKim, Mead & White was called in to design a new residence. McKim's plan strongly resembled the Langdon house in its overall shape but with all the grandeur of the Gilded Age.

McKim's 50-room plan merges a classical exterior with a European-inspired interior that befitted Frederick's wealth. It also improved his "new money" social standing by making an aesthetic connection with the past. The mansion's restrained exterior emphasizes good taste and classical decor, its three stories and square form recalling the Renaissance palazzos of the Medici family in Italy. Here, too, the application of the Corinthian order on the exterior porches and pilasters represented the height of wealth and style. As you stroll through the estate, you can sense how the house uses its porches to reach out into the landscape, taking advantage of the natural view and incorporating the extensive gardens. This clear relationship between building and landscape reflected Frederick's love of nature, and humanizes the sometimes overwhelming grandeur of the interior.

Most of the original decor and furnishings remain at Vanderbilt Mansion. The series of large-scale rooms on the first floor (with the more private family quarters upstairs) were designed by McKim's partner Stanford White in flamboyant styles modeled on European precedents. In the dining room, for example, note how White installed a massive ceiling painting amid gilded molding. In fact, the dimensions of the painting probably determined the size of the room. White purchased it during his European travels, along with many other features in the room, including the mantels and several pieces of antique furniture. Sumptuous fabrics and pilasters complete this formal chamber in European style, a taste that extends to other rooms in the house. Frederick's own bedroom, for example, features tapestries, carved moldings, a sculpted ceiling, and a bed flanked by spiral columns modeled after the Baldachino of St. Peter's Basilica in Vatican City. The rococo, Louis XV-style Gold Room likewise conveys a lavish image of wealth and class.

28 *Vanderbilt Mansion National Historic Site* 519 ALBANY POST ROAD, HYDE PARK, N.Y. 12538. (914) 229-9115. OPEN DAILY. WWW.NPS.GOV/VAMA 🅢 🔥 ♿ 🅿 🏛

NEARBY: **FDR Memorial** *(511 Albany Post Road, Hyde Park, N.Y. 914-229-8114)* The lifelong home of Franklin D. Roosevelt and the nation's first presidential library contain memorabilia from all periods of the lives of the 32nd President and his wife, Eleanor.

Mills Mansion

STAATSBURG, NEW YORK

The Hudson Valley's House of Mirth A classic example of Hudson Valley grandeur, the Mills Mansion revels in a spectacular beaux arts design. The original, 1832 Greek Revival structure belonged to Morgan Lewis and his wife, Gertrude, née Livingston. Ogden and Ruth Livingston Mills, who inherited the mansion and its 1,600 acres fronting the Hudson River in 1888, decided to engage Stanford White to enlarge and redesign their home.

White set to work, building a new classical pediment with six Ionic columns, removing the original wings and adding new, two-story wings, raising the center section an additional two stories, and completely refinishing the building's exterior. With his modifications to the bright, stuccoed exterior, the architect sought to evoke images of an 18th-century English house. Inside, the rooms recall various beaux arts styles, with marble, gilt, and oak paneling. The dining room, in Louis XIV style, extends 50 feet in length, as does the library. Among the original family furnishings on display today, you will see four 18th-century Flemish tapestries probably purchased for the house by Stanford White, as well as Chinese and Japanese ceramics collected by Mills' uncle, and French clocks collected by Mills himself.

The Mills family lived here for half the winter season, from September until January, when they moved to another of their five estates. Their lifestyle included a variety of outdoor activities—riding, boating, tennis, and golf—as well as hosting lavish parties for society friends. In 1905, the mansion gained literary immortality as the model for Bellomont in Edith Wharton's novel *The House of Mirth*. When talking to locals, do not be surprised to hear the mansion called Staatsburg, the name which the Livingstons gave it. By either name, the elaborate residence continues to recall the Gilded Age in grand style.

29 *Mills Mansion State Historic Site (Staatsburg)* OLD POST ROAD, STAATSBURG, N.Y. 12580. (914) 889-8851. OPEN APRIL THROUGH OCT. WED.-SUN., call for DEC. hours. 🅢 🔥 ♿ 🅿 🏛

Montgomery Place

ANNANDALE-ON-HUDSON, NEW YORK

A Livingston Estate for Nearly Two Centuries

On 434 scenic acres of land overlooking the Hudson River, Montgomery Place began as a dignified farmhouse and was later transformed into the romantic, classical revival residence seen today. As a home of New York's prominent Livingston family, it reflects nearly 200 years of aristocratic history and serves particularly as a monument to the women of the family, whose vision created and nurtured the estate.

Janet Livingston Montgomery, the widow of Gen. Richard Montgomery, a Revolutionary War hero killed in 1775, purchased the property in 1802. She built a simple, two-story, federal-style house of stuccoed fieldstone and became a horticultural entrepreneur, planting orchards and constructing a greenhouse and nursery. The house passed in succession to her youngest brother, Edward Livingston, his wife Louise, and their daughter, Coralie, who occupied the estate as a summer home until 1873. Louise commissioned architect Alexander Jackson Davis, famous for his picturesque country house designs along the Hudson River, to undertake two separate renovations, shaping the building into a more imposing, but still charming, country residence. While preserving the early 19th-century floor plan, Davis added three porches, a continuous veranda, and a south wing. The north porch, an open columned portico topped by a balustrade, was believed to be one of the first outdoor living spaces in the United States—a trend that grew in popularity. For the renovation of the grounds, Coralie and her husband Thomas Barton turned to Andrew Jackson Downing, the renowned 19th-century architect and landscape designer, who suggested placement for the statuary, walks, fountains, and ornamental ponds, and influenced the planning of the extensive gardens.

After Coralie's death, the house and grounds fell into decline. Later heirs to the estate, Gen. John Ross and Violetta White Delafield, brought it back to life, restoring the landscape and complementing the original plan with the addition of terraced gardens, a hedged ellipse with reflecting pool, and an artificial stream bubbling through a romantic garden.

30 *Montgomery Place Historic Estate* RIVER ROAD, ANNANDALE-ON-HUDSON, N.Y. 12504. (914) 758-5461. OPEN APRIL THROUGH OCT. WED.-MON.; NOV. TO MID-DEC. SAT.-SUN. WWW. HUDSONVALLEY.ORG 🅢 🛉 ♿ 🅿 🛖

Olana

HUDSON, NEW YORK

Moorish Fantasy on a Hudson Valley Hilltop

Olana, a Moorish-style mansion overlooking the Hudson River, seamlessly integrates landscape and architecture into a breathtaking work of art. Designed, built, and modified by the artist Frederic Edwin Church over the course of 40 years—from 1860 until his death in 1900—Olana remains his triumph. As a young painter, Church studied with Thomas Cole, whose property was located directly across the river from the 20-acre estate where Olana would be built. By 1860, then a world famous—and wealthy—artist, Church decided to build a "feudal castle" for his family on the familiar hilltop.

Rising up out of the golden landscape, Olana is a dramatic ensemble of colorful towers, balconies, recessed porches, and awnings.

Islamic-inspired archways frame the view of the Hudson River Valley from a balcony on Olana's main tower.

Church spent the first several years as a property owner reshaping the landscape—creating vistas as he would on canvas. The death of two of his children from diphtheria in 1865 induced Church to take his family abroad, first to England and then on to the Middle East. The extent to which Islamic architecture influenced the artist became clear upon his return as, with help from Calvert Vaux, he began to redesign his house. The connection was made stronger with the name of the property, Olana, after a fortified treasure-house in a region of ancient Persia reputed to be the site of the Garden of Eden.

Accented by a tower of pointed arches and vivid, multihued tiles, the exterior of the house is unmistakably Moorish, and immediately alluring. Inside, Church painstakingly mixed paints to precisely achieve the delicate tones he could see in his imagination (colors also used in some of his great paintings). Note, too, the sculpted wood screens that veil the windows and create patterns of light that fall on decorative motifs of abstracted natural and geometric forms. The furniture, carefully selected and carefully placed, carries the Moorish aesthetic throughout the house. The large center hall, called the Court Hall, showcases the artist's collection of Persian armor, Chinese and Japanese scrolls, Mexican religious art, and a pair of life-size bronze cranes.

31 *Olana State Historic Site* N.Y. 9G, Hudson, N.Y. 12534. (518) 828-0135. Open April through Oct. Wed.-Sun., call for tour reservations. 🅢 🏃 ♿ 🅿 🏛

*B*oldt Castle

ALEXANDRIA BAY, NEW YORK

A Magnificent Castle, Built for Love

Located on one of the Thousand Islands strung across the St. Lawrence River, Boldt Castle is a stunning 120-room residence reminiscent of a Rhineland castle. Towers, spires, and steeply pitched gables rise dramatically above the river. But the granite structure gives no hint of the heartbreaking story behind its construction. George C. Boldt, a Prussian immigrant, started as a restaurant worker in New York City and worked his way up to become a millionaire hotel magnate. Reported by the New York press at the time of his death as the "best hotel man in the world," he owned the Bellevue-Stratford in Philadelphia, and was proprietor of the Waldorf-Astoria in New York City, which he managed for William Waldorf Astor and his cousin, John Jacob Astor. An avid yachtsman, Boldt purchased Hart Island, changed its name to "Heart," and reconfigured the land into a heart shape—all to express his love for his wife, Louise.

In 1900 Boldt hired 300 stonemasons, carpenters, and artists to build an 11-building castle complex that included tunnels, a drawbridge, a dovecote, and Italian gardens. Then, in January 1904, with 90 percent of the work finished and 2.5 million dollars spent, Louise suddenly died. Boldt telegrammed the workers to stop construction immediately. Heartbroken, he never set foot on the island again. For more than 70 years the unfinished castle stood empty, ravaged by weather and vandals. The Thousand Islands Bridge Authority acquired the estate in 1977, and to date has spent 11.5 million dollars on improvements and rehabilitation in order to open the site to the public.

The castle is remarkable. The grand entry hall is lit by a skylight in a central dome four stories above. The reception room, filled with Louis XV-style furniture, has ornate plaster-paneled walls and a fireplace inlaid with pink marble. The billiard room, with fine oak paneling and an elaborate plasterwork ceiling, features a period Brunswick billiard table. The dining room includes the original, enormous oak table seating 18 and the family's English china, Tiffany finger bowls, and sterling silver emblazoned with the Boldt crest.

Instead of his castle, George Boldt made use of the Yacht House on neighboring Wellesley Island, an extraordinary example of shingle-style architecture built in 1899. The building, rising 64 feet above the water, would have offered Boldt a melancholy view of his abandoned dream house just across the river. In 1916, on the day of his funeral, attended by some 2,000 mourners, a New York newspaper reported the following exchange: "E. C. Bingham, for almost a score of years chief engineer of the Waldorf, looked up Chief Inspector Max Schmittberger yesterday to see about funeral arrangements. 'I suppose they'll be no objection, inspector . . . to having the funeral pass up Madison Avenue to the church?' 'Madison Avenue—hell!' cried the chief inspector, thumping his desk. 'George Boldt's body is going up the same street the President always goes up—Fifth Avenue—even if we have to hold up traffic for an hour.'"

32 *Boldt Castle* THOUSAND ISLANDS BRIDGE AUTHORITY, COLLINS LANDING, ALEXANDRIA BAY, N.Y. 13607. (315) 482-9724. OPEN DAILY. 🟢 ♿ 🍴 🏛

Following pages: An aerial view of Boldt Castle and its outbuildings, located on the 5-acre, heart-shaped, appropriately named Heart Island.

Ringwood Manor and Skylands
RINGWOOD BOROUGH, NEW JERSEY

From Iron Forges to Tranquil Gardens

The cultivated luxury displayed at Ringwood Manor and Skylands, equally genteel estates begun nearly a century apart, embodies the rising fortunes of early industrialists in the 19th and 20th centuries. Both of these grand residences are filled with antiques and surrounded by radiant gardens. They stand on their original locations, now part of Ringwood State Park in a region where iron forges and mines operated for more than 200 years, fed by rich deposits discovered in the nearby Ramapo Mountains. Elite members of society took up residence in the area, particularly after 1850, seeking country retreats for relaxation and forays into gardening.

Ringwood Manor, the older of the two, was once the largest house in America, boasting 51 rooms. This palatial residence began as a modest three-story federal-style building constructed in 1807 by Martin Ryerson, an accomplished ironmaster. Peter Cooper purchased the house and 22,000 acres of land in 1853, selling it just a year later to Abram S. Hewitt. The Hewitt family possessed one of the largest personal fortunes in the country and, not lacking in wealth or wanting in leisure, consistently expanded the home over a period of 15 years. Between 1864 and 1879, they added 41 rooms, including 15 bathrooms, 28 bedrooms, and 24 fireplaces. The family's ever larger mansion was composed of variously sized and shaped buildings with Dutch, Tudor, and Italian influences. Noted architect Stanford White contributed to the mix as well, designing the porte cochere on the south side of the house. A single roof and whitened cement stucco exterior unify the eclectic lot. Inside, the rooms are as diverse as the exterior appearance indicates, with colonial, Empire, and Gothic Revival themes throughout, reflecting the stylistic tastes of the owners. In 1936, Erskine Hewitt deeded the house and a portion of the property to the state of New Jersey, forming the core of Ringwood State Park.

Thirty years later, the state acquired Skylands, now the official home of the New Jersey Botanical Gardens. The manor and its extensively planted landscape date from the early 20th century, when Clarence Lewis, a civil engineer, purchased the land and demolished the original Victorian house on the site. Lewis commissioned John Russell Pope, architect of Franklin D. Roosevelt's home in Hyde Park, New York, to create an enormous

Ringwood Manor's grand white exterior led the mansion to be called the Second White House.

half-timbered Tudor Revival mansion set within formal and informal gardens. Pope's attention to detail within the three-story, 44-room mansion is evident in the native granite exterior walls, wavy patterned slate roof, wood-paneled rooms, and arched, ribbed ceiling in the towering great hall. Intricate chimney groupings, crenelated walls, parapets, and gables with intersecting dormers complete this picturesque arrangement. The 16th-century, English Tudor theme is continued inside, with stone and pegged-oak veneer floors, carved-stone arched doorways, and wrought-iron chandeliers designed by Samuel Yellin, a master in decorative metalwork. Forty antique stained-glass medallions from German, Bavarian, and Swiss sites may be seen in the house, many set into the seven tall and elegant windows within the great hall.

The visitor will observe that Skylands is an aptly named estate, as every window in the home has a view onto the lush countryside. Within the New Jersey Botanical Gardens, 5,000 species and varieties of plants are protected and propagated. Endangered and unique specimens populate Skylands, including the fringed gentian, adopted as the symbol of the botanical garden, and a local climbing hydrangea known as the Skylands Giant. The English-style gardens, ranging from formal areas to parklike expanses and forested areas, were set out by Vitale & Giffert under the watchful eye of Clarence Lewis, who personally tended this land for more than 30 years with the help of nearly 60 gardeners. The long cultural legacies of Ringwood Manor and Skylands can now be enjoyed by visitors to these tranquil country retreats, once distinguished homes for the Hewitt and Lewis families.

33 ***Ringwood Manor and Skylands*** Ringwood State Park, Sloatsburg Road, Ringwood, N.J. 07456. Ringwood (973) 962-7031; Skylands (973) 962-7527. Open Wed.-Sun. ⑤ 🚶 ♿ 🅿 🛗

*G*lenmont

WEST ORANGE, NEW JERSEY

Thomas
Edison's
Exuberant
Home

The splendors of the Victorian age and the legacy of an American genius endure at Glenmont, the longtime home of Thomas Alva Edison and his family. Edison, the inventor of such now everyday objects as the electric light, phonograph, and motion pictures, lived here with his wife, Mina, and their three children from 1886 until his death in 1931. The house was originally built for Henry C. Pedder, an executive at the New York department store Arnold Constable & Company. Pedder commissioned Henry Hudson Holly in 1880 to design and build a stylish Queen Anne mansion at Llewellyn Park, one of the first planned "streetcar suburbs" within commuting distance of New York City. Holly, author of two pattern books of Victorian homes and interiors, created the house as a showcase for his work. After occupying the house for only two years, Pedder was accused of embezzlement and fled the country. His employer acquired the house for a dollar, and sold it fully furnished to Thomas Edison for $125,000—about half its real value. Edison, then 39 and a widower, was delighted at the opportunity to buy the house, which he offered as a wedding gift to his new wife, Mina Miller. "To think that it was possible to buy a place like this," Edison remarked, "the idea fairly turned my head and I snapped it up. It is a great deal too nice for me, but it isn't half nice enough for my little wife here."

Glenmont is instantly recognizable as a prominent example of the Queen Anne style, with its steeply pitched cross-gable roof and high brick chimneys embellished with floral terra-cotta inserts. Every exterior surface above the first floor is covered with patterned shingles, wood clapboards, and decorative cutouts. The interior of the 29-room house reflects the shift in decorating taste away from the dark-toned, flamboyant decor of the 19th-century Victorian era. The original interior finishes were designed by Holly in cooperation with Pottier and Stymus, a premier cabinetmaking and decorating firm in New York. Note the different types of wood that characterize each room: oak in the entry hall, rosewood in the drawing room, and mahogany in the dining room. The styles of the fireplace mantels are equally diverse, following Italianate and colonial revival motifs.

A few rooms remain unchanged from the early period, including the reception hall, where you will see original Lincrusta-Walton wall coverings made of wood pulp and linseed oil, embossed with patterns and painted to match the decor. Then walk into the library where the ceiling is decorated with a multicolored border of delicate painted patterns framed by wood molding. Surprisingly, many of the books in this room did not belong to Edison, but were conveyed in the sale of the home from Pedder.

Edison preferred to read in the upstairs living room, built over the porte cochere in 1905. The family spent their evenings in this quiet area, furnished with separate desks for Edison and Mina. The Edisons also finished a downstairs den begun by Pedder, and enclosed a portion of the wraparound porch to create a serene glass-walled conservatory illuminated by unshaded bulbs. On the grounds, they constructed a number of outbuildings, including a two-story, six-car garage with a turntable.

At Glenmont the Edisons entertained many notable historic figures, including Henry Ford, Helen Keller, and Orville Wright. Edison died in 1931 in the master bedroom and is buried behind the house. In 1946, Mina left the house and grounds to a nonprofit institution

Though at first glance he thought Glenmont "a great deal too nice for me," Thomas Edison grew to love the stylish wood-brick-and-stone dwelling. The famous inventor (inset) greets his friend, Henry Ford, at Glenmont circa 1920.

as a memorial to Edison and his work. Today, Glenmont tells the story of Edison's family life while the nearby laboratories interpret his career as inventor and scientist, with the entire complex preserved by the National Park Service as the Thomas Edison National Historic Site.

34 *Glenmont* THOMAS EDISON NATIONAL HISTORIC SITE, MAIN STREET AND LAKESIDE AVENUE, WEST ORANGE, N.J. 07052. (973) 736-0550. OPEN WED.-SUN. BY GUIDED TOUR ONLY, CALL FOR HOURS. WWW.NPS.GOV/EDIS

Fonthill

DOYLESTOWN, PENNSYLVANIA

A Soaring Fantasy Castle, Fit for a Fairy Tale

Fonthill is one of the most unusual houses in Pennsylvania, expressing the signature style of its idiosyncratic and visionary owner, Henry Mercer. A leader in the Arts and Crafts movement in the United States, an archaeologist, and the developer of a line of architectural tiles, Mercer created the home over four years, beginning in 1908. The result was the whimsical realization of Mercer's dream for a 20th-century castle, a showroom for his artistic creations, and a museum for his extensive collection of tiles and prints acquired worldwide.

Funded by an inheritance from a rich aunt, Mercer set about building an entirely unique home designed from the inside out, plotting the rooms one by one as inspiration struck him—he designed the exterior only after he had planned all the interior spaces. The house is enormous, with 42 rooms (but only 5 bedrooms), 18 fireplaces, 32 stairwells connecting 7 levels, and more than 200 windows. As appropriate for a poured-in-place, reinforced concrete construction, Mercer utilized clay models rather than blueprints to work out his plans.

Inside, the house is astonishingly eclectic. Mercer fused a variety of architectural styles, including Gothic and Italianate, into a personal and distinctive house that defies ordinary description. Despite his unusual method of planning room by room, a house that could have seemed random possesses instead a remarkable unity and spontaneity. Mercer used no wallpaper—every room is instead adorned with tiles in abundance, colorfully illustrating fictional and historical stories, creating patterns over columns, walls, and mantels. Mercer's famous "Moravian" tiles (manufactured in his factory, which is still operating on the grounds) are set into the concrete along with foreign and exotic pieces amassed during his many international adventures. More than 900 prints and other objects once owned by Mercer remain in the house, testimony to his passion for collecting and his flair for unusual arrangements.

A visit to the house is akin to a tour of a troll's palace. The first-floor "saloon," or great room, boasts a beautifully tiled, vaulted ceiling. Here Mercer displayed ancient Babylonian clay tablets made some four thousand years ago. An atmosphere of mystery and magic pervades, as visitors make their way from the saloon up narrow, winding staircases, moving from the dimness of the stairs into one room after another stuffed with Mercer's fascinating collections. His study, brilliantly sunlit through high-arched windows on three sides, displays Native American tools eight to ten thousand years old. Finally, the visitor emerges onto the roof of the mansion, offering a broad view of the surrounding grounds.

Mercer inscribed the motto "Plus Ultra" over the fireplace in the library. The meaning, "more beyond," aptly sums up the visitor's experience at Fonthill, where something different always awaits discovery and the expectation of more is invariably satisfied.

35 *Fonthill Museum* East Court Street, Doylestown, Pa. 18901. (215) 348-9461. Open daily. www.libertynet.org/bchs

Fonthill's saloon, or main gathering room, where Henry Mercer entertained his guests, is an organic merging of concrete and tiles. Here a stairway—one of 32 in the house—leads up to a balcony and more rooms.

Fallingwater

MILL RUN, PENNSYLVANIA

The Happy Flowering of Genius

On a secluded spot in the Pennsylvania woodlands, Frank Lloyd Wright designed a country house, Fallingwater, which became perhaps his most famous work. Wright took full advantage of, and inspiration from, a dramatic natural feature of the site which another architect might have seen as an obstacle to be avoided—a 20-foot waterfall. Wright defied expectation by placing the house atop the waterfall, instead of overlooking it. In doing so, he brilliantly allowed the house and the waterfall to become one.

Wright built the house as a weekend retreat for department store owner Edgar Kaufmann, Sr., and his wife, Liliane. Their son, Edgar Jr., was studying architecture at Wright's studio in Taliesen and suggested that his parents employ Wright as their architect. Although Wright's cutting-edge prairie school style had revolutionized architectural practice, by this time his career had suffered numerous scandals and he was seen as an architect past his prime. Wright was fortunate in his clients, who had not only the means to build the complex project, but the taste and enthusiasm for it as well. The Kaufmann family moved into the house in 1937 after a year-long period of construction.

Fallingwater stretched the limits of design to provide a modernist yet romantic response to the international style. Wright's plans called for the four concrete slabs that form the floors to be cantilevered out from the house over the water, with an interior stairway leading to it, allowing direct interaction with the landscape and merging the natural elements of the site with the modern materials of the building. Fallingwater exemplifies, better than any other Wright building, his concept of organic architecture. Notice how the hearth makes use of the boulder around which the house is built, and how underlying rock rises up through the living room floor. The falls, not visible from any room, can nevertheless be heard throughout the house.

Though Fallingwater was clearly intended to be a work of art, the interior is not lavish. Wright designed the house's built-in and freestanding furniture, and had the floors waxed to look like stones from a stream. The living room offers views on all three sides, and contains comfortable sofas. The furniture, made of marine-quality plywood, was veneered in black walnut, so as to prevent the site's dampness from warping the wood. The kitchens and bedrooms are small and simple, and the bathrooms, tiled in cork, offer extra-large showerheads to give the feel of bathing in a waterfall. Wright considered every aspect of the house, from the indirect lighting to the wardrobes, so that the entire structure works together. Fallingwater eventually reestablished Wright at the forefront of American architecture. Equally important, the house thrilled his clients. Edgar Kaufmann, Jr., said that the family wanted, "neither lordly stateliness nor a mimicry of frontier hardihood, but a good place for city people to renew themselves in nature." The finished house, he continued, "is a happy flowering of Wright's genius."

36 *Fallingwater* PA. 381, MILL RUN, PA. 15464. (724) 329-8501. MID-MARCH TO MID-NOV. TUES.-SUN.; MID-NOV. THROUGH DEC. SAT.-SUN. BY GUIDED TOUR ONLY. WWW.PACONSERVE.ORG 🄢 🚶 ♿ 🍴 🅿 🏛

Defying convention, architect Frank Lloyd Wright cantilevered terraces over a waterfall so that the water can be plainly heard throughout the house—but not necessarily seen.

Clayton

PITTSBURGH, PENNSYLVANIA

*A Marvel
of Victorian
Clutter*

Decorated with more than 9,000 objects and works of art original to the house—paintings and drawings jostle for space on the fabric-covered walls and even the doors—Clayton is a marvel of tasteful late Victorian clutter. The residence of millionaire industrialist Henry Clay Frick and his bride, Adelaide Howard Childs, Clayton was originally a two-story Italianate house, which local architect Frederick J. Osterling transformed in 1891-92 into a 23-room, four-story mansion in the château style. The Fricks demanded the highest quality from the New York decorators they hired to oversee the fine custom-made woodwork and furnishings. On at least one occasion Frick was not pleased, writing to the design firm: "I am very much disappointed in some of the furniture and mantels. [It is] really embarrassing to me to show it to my friends and say that it was purchased in New York."

Henry Frick's Clayton was part of Millionaire's Row in the Point Breeze section of Pittsburgh—a neighborhood that included tycoons such as Carnegie, Heinz, and Westinghouse.

As in many Victorian homes, the dining room is the most sumptuous room in the house, with a mahogany table and chairs matching the elaborate woodwork and sideboards. Be sure to notice the green-and-gold embossed leather frieze adorning the walls, as well as the special-order silver-plated light fixtures and the glass transoms that add to the splendor. The less formal breakfast room features Eastlake-style chairs, table, and sideboard custom-made in the 1880s. In this room Frick held weekly poker games with his millionaire cronies, the Mellon brothers. Though the house is filled with Frick's fabulous art collection—including paintings by Monet, Hogarth, Gainsborough, and William Michael Harnett—it is clear that Clayton was also a beloved home for his two children. You can still see the special children's entrance located near the breakfast room, with a miniature sink and an oak hat rack.

Though the Fricks moved to New York in 1905, they never sold Clayton. Their daughter, Helen, even made her debut here instead of New York—much to her father's displeasure. Toward the end of her life, Helen returned to Clayton permanently, dying here in 1984 at age 96, having arranged in her will that the house be restored and opened as a house museum.

37 *Clayton* FRICK ART & HISTORICAL CENTER, 7227 REYNOLDS STREET, PITTSBURGH, PA. 15208. (412) 371-0600. OPEN TUES.-SAT.

Winterthur Museum

WILMINGTON, DELAWARE

Henry du Pont's Home and Treasure-house of American Antiquities

Winterthur Museum contains this country's foremost private collection of American decorative arts from 1640 to 1860, with more than 89,000 objects spread throughout a mansion of almost 175 rooms. This extraordinary collection came about through the efforts of Henry Francis du Pont, who transformed his family home and farm into an unparalleled showcase of American domestic history in a beautiful garden setting.

For nearly 150 years prior to becoming a museum, the house and land had gone through a succession of changes by various members of the du Pont family. It began as a modest, flat-roofed country residence. Between 1810 and 1818, Eleuthère Irénée du Pont de Nemours, who had founded the family's gunpowder works on the Brandywine River in 1802, purchased land nearby that would one day include Winterthur. Eleuthère's daughter and son-in-law, Evelina Gabrielle and James Antoine Bidermann, built the first house at Winterthur in 1837, with plans obtained from the French architect N. Vergnaud. Bidermann named the house Winterthur after the Swiss city of his ancestry. Henry du Pont purchased Winterthur from Bidermann's descendants in 1866 as a gift for his son, Col. Henry Algernon du Pont. "The Colonel" embarked upon

The Chinese Parlor at Winterthur features hand-painted, 18th-century wallpaper portraying scenes of daily life in China. In order to display the wallpaper properly, two rooms were combined.

Federal furniture complements the Montmorenci Staircase at Winterthur. Acquired from the 1822 North Carolina home of Gen. William Williams, the staircase is a marvel of sinuous elegance.

three remodeling campaigns that transformed the original house beyond recognition. In the remodeling of 1902, designed by Philadelphia architects Robeson Lea Perot and Elliston Perot Bissell, Winterthur emerged as a château reminiscent of the great reign of François I. They added a facade with elaborate dormers, balconies, a terra-cotta cornice, and tall chimneys; attached a large wing for recreational rooms; and constructed a new roof of Spanish tile—which turned out to be so heavy that the walls of the original Bidermann house had to be rebuilt. When Colonel du Pont was elected to the U.S. Senate in 1906, control of Winterthur passed to his son, Henry Francis du Pont, the prime mover behind the splendid museum and gardens seen today.

At first Henry Francis du Pont, who had studied horticulture at Harvard, mainly devoted his attention and energy to the gardens. But in the early 1920s, a visit to Beauport, Henry Sleeper's mansion in Massachusetts (see p. 35), turned his interests toward the decorative arts. His father's death in 1926 brought Henry an inheritance commensurate with his new passion for collecting the arts of the American past. After accumulating several hundred pieces of early American furniture, decorative arts, and architectural elements, he embarked on an astounding program of acquisition—purchasing furniture and entire rooms from historic houses all over the East, from such cities as Charleston, Albany, and Salem, as well as Maryland, North Carolina, and New York.

Winterthur began to change from a home to a museum as Henry's collection grew. In 1929, to accommodate the rooms he had purchased, du Pont built an addition which doubled Winterthur's size. As designed by the local architect Albert Ely Ives, the addition reached nine stories in some places, stripping the French ornament from the exterior, and leaving a plain Georgian facade with shuttered windows, simple dormers, and prominent chimneys.

The rooms, furniture, and decorative objects du Pont collected—including paintings, ceramics, pewter, glassware, silver, woodwork, and textiles—are nothing less than treasures. As a group they preserve the evolution of American decorative taste from the 17th to the 19th centuries, intact and authentic. Thus you can view high style furnishings from the New York shop of Duncan Phyfe in their proper setting then, for a revealing contrast, tour an austere Shaker room.

Henry du Pont established a nonprofit foundation in 1930 with a view toward eventually turning the house into a museum. This became reality in 1951, when the Winterthur Museum opened to the public. Since then, expansions have further increased the size of the museum, and the name Winterthur has become synonymous with exacting connoisseurship.

38 *Winterthur Museum, Garden, and Library* Del. 52, Wilmington, Del. 19735. (302) 888-4600 or (800) 448-3883. Open daily. www.winterthur.org 🖲 🖄 ♿ 🍴 🅿 🏛

Nemours Mansion
WILMINGTON, DELAWARE

A DuPont's
Heartfelt
Tribute to
France, and to
His Beloved

One of America's wealthiest men, Alfred Irénée duPont built the palatial, French-style mansion Nemours near Wilmington, Delaware, in 1909 as a home for himself and his second wife, Alicia. Even though Alfred's social and business relations with the rest of the duPont family were strained, he looked back with fondness to the ancestors who founded the American dynasty. DuPont named Nemours after a small town in France that his great-great-grandfather Pierre represented in the French Estates-General in 1789. Pierre also took the name Nemours when he received his patent of nobility from Louis XVI. The house thus combines pride in the duPont family's French origins with a grand display its New World wealth. Indeed, the massive, 102-room mansion would have amply served the needs of a French noble. Its French theme also represents Alfred's love for Alicia, who was enamored of 18th-century French culture.

To bring his Francophile vision to reality, Alfred selected New York architects John Carrère and Thomas Hastings, both of whom had trained at the École des Beaux-Arts in Paris during the 1880s. Carrère and Hastings were leading practitioners of the beaux arts manner, celebrated for a series of works that displayed practical and functional planning, restrained ornamentation, and a distinct expertise at interpreting French classical models for American clients. Although Carrère and Hastings are best known for their public buildings, such as the New York Public Library, they also excelled at country homes for wealthy clients—and Alfred I. duPont certainly fit that category.

In 1909, Alfred was the vice president and general manager of the Du Pont Company and an heir of the family dynasty, founded in this country in 1799 when Pierre Samuel du Pont de Nemours emigrated from France. Pierre and his son Eleuthère opened a gunpowder works on the Brandywine River in Delaware. By the time Alfred I. duPont was born in 1864, the family was already fabulously wealthy. Along with his financial fortune, he inherited great-great-grandfather Pierre's scientific aptitude and went on to contribute many innovations to the family business. One of his inventions, a waterwheel designed in 1931, can be seen in the pump house at Nemours.

When construction on Nemours began during the summer of 1909, Alfred took an active role in the process, suggesting a recessed portico on the garden facade, which was built against the judgment of Carrère and Hastings. By December 1910 the lavish house was ready for the duPonts. Although the total cost of Nemours is unknown (Alfred directed his contractor to destroy all account books after the final bill was paid), one conservative estimate is two million dollars. Whatever the cost, the result is a mansion that subtly proclaims its magnificence, unlike the overpowering manner adopted by many contemporary country estates.

Although a 1913 article in *Town & Country* described Nemours as "one of the purest examples of French architecture to be found in this country," the mansion is actually an eclectic combination of French classicism and 20th-century beaux arts styles, all governed by the formality and rational planning that characterized Carrère's and Hastings' approach to architecture. The strong influence of French classicism can be seen in the house's symmetrical balanced form, mansard roof, balustraded roofline, and double Corinthian columns. The architects intended the facade to be a variation of one of France's great architectural landmarks—the Petit Trianon at Versailles—but Alfred's insistence on a recessed portico made the rendition less accurate. For the gardenside facade the architects turned to another French model, the château at Blois. The 102 rooms inside were decorated in a series of contrasting styles with a French theme predominating. Much of the original antique furniture, tapestries, and paintings dating from the 15th century are also on view, making a tour a good idea. By taking the mansion in room by room you can quickly enter into the life of this enormously wealthy family. In the dining room, for example, hangs a larger-than-life-size portrait of Louis XVI, who was so important in the life of Alfred's great-great-grandfather.

Alfred's interest in science and mechanics is visible throughout the mansion. Light fixtures are prominently placed, reflecting his fascination with electricity—the inventor Thomas Edison was one of his close friends. Nemours also contained a state-of-the-art solarium, a machine for making 30-pound blocks of ice, and another for bottling mineral water. All the mechanical devices at Nemours were the best money could buy, and Alfred often bought two of each, in case of breakdowns. In addition to the main house, an automobile garage, also in French classical style, was built on the property in 1914. Five years later, the mansion's staff wing was taken down and extended, a new laundry built, and a French medieval water tower constructed.

However magnificent, the mansion added fuel to a simmering feud between Alfred and the rest of the duPont family. The troubles had begun with Alfred's takeover of the Du Pont Company in 1902 with cousins Coleman and Pierre. Four years later, Alfred divorced his first wife, Bessie, and soon thereafter he outraged the family by marrying his cousin Alicia Bradford Maddox. Then came the construction of Nemours, on 300 acres of land, as a present for his new bride. The lavishness of the house shocked the conservative duPonts, and led to strained family relations that would last for the rest of Alfred's life.

Alfred intended Nemours to be a private retreat from the rigors of the business world and the turmoil of the duPont family feud. In order to maintain this solitude, he ordered a 9-foot wall topped with jagged glass built around the property's perimeter. Armed guards were stationed at all entry points. The estate behind the wall included an elaborate sunken garden, designed by duPont's son Alfred Victor duPont and his partner, Gabriel Massena, whom he met while studying architecture at the École des Beaux-Arts in Paris. In 1929, Alfred duPont commissioned his son's brand new firm after becoming dissatisfied with Thomas Hastings' garden plan, and Alfred Victor cut short his architectural studies to return to America and supervise construction. Massena and duPont also built a 200-foot carillon tower on the

Jets of water dapple the surface of the reflecting pool at Nemours. An acre in size, the pool graces the approach to the grand mansion built by Alfred Irénée duPont.

grounds in 1936, designed to hold 31 cast-iron bells. However, the majority of the gardens are as designed by Carrère and Hastings, combining elements of Italian Renaissance and French classical styles and interspersed with pools, fountains, marble stairways, and open green spaces, all laid out along a single tree-lined axis. Water features prominently throughout the landscape, which also includes a pavilion based on Marie Antoinette's Temple of Love from Versailles, a maze, and a parterre garden.

When Alfred duPont died in 1935, his will created the Nemours Foundation with a mandate to maintain the house and grounds for public enjoyment and to apply much of Alfred's wealth for the care of handicapped children and the indigent elderly. Alfred's third wife, Jessie Ball duPont, hired Massena and duPont to construct a children's hospital on the grounds in 1940—today it is a world-renowned medical facility. Jessie lived at Nemours until her death in 1970, and is buried alongside Alfred beneath the carillon tower. The house and garden were opened to the public, pursuant to Alfred's wishes, in 1977.

39 *Nemours Mansion & Gardens* 1600 Rockland Road, Wilmington, Del. 19899. (302) 651-6912. Open May through Nov. Tues.-Sun. Visitors must be more than 16 years old.

William Paca House

ANNAPOLIS, MARYLAND

*Colonial
Living at
its Peak*

A showcase of prerevolutionary style, the William Paca House demonstrated how an English Georgian house could fit into a colonial urban landscape, merging spectacular gardens with magnificent architecture. Built between 1763 and 1765, the Paca House represents an early use of the Maryland five-part plan. It also marked the start of a decade-long building boom among the wealthiest families of Annapolis. The house was built for—and probably designed by—William Paca, one of the capital city's foremost lawyers and patriots, and a signer of the Declaration of Independence.

The house's five-part plan includes a massive, multistory main block flanked by two considerably smaller wings. Passageways called hyphens connect the wings to the main building, while also allowing a separation between them. The hyphens provided an important measure of fire protection and served as a practical buffer space between, for example, the kitchen and the main house. Most of the Paca family's domestic activity occurred in the house's main block, which is decorated with refined Georgian woodwork and molded plaster. With the exception of the parlor, painted a vibrant Prussian blue, the rooms are whitewashed and

accented with trim of various colors. True to period inventories, the house's furnishings reflect the tastes of an 18th-century Annapolis gentleman and include many pieces in the Chinese Chippendale style, then fashionable in England.

The Paca House and garden have been carefully restored, revealing how colonial architecture and landscape design created a style of living comparable to that of the English gentry. Take the time to wander through the recon-

An arching bridge leads to the formal garden behind the William Paca House. Edged in boxwood, the 18th-century terraced garden has been restored to its original elegance.

structed garden, widely considered the most elegant in Annapolis, and see how it matches the house in grandeur and style. While strolling you will note, for example, how the terraced landscape combines elements of formal European design, such as geometric hedges, with elements of picturesque "wilderness" gardens, such as a fishpond, a latticework bridge, and a summerhouse. Paca so loved this garden that he chose it as the background for his portrait, painted by Charles Willson Peale.

40 *William Paca House and Garden* 186 PRINCE GEORGE STREET, ANNAPOLIS, MD. 21401. (410) 263-5553. OPEN MARCH THROUGH DEC. DAILY; JAN. THROUGH FEB. SAT.-SUN. WWW.ANNAPOLIS.ORG

*H*ammond-Harwood House

ANNAPOLIS, MARYLAND

Annapolis Showcase of a Master Carpenter

Prominently located near the Maryland State House, the Hammond-Harwood House reveals the graciousness of late colonial taste and the superlative skill of the joiner and carpenter William Buckland. An Englishman, Buckland had helped create the elaborate carvings for Gunston Hall in Virginia (see p. 108), but he designed this house in its entirety, inspired by the work of the Italian Renaissance architect Andrea Palladio. The residence was planned and begun by Mathias Hammond, a young lawyer who intended it to be a home for himself and his fiancée. He commissioned Buckland to begin the work in 1774. Though the house borrowed heavily from Palladio's work, it retained a local flavor in the five-part facade, typical of upper-class Maryland houses.

Buckland relied on pattern books such as Abraham Swan's *British Architect,* as a source of inspiration for his designs, but added his own original and imaginative flair. The result was a handsome house that stood out from other Annapolis structures. Buckland subtly emphasized the center of the facade through his placement of a slightly projecting pediment, an elaborately trimmed second-story window, and a framed door composed of Ionic columns, classical entablatures, and a pediment. He also devised an irregular interior floor plan, while preserving symmetry through false doors or a large window that functioned as a door.

Buckland did not live to see the completion of the house, dying mysteriously on Maryland's Eastern Shore. His patron, Mathias Hammond, never lived in the house but ironically the house eventually came into the hands of Buckland's great-grandson, William Harwood, whose family retained ownership until 1924. In 1940, the Hammond-Harwood House Association acquired the property and restored it to the Georgian period, with furnishings from Hammond's period and several pieces from the Harwood family. Of special interest is a series of paintings by the noted Maryland artist Charles Willson Peale, and an original dining room table and set of chairs.

41 *Hammond-Harwood House* 19 MARYLAND AVENUE, ANNAPOLIS, MD. 21401. (410) 263-4683. OPEN DAILY.

NEARBY: **Chase Lloyd House** *(22 Maryland Avenue, Annapolis, Md. 410-263-2723)* Begun in 1769, this three-story brick house lies just across Maryland Avenue from the Hammond-Harwood House.

omewood

BALTIMORE, MARYLAND

A Country House for an Extravagant Son

A secluded country retreat for one of Maryland's leading families in the early 19th century, Homewood began in 1801 on 130 acres of rolling farmland sited almost an hour away from town by horse and carriage. Charles Carroll, a signer of the Declaration of Independence, gave the land as a wedding present to his only son, Charles Jr., and his bride, Harriet Chew, along with $10,000 to build and furnish the house as a summer residence. Despite his father's attempts to restrain expenditures, Charles Jr. spent nearly $40,000 on the house as he undertook numerous changes and additions over a span of five years.

The regally proportioned, federal-style manor was designed in the traditional five-part plan consisting of a main block framed on either side by matching wings and connecting halls, called hyphens. The center portion of the house is distinguished by a projecting portico supported by four slender wood columns carved from locally cut poplar trees painted a delicate off-white. Observe, too, how the gable end of the pediment, or tympanum, is

Its grandeur notwithstanding, Homewood was merely a summer home for Charles Carroll, Jr., and his new bride, Harriet. Charles Jr. probably designed the house himself, going some $30,000 over budget.

ornamented with an unusual shield-shaped window encircled by bas-relief swags. Detailing here and within the interior is typical of the Adamesque style, characterized by finely crafted plasterwork ornament and classically inspired decorative motifs.

Homewood was held by the Carroll family until 1838. The Wymans, subsequent owners of the estate, donated it to the Johns Hopkins University in 1902, and it is now incorporated into the university campus. The interior of the residence, restored in 1987, is filled with a superb collection of English and American furnishings dating from the 18th and 19th centuries. Many pieces were once owned by the Carroll family, including an unusual "night table," or commode disguised as a chest of drawers, equipped with an early flush mechanism to rinse the chamber pot. The floors are covered with painted floorcloths and Brussells carpets, the latter reproduced for the house from archival point patterns dated 1807.

42 *Homewood House Museum* Johns Hopkins University, 3400 North Charles Street, Baltimore, Md. 21218. (410) 516-5589. Open Tues.-Sun.

NEARBY: **Mount Clare Mansion** *(Carroll Park, 1500 Washington Boulevard, Baltimore, Md. 410-837-3262)* Built in 1760, this five-part Georgian mansion was once the center of an 800-acre plantation and still displays original furnishings, including rare Chippendale and Hepplewhite pieces. **Ladew** *(3535 Jarretsville Pike, Monkton, Md. 410-557-9466)* Although this estate is best known for its whimsical topiary, Ladew's mansion features English antiques and fox-hunting memorabilia, and is particularly noted for its Oval Library.

$\mathcal{E}$vergreen House

BALTIMORE, MARYLAND

A Happy
Couple's
Palatial Estate

This opulent Greek Revival mansion, built in 1858, enjoyed its heyday in the early 20th century as the residence of John and Alice Garrett. The house was purchased in 1878 by John's grandfather, president of the Baltimore & Ohio Railroad, for his son T. Harrison Garrett. He in turn left it to his diplomat son, John Work Garrett. John and his wife, Alice, dedicated patrons of the arts and active socialites, made Evergreen what it is today—a luxurious home filled with rare antiques, paintings, and fine furniture. Although Alice remodeled the palatial house in 1921, she kept a number of rooms from the Victorian period intact. Upon entering the elaborate stair hall, dated 1895, you immediately note its finely

John Work Garrett and his wife, Alice (above), pictured at a party in Baltimore in the 1930s, extensively renovated Evergreen House (right) and created a private theater (following pages) in a wing of the house.

carved and polished woods. Bold coffering defines the ceiling, set high over paneled walls and a heavy balustrade. Look farther to see the carved lions and dragons with shields atop the newel-posts, the whole illuminated by a series of simple stained-glass windows. John's two-story boyhood bedroom remains as he left it, a space noted for its wrought-iron bookcases and catwalk floored in translucent glass panels. Be sure not to miss the Gold Bathroom, finished in the 1880s and unique among American mansions. The woodwork and fixtures in this room are gilded with 23-karat gold, set against a background of intricate tile mosaics laid over the walls, mantel, and floor.

A number of Evergreen's distinctive rooms date from the 20th-century remodeling. In the dining room, for example, Alice Garrett commissioned the famous set designer, Leon Bakst, to decorate with red Chinese silk and rice paper panels against golden yellow walls. Bakst also embellished the private theater, converted from a gymnasium into a popular setting for plays and musical concerts using simple, colorful stencils inspired by his Russian heritage to ornament the columns and ceiling. But perhaps the couple's favorite space was the walnut-paneled Great Library, holding 8,000 volumes arranged in custom-made cases separated by high, arched windows. Double doors lead from the library through a line of dignified rooms, including the reading room, marked by scenic murals, and the drawing room, decorated with artwork by great painters including Modigliani, Picasso, and Vuillard.

43 *Evergreen House* Johns Hopkins University, 4545 North Charles Street, Baltimore, Md. 21210. (410) 516-0341. Open daily. www.jhu.edu/~evrgreen/

The White House

WASHINGTON, D.C.

*Home to Two
Centuries
of First
Families*

Sitting in the heart of busy Washington, surrounded by a simple iron fence, the White House is perhaps the most accessible residence of any head of state. About 1.5 million people visit every year to view its architecture and antique furnishings and to hear the histories of the first families—stories that form a microcosm of America's history.

Every President but George Washington has slept here, though it was Washington who chose the site and sponsored the competition to pick its design. Irish immigrant James Hoban won the contest with his rendition of a classical manor near Dublin. Construction began in 1792 and still was not complete when, in November 1800, John Adams moved in with his wife, Abigail, who complained in a letter: "not one room or chamber finished of the whole [house]; the principal stairs are not up ...."

During the War of 1812, a fire set by British troops gutted the house, though Dolley Madison bravely rescued a carriage load of papers and a portrait of George Washington (now

hanging in the East Room). James Hoban oversaw the postwar reconstruction, which included repainting the charred sandstone walls white. In the 1820s Hoban built the distinctive porticoes on the northern and southern facades, using a design by Benjamin Henry Latrobe.

As domestic technology advanced in the 19th century, the White House benefited from the installation of gas lighting (1848), central plumbing (1853), and electricity (circa 1890). Presidents and their families decorated the White House according to prevailing tastes, dispersing many of the original furnishings. In 1902 Theodore Roosevelt hired renowned architect Charles McKim to renovate the house, which was showing signs of potentially dangerous deterioration. McKim removed Victorian-era decorations to restore the spirit of Hoban's neoclassic design, and added an executive office wing to preserve the residential portion of the house for domestic and ceremonial uses. Further deterioration required an extensive, four-year reconstruction from 1948 to 1952, during the Truman Presidency, when the interior was dismantled and then reassembled within a new steel frame. In the early 1960s, Jacqueline Kennedy began the ongoing project of furnishing the interior with original items that could still be recovered and with fine antiques, turning the White House into the museum showplace it is today.

Your first stop should be the visitor center, where a video and exhibits will orient you for

the guided tour. The tour includes the gold-and-white East Room, decorated in late 18th-century classical style. While here, be sure to take note of the oak floor of Fontainebleau parquetry and stunning Bohemian cut-glass chandeliers. You will also visit the East Room, traditionally used for such large gatherings as weddings, wakes (including those of Presidents Lincoln and Kennedy), and bill-signing ceremonies. Theodore Roosevelt's children enjoyed roller-skating here.

The Green Room, named for the green silks chosen by the Monroes, represents a federal-style parlor with furniture by the famed New York cabinetmaker Duncan Phyfe. Next comes the elliptical Blue Room, considered the most elegant architectural feature of Hoban's plan, to which an oval portico with curving stairs was added in 1824. It is decorated in the French Empire style, as originally planned by James Monroe in 1817. The American Empire-style Red Room showcases richly carved furniture by Charles-Honoré Lannuier, including a magnificent mahogany secretary and elegant sofa with gilded dolphin feet.

The State Dining Room, enlarged by Charles McKim in the neoclassic look of late 18th-century English houses, features natural oak paneling with Corinthian pilasters. Be sure to read the inscription carved into the mantel, taken from a letter John Adams wrote on his second night in the White House: "I Pray Heaven to Bestow the Best of Blessings on THIS HOUSE and on All that hereafter Inhabit it. May none but Honest and Wise Men ever rule under this Roof."

44 *The White House* 1600 PENNSYLVANIA AVENUE, WASHINGTON, D. C. 20036. (202) 456-7041. OPEN TUES.-SAT. FREE, SAME-DAY TICKETS, REQUIRED MID-MARCH THROUGH LATE AUG. AND DEC., AVAILABLE FROM VISITOR CENTER (15TH STREET NEAR E STREET, NW) OR CONTACT YOUR CONGRESSIONAL OFFICE TO ARRANGE A VIP TOUR, WHICH INCLUDES ROOMS NOT OPEN TO THE PUBLIC ON A REGULAR BASIS. WWW.WHITEHOUSE.GOV

The South Portico of the White House is dramatically lit at night.

Anderson House

WASHINGTON, D.C.

Lavish
Tribute
to the Patriots
of the
Revolution

Fronted by great arched gates and a formal courtyard, Anderson House simultaneously evokes the privileged atmosphere of the Gilded Age as well as the august heritage of Revolutionary War heroes. Built in 1902-05 for career diplomat Larz Anderson III and his heiress wife, Isabel, this 50-room Italianate palace is both a house museum and the headquarters of the Society of the Cincinnati, descendants of Revolutionary officers. Larz Anderson was the great-grandson of one of the society's founders.

Anderson envisioned the house as a setting for entertaining foreign dignitaries, diplomats, and presidents during the high society season of winter. At a cost of $800,000, Boston's Little & Browne created one of Washington's most opulent houses. Keep a lookout for such lavish details as the 18 different colors of marble, intricate 23-karat gold trim with the Andersons' initials, elaborate frescoes containing personal insignia and faces of family members, and coffered ceilings. Four twisted salmon-colored marble columns support the Musician's Gallery in the two-story ballroom, while the long, narrow Olmsted Gallery, paneled in American brown oak, was designed specifically to showcase the Andersons' treasures.

The Andersons traveled extensively, searching far corners for art objects and exotica. After serving for six months in 1912 and 1913 as "Ambassador extraordinary and plenipotentiary" to Japan, Anderson returned to the United States with some of the first bonsai trees ever brought to this country. Among the first Americans to visit Tibet, around the turn of the century, the couple purchased a gilded bronze helmet, made around 1610, from a monk who claimed it had magical properties. You can see it displayed in the French Drawing Room, along with late 19th-century Chinese "jade" trees made of precious and semiprecious stones and lovely 17th-century Belgium tapestries. The English Drawing Room showcases a fine collection of English paintings, and a pair of Ch' ing Dynasty porcelain ginger jars. To get a sense of the people behind the art, see the full-length portraits of Larz and Isabel in the dining room—him formal and stern, her ephemeral in a gauzy white dress and Indian emerald turban brooch, said to have been a gift from a maharaja admirer.

While the family's collection of decorative arts is stunning, this hidden showpiece has more of a story to tell. From the very start, Anderson intended that his house and all its furnishings be bequeathed to the Society of the Cincinnati. Formed in 1783 by a group of Revolutionary War officers to uphold the ideals that had united them, the society was named for the Roman war general and farmer Cincinnatus, to whom George Washington, the society's first president general, is often compared. Reminders of this and of Anderson's other patriotic associations are prevalent throughout the house, especially in the masterful historical murals that grace several rooms. Anderson House's art collection also includes works by some of the country's most important painters, such as Gilbert Stuart, John Trumbull, and George Catlin.

45 *Society of the Cincinnati: Headquarters, Library, and Museum at Anderson House*
2118 MASSACHUSETTS AVENUE NW, WASHINGTON, D. C. 20008. (202) 785-2040. OPEN TUES.-SAT. 🚹 ♿

Plaster urns decorate the railing of the great staircase at Anderson House. Looking up the stairs from the first landing, one can see a series of formal reception rooms in the west wing of the mansion.

udor Place

WASHINGTON, D.C.

Washington Showplace Where Lafayette Dined

Among the greatest works of Dr. William Thornton, the U.S. Capitol's first architect, Tudor House preserves the life and times of the Peter family, who resided here for 178 years. In 1805 Martha Parke Custis Peter bought an entire city block in fashionable Georgetown with an $8,000 inheritance from her stepgrandfather, George Washington. She and her husband, Thomas, hired Thornton to create a mansion that would rival other family homes, including Mount Vernon (see p. 105), Woodlawn, and Arlington House (see p. 109). Thornton remodeled an existing residence and carriage house into the wings of an original, 26-room, neoclassic showplace, complete with buff-colored stucco, exaggerated proportions, floor-to-ceiling windows, and a domed circular portico recessing into the salon—all features unheard of just a few years before. The plain north front, with an unadorned doorway and windows, effectively sets off the circular carriage driveway and elegant gardens.

Most of the rooms remain arranged as they were during the lifetime of the house's last owner, Armistead Peter III, who died in 1983. The variety of furniture, portraits, silver, porcelain, glass, photographs, and books reflects the different styles and histories of six successive generations of family residents. Among the treasures for you to see are an engraving presented to Martha Peter by the Marquis de Lafayette, who was feted in the formal drawing room; a desk that belonged to Francis Scott Key, composer of "The Star-Spangled Banner"; and a number of items from Mount Vernon, including a pair of andirons and the stool George Washington used during the Revolutionary War. The house also preserves the office of Armistead Peter, who worked here as a doctor from 1914 to 1925.

The extensive gardens, embracing a sweep of green lawn, parterres, 19th-century specimen trees, and English boxwood, were begun by Martha Peter and enhanced by successive family members. Martha is said to have planted the China rose, Old Blush, which still blooms along the south front.

46 *Tudor Place* 1655 31ST STREET NW, WASHINGTON, D. C. 20007. (202) 965-0400. OPEN DAILY. WWW.TUDORPLACE.ORG

illwood

WASHINGTON, D.C.

French Gardens and Russian Art

Designed by John Diebert in the neo-Georgian style and built in 1926, Hillwood overlooks Washington's Rock Creek Park from a countrylike setting just minutes from busy Connecticut Avenue. Its sweeping view takes in the Washington Monument 6 miles away. Marjorie Merriweather Post, the only daughter of C.W. Post, founder of the cereal empire, purchased the house in 1955. Heiress to a great fortune, Post was also an astute businesswoman, a philanthropist, and an extraordinary collector. After purchasing Hillwood, Post oversaw the house's complete reconstruction and enlargement, as well as an extensive relandscaping of the

An 1857 portrait of the Empress Eugénie hangs above the fireplace in Hillwood's French drawing room, which is lavishly decorated with Louis XVI-period furnishings. Some of Marjorie Merriweather Post's collection of gold boxes can be seen in the display case in the foreground.

grounds. She hired the fashionable firm of Innocent and Webbed to carry out her grand vision of creating a landscape of pleasure gardens—including a formal French garden extending from the house's Louis XVI drawing room. Post intended that one day Hillwood would be a public showcase for her cherished treasures, a superlative collection of 18th-century French and imperial Russian decorative arts.

As a young woman in the early 1900s, Post developed a passion for French decorative arts, and over the years collected Sevres porcelain, exquisite tapestries, and rare furnishings. It was only later, when she moved to Moscow in the 1930s with her third husband, Joseph Davies, Ambassador to the Soviet Union, that she discovered Russian art. At a time when many of the treasures of imperial Russia were being sold off, she acted quickly, purchasing icons, chalices, textiles, porcelains, and furniture that eventually formed the basis of the Hillwood collection. Over the next 50 years, she continued to acquire Russian art, including some 90 pieces from the workshop of Fabergé. By the time of her death in 1973, Post had amassed the largest assemblage of Russian decorative art outside Russia.

Closed in December 1997 for extensive renovations, the museum plans to reopen in the spring of 2000.

47 *Hillwood* 4155 Linnean Avenue NW, Washington, D. C. 20008. (202) 686-8500. Closed for renovations until 2000. www.hillwoodmuseum.org

The South

VIRGINIA • WEST VIRGINIA

KENTUCKY • TENNESSEE

NORTH CAROLINA

SOUTH CAROLINA

GEORGIA • FLORIDA • ALABAMA

MISSISSIPPI • LOUISIANA

Long, tree-lined drives; wide, welcoming verandas; white columns gleaming in the sun—all these symbolize the South and its heritage. Here great wealth derived from tobacco, cotton, and sugar—cash crops raised by slave labor—funded an architecture of pride and grandeur. From the Potomac to the Gulf, the mansions of the planters proudly present magnificent colonnades inspired by the architecture of ancient Greece.

The imposing facade of Stanton Hall, Mississippi

The South

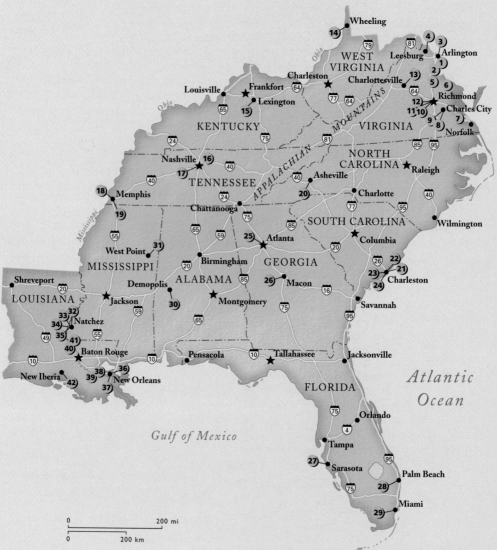

Wheeling

14

WEST
VIRGINIA

79

81

4
3
Arlington
Leesburg
1
2
6
5
Richmond
Charles City
7

Charleston
Charlottesville
13
12
11 10
9 8
Norfolk

Louisville
Frankfort
Lexington
15

64
77
64

65

KENTUCKY

75

81

VIRGINIA

NORTH
CAROLINA

85
95

Raleigh

Nashville
16
17
TENNESSEE

40

24

Asheville
20

40

Charlotte

77
95
40

Memphis
18
19

40

Chattanooga

75

85

SOUTH CAROLINA

Columbia

Wilmington

West Point
31

55
65

59

25
Atlanta

20

26
22
23
21
24
Charleston

MISSISSIPPI

20

Birmingham
ALABAMA

GEORGIA

Macon
26

16

Savannah

Shreveport

20

LOUISIANA

Jackson

32
33
34
Natchez
35

49

55

59

Demopolis

30

Montgomery

65

95

Mississippi

41
40
Baton Rouge

10

38 36
39
37
New Orleans

42
New Iberia

10

Pensacola

10

Tallahassee

Jacksonville

FLORIDA

*Atlantic
Ocean*

Gulf of Mexico

75

Orlando

4

Tampa

95

27
Sarasota

Palm Beach
28

75

Miami

29

0   200 mi

0   200 km

Mount Vernon

ALEXANDRIA, VIRGINIA

The First President's Estate on the Potomac

George Washington's enduring fame as a general and statesman has overshadowed his achievement as an amateur architect. In 1761, he inherited the modest farmhouse built by his father on the family's Mount Vernon plantation, located on a bluff over the Potomac River. In stages Washington transformed the plain structure into a grand manor, imposing on the outside and boasting one of the most elegant interiors in Virginia.

Though Washington himself referred to his plain, "republican style of living," he had a taste for grandeur and large-scale architectural statements. Arriving at Mount Vernon's gate, visitors gaze across an expansive lawn toward a broad white mansion that evokes, as the architect Benjamin Henry Latrobe put it, "a plain English country gentleman's house . . . of the old school." Two curving colonnades embrace the house, framing the view. From the gateway the mansion appears to be made of painted stone, an effect Washington achieved by having the pine weatherboarding of the main house cut, painted, and dusted with sand to resemble stone blocks. Desiring a pleasant spot for his afternoon tea and for reading, Washington also designed an eight-columned piazza that extends more than 90 feet. This shaded outdoor room, cooled by river breezes, offers a stunning view overlooking the Potomac.

The main entrance leads to the passage, or stair hall, where the Washingtons held informal social events. Handsomely paneled, with doorways featuring broken pediments, the passage has openings on the land and river sides, making it a breezy place to entertain visitors. On display is the key to the Bastille sent by the Marquis de Lafayette to Washington in tribute to him "as a missionary of liberty to its patriarch" during the French Revolution.

Washington consulted British builders' guidebooks such as Abraham Swan's *British Architect* and Batty Langley's *Treasury of Designs* to find the plans for interior embellishments. Elegant wood paneling encloses the west parlor, which Washington once declared to be the best room in the house. It served as a family portrait gallery, tearoom, and gentlemen's card room. Among the copies of 13 family portraits here, you can view large canvases depicting Martha Washington and her two children along with a portrait of Washington originally painted by Charles Willson Peale in 1772.

It is often thought that 18th-century interiors were painted a pale, comforting shade of beige. In fact they were quite vivid, with a brightness and sheen surprising to the modern eye. Meticulous analysis of remnants of the original paint throughout the house revealed Washington's preference for "prussian blue" and "verdigris green," paints that were costly to produce and difficult to apply. The choice of colors and techniques had a practical as well as decorative purpose—the vibrant hues and reflective glazes seen in Mount Vernon's rooms would have considerably brightened a candlelit interior.

The house has two dining rooms. The first, smaller dining room is painted a bright green and displays numerous portraits. The focus here is on a small oval dining table set for the last course of a dinner described in a letter written by an English visitor in 1799. While visiting this room, be sure to seek out the unusual spirits case, designed to hold 16

Mount Vernon, George Washington's architectural masterpiece, was described by an 18th-century traveler as "a country house of an elegant and majestic simplicity."

one-gallon bottles of liquor. When Washington ordered the case in 1760, he complained to his London supplier that he found the price "as great an Imposition as ever was offered by a Tradesman."

Even before the Revolutionary War brought international fame and hordes of visitors, Washington found Mount Vernon too small. The large dining room represents Washington's most ambitious expansion of the house, which he began in 1775 only to have it interrupted by the war. It soars two stories high, with a grand Palladian window dominating one wall. Washington himself chose the color scheme—two tones of green with delicate off-white decorative elements under an off-white ceiling—and was particular about the quality of the painting. He wrote to his nephew, who was supervising the work, that "it will require Small brushes and considerable attention to paint the mouldings, to prevent their filling too much with paint." This is where you can see one of the finest decorative elements in the house— the Vaughn mantel, a gift to Washington from an English admirer, Samuel Vaughn, who had the mantel removed from his own house in England and shipped to Mount Vernon. Fashioned of marble with fluted columns of brown jasper, the mantel features three panels carved with farming scenes. Although the mantel was a gift, it perfectly harmonizes with other elements of the room's decorative scheme, such as the farming motifs depicted on the ceiling. The original furnishings include mahogany and ash side chairs made by the Philadelphia cabinetmaker John Aitken, a mahogany sideboard also by Aitken, and a large looking glass that Washington purchased from a French diplomat. In this room, Washington received the official notification that he had been elected first President of the United States. After Washington's death, his body lay in state here for three days, in accordance with his wishes.

Cross to the opposite side of the house, where Washington's study reveals his multifaceted duties and interests. Here Washington conducted his political correspondence, making this room, as one 18th-century observer put it, "the focus of political intelligence for the new world." Since he began work at his desk first thing in the morning, one of the original pieces of furniture here is his dressing table, where he washed and shaved. In the midsummer heat he read sitting in a fan chair, operating an overhead fan with foot pedals. Indicative of Washington's concerns with statecraft and foreign policy is a globe, which he ordered from London. Note, too, the book press that holds part of his library of 884 volumes. The study also contains the leather chair that Washington used throughout the eight years of his Presidency, and the item regarded as the finest piece of American furniture Washington owned—the tambour secretary-bookcase of mahogany, made by Aitken. Personal items include a walking staff, a duck gun, and a whip handle.

The second floor of the house contains five guest bedrooms and the master bedchamber from which Martha Washington managed the household. The four-poster bed with dimity hangings is where Washington died on December 14, 1799, after contracting a throat infection during a sudden snowstorm. After her husband's death, Martha Washington never used the bedroom again. She died in her third-floor bedroom on May 22, 1802.

Mount Vernon itself was not a working plantation but rather the home farm, headquarters for an agricultural operation that took place on four nearby farms. However, numerous outbuildings reflect the multiplicity of labors required to maintain the estate. Among these, original or reconstructed, are the kitchen, storehouse, smokehouse, washhouse, stable, coach house, overseer's quarters, icehouse, and greenhouse. A practical man, Washington took a hand in many building and repair projects around the estate. "The General has a great turn for mechanics," one visitor noted. "It's astounding with what niceness he directs everything

Nine of the original 24 side chairs made by the master cabinetmaker John Aitken for Mount Vernon's large dining room stand beneath the room's Palladian window.

in the building way, condescending even to measure the things himself, that all may be perfectly uniform."

Much of the work at Mount Vernon was carried out by African-American slaves. A marker designed by architecture students at Howard University in Washington, D.C., serves as a memorial to Mount Vernon's enslaved people, some of whom lay buried in a cemetery overlooking the river, although their grave markers have disappeared.

George and Martha Washington are buried in a vault on the grounds, behind a dignified brick gateway. Although Mrs. Washington agreed to have the general's remains interred in a crypt at the United States Capitol, she died before it was completed. Washington's grandnephew decided to honor his wish that his remains rest at Mount Vernon.

1 *George Washington's Mount Vernon Estate & Gardens* GEORGE WASHINGTON MEMORIAL PARKWAY, ALEXANDRIA, VA. 22121. (703) 780-2000. OPEN DAILY. WWW.MOUNTVERNON.ORG

Gunston Hall

MASON NECK, VIRGINIA

Exquisite Carving in the Home of a Virginia Patriot

Gunston Hall's plain brick facade contains a jewel-box interior of exquisite paneling and furnishings. George Mason, a driving intellectual force behind American independence, began work on the house about 1755 and completed it four years later. He hired an English carpenter-joiner, William Buckland, as an indentured servant to design the interior and supervise construction. Research indicates that a second craftsman, another English indentured servant named William Bernard Sears, carved Gunston Hall's extraordinary woodwork, exhibiting great imagination and meticulous attention to detail. You can readily admire the superb artistry of Buckland and Sears in the Palladian parlor, where bold classical forms combine with subtle rococo detail to create a pleasing visual richness. Equally striking is the Chinese-inspired carving in the dining room.

Amid these elegant surroundings, Virginians such as George Washington and Thomas Jefferson met to discuss politics with Mason, who wrote the Virginia Declaration of Rights in May 1776. This included the statement: "All Men are by nature equally free and independent, and have certain inherent Rights ... namely, the Enjoyment of Life and Liberty, with

Gunston Hall's elaborately decorated center hall served as both a passageway to the back of the house and a reception area where dances were held.

the Means of acquiring and possessing Property, and pursueing and obtaining Happiness and Safety"—words that found an echo several weeks later in Jefferson's Declaration of Independence.

Gunston Hall passed through several owners who made many changes, and since the mid-1980s the house has been undergoing an ambitious restoration to the time of Mason's residence. Architectural detective work has revealed that a staircase originally ran from cellar to attic; its presence was confirmed with the removal of 20th-century plaster and woodwork. The estate's extensive grounds are also undergoing restoration—scholars of 18th-century garden design believe that the outlines of Gunston Hall's gardens survive from Mason's time, including the central allée of boxwood.

2 **Gunston Hall Plantation** 10709 GUNSTON ROAD, MASON NECK, VA. 22079. (703) 550-9220. OPEN DAILY. WWW.GUNSTONHALL.ORG ⬤ ⬤ ⬤ ⬤ ⬤ ⬤ ⬤

Arlington House

ARLINGTON, VIRGINIA

A Tribute to Two Great Generals

An enormous Greek temple on a hill, Arlington House looks across the Potomac River toward Washington, D.C. It was built between 1802 and 1817 by George Washington Parke Custis, Martha Washington's grandson, whom George Washington adopted. Custis intended the house to be an architectural proclamation of the first President's unique importance in the history of the nation, but it has become better known on two other historical counts: Before the Civil War it was the residence of Robert E. Lee, who married Custis' only child, Mary; and during the Civil War the grounds were used as a Federal cemetery. Today Arlington National Cemetery surrounds the house.

Referring to the mansion's grand scale, Robert E. Lee called it "a house that any one might see with half an eye." Massive Doric columns, 5 feet thick at the base, stand at the building's entrance. While the facade and columns appear to be constructed of marble, they are in reality bricks artfully coated with cement. Custis, who had grown up at Mount Vernon, hired the well-known British architect George Hadfield to design Arlington House. Inside he displayed furniture and personal items inherited from Washington. Custis also inherited his grandmother's slaves, several of whom had been by Washington's side at his death—an event Custis had them recount for visitors. One room displays a monumental painting, done by Custis himself, depicting George Washington's victory at the Battle of Monmouth. Custis also painted murals of hunting scenes in the mansion's back hall. On his visit here in 1824, the Marquis de Lafayette looked through the doorway toward the capital and proclaimed what lay before him as "the finest view in the world."

Robert E. Lee and Mary Custis were married here in the family parlor in 1831. Although Lee subsequently spent little time at the house because of the demands of his military duties, he regarded Arlington as his permanent home, where "my affections and attachments are more strongly placed than at any other place in the world." During the Civil War, the federal government confiscated the property after Mrs. Lee, an invalid, was unable to pay the taxes in person—a newly passed wartime requirement. The War Department acquired the property at auction for use as a cemetery—a decision apparently made out of pressing need and not, as some have alleged, as a gesture of contempt toward Lee. In 1933, ownership passed from the War Department to the National Park Service. Congress later designated the house as a memorial to Robert E. Lee.

Arlington's furnishings reflect the Lee period of ownership, when their seven children lived here. One of the most charming rooms is the girls' dressing room, with miniature furniture. In an upstairs bedchamber on April 19, 1861, Robert E. Lee agonized over the choice of accepting command of the Federal Army that would soon invade the South or resigning to join the Confederacy. After a long night awake and alone, he composed a letter of resignation from the U.S. Army, deciding to serve instead in the armed forces of Virginia. Two days later he left Arlington. Although he was seen visiting the cemetery in 1869, Lee never entered his old home again.

3 *Arlington House: The Robert E. Lee Memorial* George Washington Memorial Parkway, Arlington, Va. 22201. (703) 557-0613. Open daily. www.nps.gov/gwmp/arl_hse.html

Oatlands

LEESBURG, VIRGINIA

Antebellum Survivor in a War-torn State

One of the finest houses in Virginia's hunt country, Oatlands gracefully combines several architectural and decorative styles into a handsome, imposing plantation house. The great-grandson of Robert "King" Carter, the wealthiest man in colonial Virginia, George Carter inherited Oatlands Plantation in the 1790s when his father divided up the family lands (a complex transaction, given that George was one of 17 children). In 1804, George Carter began building the first portion of the manor house in the architecturally plain Georgian style. In the late 1820s, when the Greek Revival style was in vogue, Carter added two semioctagonal wings on the sides of the house to enclose new stairways, as well as a monumental, two-story portico with six Corinthian columns carved in New York, and a parapet roof. He also had the original brick facades covered with more fashionable stucco and redecorated the interior with fine plasterwork in the Adamesque style. These additions and stylistic flourishes reflected the owner's prosperity.

Indeed, the 3,400-acre plantation flourished in the antebellum period and survived the Civil War without damage, while other properties in the region were completely destroyed. After the Civil War, however, George's son and namesake faced such financial strain that he and his wife were compelled to operate Oatlands as a boardinghouse. They sold the property in 1898 to Stilson Hutchins, founder of the *Washington Post,* who in turn sold it in 1903 to William Corcoran Eustis and his wife, Edith, scions of prominent Washington, D.C., families. Eustis, whose family established Washington's Corcoran Gallery of Art, served as an interpreter on the staff of Gen. John "Black Jack" Pershing in World War I. Mrs. Eustis, the daughter of Vice President Levi P. Morton (under President Benjamin Harrison), entertained such luminaries as Senator Henry Cabot Lodge, Gen. George C. Marshall, and President and Mrs. Franklin D. Roosevelt.

Oatlands' furnishings mainly reflect the Eustis period of ownership, although the dining room contains interesting items from the George Carter period. Note, for example, a sideboard made in Baltimore displaying two unusual knife holders crafted in 1824. Circular, rather than the usual square, each has slots for 52 knives arranged in concentric rings. Gardening interested George Carter as much as architecture did, and he laid out a beautiful 4-acre English garden in a progression of falling terraces alongside the house. Also of interest is the propagation greenhouse—the second oldest such greenhouse in America—where Carter was able to raise fruits and vegetables out of season, including such exotica as bananas and pineapples.

4 *Oatlands Plantation* 20850 OATLANDS PLANTATION LANE (US 15), LEESBURG, VA. 20175. (703) 777-3174. OPEN DAILY. WWW.OATLANDS.ORG 🆂 🚶 ♿ 🅿 🏛

Oatlands Plantation, the grand antebellum symbol of the Carter family's preeminence in piedmont Virginia, became a refuge for homeless relatives, friends, and freed slaves after the Civil War.

*K*enmore

FREDERICKSBURG, VIRGINIA

Prosperity and Beauty, Sacrificed for Liberty

Kenmore long ago gained renown among connoisseurs of 18th-century design for the extraordinary beauty and lavishness of its plasterwork. However, it deserves equal fame for its history. Kenmore was the home of Fielding Lewis and his wife, Betty Washington Lewis, the only sister of George Washington. Their house reveals the lifestyle of these patriots dedicated to the cause of liberty. It also bears scars of the Civil War. Look for the cannonball lodged on the east face of the house, just to the right of the portico.

The Lewises built Kenmore in 1775, on land surveyed for them 25 years earlier by George Washington. The fashion for plaster ornamentation, popular in Italy and England, was just reaching America in the 1770s—carved and paneled walls had been the decoration of choice in high-style houses. But at Kenmore, the drawing room, dining room, and master bedroom are covered almost entirely with the elaborate plasterwork designs of an itinerant Frenchman, a "stucco man" who favored floral motifs. In the dining room, for example, the artist made a medallion of long leaves radiating from the ceiling's center point. He surrounded the medallion with a circle of eight flower baskets, enclosed the circle in a panel of swirling vines, placed four cornucopias around the panel, and added six more leaf medallions at the sides. The drawing room ceiling features emblems of the seasons, including delicate crossed palms symbolic of spring. The stucco artist, whose name is unfortunately unknown, also created overmantels for the dining and drawing rooms. The latter depicts a scene from Aesop's fable of the fox and the crow, which dramatizes the moral "beware of flattery." According to family tradition, George Washington himself suggested the scene to the Lewises.

In contrast to the lavish decoration inside, Kenmore's brick facade is in the simple, barely adorned, late Georgian style, a lack of decoration not unusual for a colonial Virginia house. Before the Revolutionary War the Lewises prospered in a variety of businesses such as shipping, tobacco and wheat farming, and importing farm equipment and luxury items. (Taking on a role that was highly unusual for the era, Betty participated as a partner with her husband in their business ventures.) Kenmore reflects the affluence they put at risk when the war broke out. The Lewises financed and managed a gun factory, built and provisioned ships, and provided gunpowder, clothing, food, and other supplies to Washington's army. Exhausted by constant work, Fielding died impoverished after George Washington's victory at Yorktown in 1781. Several years later, facing financial ruin, Betty left Kenmore for a small farm and carried on. Ironically, she died in 1797 almost the same way her famous brother would two years later—both succumbed to illnesses contracted while working outdoors in harsh winter weather.

Kenmore has been furnished according to a 1781 inventory of the Lewises' possessions and other records. The plaster ceilings remain in remarkably fine condition, having survived two centuries of Virginia humidity.

5 *Kenmore Plantation and Gardens* 1201 WASHINGTON AVENUE, FREDERICKSBURG, VA. 22401. (540) 373-3381. OPEN DAILY. WWW.KENMORE.ORG 🅢 🏃 ♿ 🅟 🏛

Intricately designed, hand-molded plaster reliefs grace a ceiling at Kenmore. The plasterwork was painstakingly crafted in 1775 by an itinerant artisan who also decorated two rooms at Mount Vernon.

Stratford Hall

STRATFORD, VIRGINIA

Fortresslike
Home of a
Virginia
Dynasty

One of the South's finest colonial-era mansions, Stratford Hall holds unusually rich architectural and historical associations. While widely known as the birthplace of Confederate Gen. Robert E. Lee, its history is older than the general's, and its architecture harkens to the manor houses of England. Built in the late 1730s by Thomas Lee, Stratford Hall presents the appearance of a brick bastion in the wilderness with its severely plain brick walls, massive chimneys, and broad stairway that brings to mind a drawbridge. It is likely that the plans for this sophisticated house were drawn up in England, but the identity of the architect is unknown.

The interior is equally aristocratic, with a spacious, beautifully paneled Great Hall occupying the center of the second story. Home of the wealthy, politically powerful Lees, Stratford Hall was designed for the lavish entertainments of which upper-class Virginians were so fond—entertainments that could last for days and included horse races, gambling at cards, festive music, and dancing. According to a family story, one of the Lees built a balustraded platform on the roof so guests could dance under the stars in summer.

The builder, Thomas Lee, served in Virginia's House of Burgesses and as the colony's acting governor. In 1744 he was one of Britain's chief negotiators in talks with the Six Nations

Stratford Hall, the Lee family's imposing 18th-century brick mansion, is topped by a pair of arcaded quadruple chimneys that lead to 16 fireplaces within the house.

of the Iroquois that resulted in the acquisition of enormous territories in the West—lands that later formed six states and part of a seventh. His sons stood in the forefront of the patriots' cause in the era of the Revolution. John Adams called the Lees, "this band of brothers, intrepid and unchangeable." Richard Henry Lee and Francis Lightfoot Lee signed the Declaration of Independence—the only brothers among the signers. William Lee and Arthur Lee served as diplomats in Europe and Thomas Lee held a post in Virginia's Revolutionary government. Through marriage, Stratford Hall came into the possession of a cousin, Henry "Light Horse Harry" Lee, one of the great cavalry heroes of the Revolution. His second wife, Ann Carter (of Shirley Plantation, see p. 118), gave birth to five children, including Robert Edward Lee in 1807. The future general spent his early childhood here, but the family departed when failed land speculations ruined Harry Lee financially, compelling him to chain the doors of the house to keep out the collectors. He was eventually imprisoned for his debts. After passing through several owners in the 19th

The kitchen at Stratford Hall features a gleaming late 18th-century medicinal still (foreground) and an ingenious device mounted on the wall to turn the roasting spit automatically.

century, the property was acquired in 1929 by the Robert E. Lee Memorial Foundation, a group of women who undertook the restoration of the main house and outlying buildings.

Designed in the shape of an H, Stratford Hall contains work rooms and bedchambers on the ground floor and formal rooms on the upper floor, notably the 29-square-foot Great Hall, which offers sweeping views of the estate. Visitors are invited to wander the eight rooms on the upper floor, furnished with antiques that reflect the house during the mid- to late 1700s, when the Lees were at the height of their prosperity. The rooms further convey information about family and society at the time. The nursery, for example, was a library until the mid-1700s, when a new trend dictated that even very young children should participate in family life rather than be handed off to the care of a wet nurse. If time allows, stroll the gardens where some of the plantation's outbuildings have been reconstructed or restored, including slave quarters, springhouses, a working mill, and the Lee family burial vault.

6 *Stratford Hall Plantation* VA. 214 (OFF VA. 3), STRATFORD, VA. 22558. (804) 493-8038. OPEN DAILY.
WWW.STRATFORDHALL.ORG

James River Plantations

Carter's Grove, Sherwood Forest Plantation, Shirley Plantation, Wilton, Virginia House, Maymont

The James River has served as one of the most important arteries of Virginia's commerce and communication. All three of Virginia's capitals—Jamestown, Williamsburg, and Richmond—are located near its banks. The James also saw an architectural flowering engendered by the colony's tobacco wealth. From Williamsburg to the edge of Richmond, the river banks are dotted with the mansions of tobacco aristocrats, whose families made their marks not only in the history of American wealth, but in politics and military service as well. All together, the James River plantations form one of the finest ensembles of American architecture in the country.

Carter's Grove

WILLIAMSBURG, VIRGINIA

Two Centuries Meet in a Riverside Mansion

An amalgam of the 18th and 20th centuries, Carter's Grove presents a colonial revival interior of the 1930s within the walls of a grand mansion of the 1750s. Operated by Colonial Williamsburg, located just a short drive away, Carter's Grove was begun in the 1730s by Carter Burwell. His grandfather Robert "King" Carter had purchased this spot on the James River, along with a thousand-acre plantation, for his daughter (Burwell's mother).

Completed at the end of 1755, the massive house features sumptuous walnut and pine paneling by a London artisan named Richard Baylis. His extraordinary work makes the 28-foot-wide stair hall, where a broad archway frames the staircase, one of the most imposing rooms in Virginia. Records suggest that the balusters and newel-post may have been made by a slave named Sumpter. Take a close look at the stair rail—legend has it that the slash marks visible date back to the Revolutionary War, when the famed British officer Banastre Tarleton rode his horse up the stairs, banging the rail with his sword to awaken his slumbering troops.

In 1838 the Burwell family sold the property, which passed through nine owners until acquired in 1928 by Pittsburgh industrialist Archibald McCrea. His wife, Mollie, was the widow of a collateral descendant of the Burwells. Their passionate interest in Carter's Grove coincided with the nationwide colonial revival movement of the 1920s and 1930s. Their efforts included enlarging the house by raising the roof and linking the main block to the outlying kitchen and office structures. The elegant furnishings in the house today, including paintings, silver, china, and glassware, reflect the McCreas' vision of the house as a relic of prerevolutionary aristocratic life.

7 *Carter's Grove* US 60, WILLIAMSBURG, VA. 23187. (757) 229-1000. OPEN DAILY MID-MARCH THROUGH DEC. WWW.COLONIALWILLIAMSBURG.ORG 🔅🏛️♿🍴🅿️🏛️

Dormer windows peer out from the steeply pitched roof at Carter's Grove. In order to expand the house in the 20th century, a new roof was added 7 feet higher than the colonial original.

Sherwood Forest Plantation

CHARLES CITY, VIRGINIA

A Presidential Long House

The home of President John Tyler and his family, Sherwood Forest nestles comfortably in its wooded setting. Tyler was still in the White House in 1842 when he purchased the house and 1,600 acres from a cousin. He renamed the house Sherwood Forest, referring to his reputation as a political outlaw. Measuring more than 300 feet across, Sherwood Forest is the longest frame house in America—but it is only one room deep. The very narrowness of the house makes it feel a part of the lush landscape and creates a charming coziness along with some pleasing architectural anomalies. A succession of small rooms, for example, leads abruptly to an elongated ballroom, its sudden spaciousness an open invitation to festivity. Tyler added the ballroom at the suggestion of his wife, Julia Gardiner Tyler, who also chose many of the Greek Revival embellishments in the house. The Tylers enjoyed entertaining, and their long, narrow ballroom proved the perfect setting in which to dance the Virginia reel.

The house remains the property of the President's descendants, and its furnishings span several generations. When in the dining room, note the original gilded valences over the windows, selected by Julia Tyler, who corresponded with her mother in New York about the purchase. (Having asked her mother's advice, Julia ignored it and chose the most expensive samples.) The dining room displays Paris china believed to have been used at the White House. Several other items in the house are associated with Tyler's tenure as President, including a silver-headed walking stick given him on the occasion of the annexation of Texas, and a tea service presented by a Chinese envoy to mark a treaty signing. Outside, the 25 acres of terraced grounds and gardens include a gingko tree brought from Asia in the 1850s by Capt. Matthew Perry, who opened Japan to trade with the United States.

8 *Sherwood Forest Plantation* 14501 JOHN TYLER HIGHWAY (VA. 5), CHARLES CITY, VA. 23030. (804) 829-5377. OPEN DAILY. WWW.SHERWOODFOREST.ORG ⑤ 🚶 ♿ 🍴 🅿 🏛

Shirley Plantation

CHARLES CITY, VIRGINIA

Horse Races and Hospitality for Eleven Generations

In a rare feat of historical survival, Shirley Plantation has remained a working farm owned by the same family since 1660. The 1738 mansion, which serves as the plantation headquarters, displays 18th- and 19th-century furnishings that remain in daily use. The current occupants represent the tenth and eleventh generations of Carters on this land.

Shirley's architecture reveals how Virginia's builders could imbue the simplest of forms with grace. The house is essentially a square brick box, but its hipped roof, rows of dormer windows, and most of all its two-story Palladian porticoes combine to impart a lively and welcoming air. Be sure to look up, as topping it all a carved pineapple, symbolizing hospitality, ornaments the roof. While the original main entrance to the house was on the water side, modern visitors make a much grander entry from the land side into a delightful hall dominated by Shirley's famed "flying" staircase. Thanks to a carefully concealed system of cantilevers, the stairs zigzag three stories overhead with no visible means of support. At Shirley's social events, it is likely that musicians stood on a landing over the stair hall while guests danced below.

The four downstairs rooms—stair hall, bedchamber, parlor, and dining room—are a compact treasure trove of antiques and history. (The upper floors remain the family's private residence.) Family lore attaches to almost every item, even humble panes of glass. In the mid-1700s, a young Carter woman scratched her initials—still visible—into a dining room pane using the engagement ring her suitor had just handed her. Doubting his sincerity, she wished to see if the diamond was genuine, and this testing of the ring on a window became a family tradition, as shown in several windows around the house.

The plantation reached a peak of prosperity under Charles Carter, and in 1793 his daughter Ann married Henry "Light Horse Harry" Lee in the parlor. They lived for a time at Stratford Hall (see p. 114) where their son Robert E. Lee was born, but in the midst of Harry's financial woes Ann brought the children to live at Shirley. Don't miss the dining room where some of the 60 items of silver her father acquired for his entertainments are on display. Like many Virginians Charles was mad for horse racing, as evidenced by the table's centerpiece—a large silver punch bowl engraved with a portrait of Charles' champion racehorse, Nestor. After victories, the bowl was filled with champagne for Nestor to drink.

Shirley survived the centuries with so few changes thanks to the Carter family's inbred

A portrait of Elizabeth Carter hangs on the dining room wall at Shirley Plantation. In the mid-1700s she agreed to marry William Byrd III—but only after ascertaining that his diamond engagement ring was real by testing it on a window pane in the room.

conservatism. Their resistance to change provoked comment even in the 1850s, when John and Julia Tyler visited from Sherwood Forest (see p. 118). Julia Tyler later wrote, "Shirley is indeed a fine old place, but if it were mine I would arrange it so differently. I should at least have the parlor . . . in conformity with modern fashion."

Visitors are free to stroll the grounds and view the seven 18th-century brick outbuildings on the land side of the house. Four of these buildings enclose a Queen Anne courtyard, perhaps the only surviving example of this architectural feature in the country. The forecourt is formed by a large, two-story kitchen building, a laundry house, and two L-shaped barns, one containing an ice cellar. On the other side of the house, a short stroll brings you to the edge of the James River. The gently sloping lawn must have presented a melancholy sight when, during the Civil War, the grounds and outbuildings were converted into a hospital by the invading Union Army. Distressed by the suffering of the young soldiers, the Carter women put aside their enmity and tended the Yankee wounded, earning a commendation from the grateful Federal commander, Gen. George McClellan.

9 *Shirley Plantation* 501 SHIRLEY PLANTATION ROAD (OFF VA. 5), CHARLES CITY, VA. 23030. (804) 829-5121. OPEN DAILY. WWW.SHIRLEYPLANTATION.COM

NEARBY: **Berkeley Plantation** *(Va. 5, 3 miles W of Shirley Plantation. 804-829-6018)* The birthplace of President William Henry Harrison, Berkeley was built in 1726 in the Georgian style. Its grounds feature extensive gardens and a small Civil War museum. **Westover** *(Va. 5 near Berkeley. 804-829-2882)* This magnificent 1730s Georgian house, built by William Byrd II, is private although the grounds are open daily.

Wilton

RICHMOND, VIRGINIA

The Essence of True Elegance William Randolph III, scion of one of Virginia's most prominent families, built Wilton in 1753. One of 12 mansions the family built in Virginia, Wilton is a superb example of the symmetrical Georgian style and reflects the dignified conservatism of the colonial aristocracy. The house is capped by a low-pitched, hipped roof, its brick facade enlivened by edgings of vermilion-rubbed brick at the corners and around the windows and doorway. For the interior, Randolph commissioned superb floor-to-ceiling paneling for every room of the house, including the closets, which were themselves something of an extravagance at the time. Lavish in its extent, but subtle in its design, Wilton's paneling hints at wealth without proclaiming it too loudly. "Methodical nicety . . . is the essence of true elegance," wrote a Randolph woman in *The Virginia Housewife*, a book about household management. That sentiment describes Wilton exactly.

The parlor paneling recalls the late baroque style of the British architect Sir Christopher Wren and his master carver, Grinling Gibbons. Note how such architectural details as fluted pilasters, arched alcoves, and a finely carved cornice combine to create a sense of movement. Understandably, Randolph's artisans were proud enough to sign their work; during restoration,

The original front entrance to Shirley Plantation overlooks the James River. After one Civil War battle the lawn stretching in front of the portico was covered with Union wounded, and the Carter women— though staunch Confederates—tended to the injured men.

curators discovered a penciled graffito left by one of the original carpenters: "Samson Darril put up this cornish in the year of our Lord 1753."

George Washington stayed as a guest at Wilton in 1775 after attending the Richmond Convention where Patrick Henry delivered his fiery challenge, "Give me Liberty, or give me death!" During a campaign late in the Revolutionary War, Lafayette's army encamped around Wilton, with the marquis himself using the house as his headquarters.

Wilton has been restored and holds an excellent collection of period furnishings by northern and southern craftsmen. Be sure to see one outstanding piece, a tall case clock, 9.5 feet high, by one of the premier clockmakers in America, Simon Willard of Massachusetts.

10 *Wilton House Museum* 215 SOUTH WILTON ROAD, RICHMOND, VA. 23226. (804) 282-5936. OPEN TUES.-SUN.

⑤ 🚹 🍴 🅿 🏛

Virginia House

RICHMOND, VIRGINIA

Old England in the Old Dominion

Virginia House—named not for the commonwealth but for Virginia Chase Steedman Weddell, one of its American owners—incorporates stones from a 12th-century English religious house. Completed in 1119, the Priory of St. Sepulchre in Warwickshire was in operation for more than 400 years, becoming a private manor house when King Henry VIII dissolved all Catholic monasteries in the 1500s. Alexander and Virginia Weddell purchased the building in 1925 when it was threatened with demolition and shipped a portion of it, dismantled and packed in crates, to this hillside overlooking the James River. The redesign and assembly of the building took three years.

Some common household items of the 1930s and 1940s may be found amid the medieval furnishings and artworks—reflecting the curators' interpretation of the house as an expression of the upper-class American drive to create aristocratic surroundings in the New World out of Old World materials. Nonetheless, the prevailing atmosphere is ancient, with weathered timbers, leaded windows, staircases with oak balustrades, and massive oak doors.

The entrance leads to the Great Hall, where you will find a 300-year-old tapestry hanging over a 17th-century stairway ornamented with impressive openwork carving. A suit of armor, purchased by the Weddells from the Tower of London, stands guard at the foot of the stairs. The sunroom, known as the Withdrawing Room, features linenfold paneling from a home in Warwickshire and a ceiling based on a design in a 15th-century castle. Hanging here is a painting of St. Peter that Alexander Weddell purchased in Spain, believing it to be an El Greco. Modern research discovered it to be a skillful forgery, but it remains on display as an example of the Weddells' taste and of the pitfalls that beset hopeful collectors. The east drawing room reflects the eclectic spirit of American country house decor, with furnishings from around the world. Look around and note a Florentine fireplace, an English oak tavern table, brass Buddhas from India, Chinese slippers, Greek terra-cotta bowls, Russian snuffboxes, and pre-Columbian artifacts. Interspersed with these are portraits of the Weddells' distinguished friends, including Anna Pavlova, Jascha Heifetz, Ignacy Paderewski, and Lily Pons.

Upstairs, the library contains roughly 7,000 volumes, including large, illuminated folios bound in leather and steel. A highlight of the Weddell collection is the royal arms of James I,

Virginia House opens into the Great Hall, which, with its tapestries, suit of armor, and wood paneling, recalls Tudor England.

dated 1615 and purchased from William Randolph Hearst when he was staving off bankruptcy. Also of interest is the secret passage Weddell asked his architect, Henry Grant Morse, to contrive in the library. It enabled him to appear in the room as if by magic, to the bafflement of his young nieces and nephews. Virginia House also incorporates elements of two other English country houses. The west wing mimics part of Sulgrave Manor, ancestral home of George Washington's family in Northamptonshire. The tower wing recalls the gatehouse lodge of Wormleighton, ancestral home of Winston Churchill's forebears, the Spencers.

For the grounds the Weddells turned to famed landscape architect Charles Gillette to create a suitable setting for Virginia House. His 8-acre creation, which took 20 years to complete, features Gothic archways, flagstone paths and courtyards, a canal garden, a cloister

garden, terraces, and sunken gardens. Sadly, at the time their garden was reaching its maturity, the Weddells died in a train accident in Missouri. As they had planned, the house passed to the Virginia Historical Society, which owns and maintains the property today.

11 *Virginia House* 4301 SULGRAVE ROAD, RICHMOND, VA. 23221. (804) 353-4251. OPEN TUES.-SUN. WWW.VAHISTORICAL.ORG 🔲🔲🔲🔲🔲

NEARBY: **Agecroft Hall** *(4305 Sulgrave Road, Richmond, Va. 804-353-4241)* Originally built 500 years ago in England, Agecroft Hall was moved to Richmond in 1925. The house serves as an interpretive museum of life in an English manor house during the 16th and 17th centuries.

Maymont

RICHMOND, VIRGINIA

Pink Damask, Narwhal Tusks, and a Swan-shaped Bed

A flamboyant Gilded Age confection, Maymont stands on a riverfront site in the heart of Richmond. Romanesque Revival in style, with walls of rough sandstone, round and octagonal turrets, a wraparound porch with pillars of pink granite, and an arched porte cochere, the house conjures up images of French châteaus, medieval cloisters, and baronial castles. Maj. James H. Dooley, a millionaire financier and railroad investor, built Maymont in the 1890s and named it for his wife, Sallie May. The design was the work of a young Richmond architect, Edgerton Rogers.

Twelve of the mansion's 30 rooms are open to the public, presenting a festive pageant of Gilded Age wealth. The furnishings represent a variety of styles in keeping with the era. The pink drawing room, for example, evokes the French salons of Louis XV, with pink damask-covered walls rising to a painted ceiling. After a meal in the baronial dining hall, with its beamed ceiling and painted tapestries, the gentlemen could retire to the Middle Eastern-style den to enjoy their cigars. For her bedroom Mrs. Dooley commissioned a bed in the shape of an enormous swan. Don't miss her Tiffany & Company dressing table, its surface fashioned of sterling silver inlaid with ivory, embellished with narwhal tusks. The dining room displays another of the Dooleys' treasures, a carved rosewood china cabinet, almost 13 feet high, exhibited at the Paris Universal Exposition in 1855. The rococo revival cabinet contains a duplicate set of White House china made by Haviland for President Rutherford B. Hayes.

The house presides over 100 acres of grounds, with an Italian garden planned by the Richmond firm of Noland and Baskerville, an arboretum, and a series of outbuildings designed to create the impression of a village. In 1975 Maymont began to acquire a set of historical carriages and other vehicles of the Dooleys' era. Preserved in the 1904 carriage house, the 23-vehicle collection includes surreys, a sleigh, a lady's phaeton, a formal landau, a governess' cart, and a road coach.

12 *Maymont* 1700 HAMPTON STREET, RICHMOND, VA. 23221. (804) 358-7166. OPEN TUES.-SUN. 🔲🔲🔲🔲🔲

Maymont's ornate pink drawing room, modeled after an 18th-century French salon, captures the exuberant spirit of the Gilded Age.

Monticello

CHARLOTTESVILLE, VIRGINIA

Thomas Jefferson's Masterpiece on a Mountaintop

Thomas Jefferson spent years constructing, tearing down, and reconstructing his revolutionary vision of a house, Monticello. He had pored over architectural pattern books and prints of the great buildings of the classical world; in Europe he had gazed in admiration at Roman ruins. His genius led him to absorb all this and make something fresh—an architecture that expressed the ideals of the new republic and looked ahead, not back. "I like the dreams of the future," Jefferson wrote, "better than the history of the past."

Jefferson began building Monticello in 1769 when he was 26 years old and partly completed a two-story house derived from designs in Andrea Palladio's *Four Books of Architecture,* a work of the Italian Renaissance inspired by Roman models. But when the new American government sent him to France for five years, he got his first chance to see Roman architecture with his own eyes. He also, in his words, became "violently smitten" by a newly built residence in Paris, the Hôtel de Salm. "All the new and good houses," Jefferson wrote of the places he had seen in France, "are of a single story." After his return to Virginia, he tore apart much of what he had built and undertook the creation of a new Monticello—a three-story building situated on a hilltop, with sweeping views of the central Virginia countryside, which appears from the outside to have only one floor. The first house in America to be covered by a dome, this neoclassic building's Roman motifs declare America as the newest heir to the wisdom of the classical world.

Jefferson disdained what he regarded as the crude simplicity of colonial Virginia's brick buildings, which reminded him of British rule. For Monticello he devised a complex but harmonious geometry of circles, triangles, and octagons. As you walk around the exterior, notice how the walls form an irregular rectangle without sharply defined corners. Inside, you will find more geometric innovation in rooms of varying shape, size, and height—and you will also notice there is something missing: The house has no grand stairway because Jefferson regarded such things as a waste of space.

Enter the house via a hall Jefferson described as his museum, where he displayed busts of European thinkers, maps of America, copies of Old Master paintings, and artifacts sent from the West by the Lewis and Clark expedition, including a Mandan buffalo-hide rug painted with a depiction of a battle. (The hide on display today is a reproduction; the original resides at a Harvard University museum.) Fossils, bones, and antlers reveal Jefferson's interest in documenting the natural life of the New World. One of the house's treasures is the entrance hall's great clock, built to Jefferson's specifications by a Philadelphia clockmaker in the 1790s. The clock, attached to a gong on the roof, was audible for 3 miles. The weights that power the clock serve double duty—as they descend they pass plaques on the wall marking the day of the week.

Beyond the entrance hall lies the mansion's splendid parlor, flooded with light from tall glass doors that offer a stunning view of Monticello's west lawn and Carters Mountain. Jefferson commissioned one of the country's first parquet floors for this room—his Irish

Antlers from Lewis and Clark's expedition grace the entrance hall at Monticello, while an aerial view (pages 128–129) of Jefferson's mountaintop home reveals its grandeur.

carpenter had never made anything like it, and grumbled that he never again would do the same job for $200. The walls display paintings of religious scenes and portraits of explorers, philosophers, and heroes of the Revolution. But this elegant parlor was also a cozy family room. Jefferson's daughter Martha Randolph and her 11 children lived at Monticello with Jefferson after he retired from the Presidency. He doted on his grandchildren, playing chess and perhaps helping them make silhouettes with a camera obscura like the one on display here today. At twilight the family gathered in the parlor to read and in the evenings there were musicales with Jefferson playing the violin, joined by his daughter and her children on the pianoforte, harpsichord, and guitar.

Jefferson's private suite—which one visitor called the "sanctum sanctorum" because so few people were ever admitted to it—includes his bedroom, his "cabinet" or study, his book room, and an attached greenhouse. Jefferson placed his bed in an alcove with open sides: on one side lay his dressing room, on the other his study. Filled with scientific and writing instruments, the study reflects Jefferson's wide-ranging interests and his talents as a designer of practical contrivances. Notice the revolving book stand, which allowed him to consult five open volumes at once. The instruments on display include telescopes, a microscope, thermometers, surveying equipment, and an astronomical clock. Modern visitors are always fascinated by Jefferson's polygraph, a device invented in England for making a duplicate of a letter as it is being written.

The book room, adjacent to the study, displays some books originally owned by Jefferson. He sold his first library of 6,700 volumes to the Library of Congress to replace the books burned by the British in the War of 1812, and later assembled a smaller collection of about a thousand volumes. To find respite from "drudging at the writing table," Jefferson could step from his library into the greenhouse, where he may have maintained an aviary.

In the handsome dining room, lit by a skylight, you will see evidence of Jefferson's propensity for using mechanical aids in his everyday life. A dumbwaiter concealed in the side of the fireplace is connected to the wine cellar in the basement—Jefferson could place an empty bottle in the compartment, lower it, have it replaced, and draw up a fresh bottle. Since the room faces the western side of the house, which receives the strongest winds, Jefferson insulated it with triple-paned glass. Next to the dining room, the tearoom displays busts of political and intellectual figures whom Jefferson admired. He called the room his "most honorable suite."

An enthusiastic farmer, gardener, and landscape designer, Jefferson surrounded his mansion with beautiful decorative plantings, a grove, an orchard, a vineyard, and an extensive vegetable garden. In a 1,000-foot-long terrace along the eastern side of the hilltop, he cultivated 250 varieties of vegetables, including many exotic imported varieties. In his 8-acre orchard he raised 170 varieties of fruit. The expansive west lawn, where Jefferson often romped with his grandchildren, is bordered by a winding walk fringed with flowers. From almost any point on the grounds the view is spectacular. Monticello—Italian for "little mountain"—stands atop an 875-foot-high hill. To the east a broad, flat plain unrolls into the distance, while to the west the hilltop affords a bird's-eye view of Charlottesville and a stunning, 60-mile panorama of the Blue Ridge.

Before or after the house tour, be certain to see another architectural innovation Jefferson designed—the semisubterranean complex that houses the service rooms. You will find some tucked into the hillside facing east, while others line a tunnel that runs the width of the house. In addition, more work buildings and slave cabins once stood along Mulberry Row. In recent years Monticello's curators and historians have devoted a great deal of effort to investigating the lives of the plantation's enslaved blacks, and Plantation Life tours recount the daily lives, work schedules, and personal stories of the estate's large African-American community.

Jefferson died at Monticello on July 4, 1826, exactly 50 years after the Declaration of Independence was adopted by the Continental Congress. He was buried here under a granite obelisk inscribed with what he considered his most important achievements—writing the Declaration of Independence and the Virginia Statute for Religious Freedom, and founding the University of Virginia. The family graveyard, still owned by Jefferson's descendants, lies just beyond the west lawn below the crest of the hill. At his death Jefferson was deeply in debt, a situation that forced the sale of his slaves, personal property, and house. In 1834 a naval officer who admired Jefferson, Uriah P. Levy, purchased the house and some of its land. His nephew sold Monticello to the Thomas Jefferson Memorial Foundation in 1923.

13 *Monticello* VA. 53, 2 MILES SE OF CHARLOTTESVILLE, VA. 22902. (804) 984-9822. OPEN DAILY. WWW.MONTICELLO.ORG

NEARBY: **Ash Lawn**, also known as **Highland** *(Va. 795, 2.5 miles SE of Monticello. 804-293-9539)* A simple piedmont farmhouse owned by President James Monroe, Ash Lawn-Highland displays many original furnishings bought by the Monroes during their years in Europe.

Mansion Museum

WHEELING, WEST VIRGINIA

An Industrialist's Retreat, Transformed into a Museum

Formerly the residence of the wealthy industrialist Earl W. Oglebay, the Mansion Museum interprets the domestic life of Ohio Valley residents from 1790 to 1890. Originally an eight-room farmhouse built in 1846, the house was extensively remodeled by Colonel Oglebay, a Wheeling native who amassed a mining and shipping fortune in Cleveland. After purchasing the house and grounds as a summer retreat in 1900, Oglebay hired a well-known local architect, E.B. Franzheim, to redesign the house in neoclassic style, adding a large front portico, a two-story wing, and rambling side porches.

The mansion's 13 period rooms feature furniture, paintings, china, and pewter. The game room re-creates the oldest period, 1740-1810, with a folding chess table, Queen Anne-style chairs, and a portrait of Cynthia Zane, the daughter of one of Wheeling's founders. The Victorian parlor includes a chair by John Henry Belter, a papier-mâché chess table inlaid with mother-of-pearl, and a tea table with Mrs. Oglebay's silver tea service. The dining room best captures the spirit of the Oglebays' taste, with such federal-period furnishings as a Sheraton banquet table and side table, a Hepplewhite buffet and drop-leaf table, and the family's 19th-century china and silver. The kitchen displays a historical curiosity—a cast-iron stove bearing the stamp "Wheeling Virginia 1866"—that reflects the area's Civil War legacy. Unionist West Virginia had separated from Confederate Virginia in 1863 in a wartime political maneuver that some diehards continue to question, since the U.S. Constitution forbids forming a new state out of an existing one. The stovemaker may have been expressing his political sentiments by steadfastly refusing to alter his mark, even three years after the disputed split.

14 *Mansion Museum* OGLEBAY INSTITUTE, OGLEBAY PARK EXIT OFF I-70, WHEELING, W.VA. 26003. (304) 242-7272. OPEN DAILY.

Ashland

LEXINGTON, KENTUCKY

Statesman's
House of
Nine Lives

A charming and fascinating house, Ashland has had several lives—first as the residence of statesman Henry Clay and later, after a total reconstruction, as home to his descendants, a college official, and finally a museum.

Henry and Lucretia Clay built the first Ashland in a beautiful rural setting surrounded by towering ash trees, around 1806. Ten years later they built wings designed by Benjamin Henry Latrobe, one of America's greatest architects, whose many achievements included work on the U.S. Capitol. Perhaps weakened by earthquakes in 1811 and 1812, the walls settled dangerously over the years, forcing the demolition of the house after Clay's death in 1852. His son James Clay rebuilt the house on the same foundation, following the original, appealingly irregular floor plan with three octagonal rooms, one of them an entrance hall featuring an elliptical stairway. Unfortunately this stair was later removed to make way for a more fashionable, straight staircase.

Kentucky University (later the University of Kentucky) owned Ashland from 1866 to 1882, when it was purchased by Clay's granddaughter Anne Clay McDowell and her husband. Although the ground floor opened to the public in 1950, a series of Clay descendants occupied the second floor until 1958.

Most of the furnishings are family pieces, including Henry Clay's canopied bed and a quilt given to him by the Whig Ladies of Philadelphia in 1844, when Clay was running for President as the Whig Party candidate. The red parlor features a rosewood suite by John Henry Belter; a large, handsome mirror in the drawing room dates from James Clay's occupancy. Still visible nearby are remnants of a Springfield gas machine that converted gasoline into fuel to light the house. The surrounding grounds retain the beauty of Henry Clay's era when, it is said, he would pace the walkways while composing his speeches.

15 *Ashland: The Henry Clay Estate* 120 Sycamore Street, Lexington, Ky. 40502. (606) 266-8581. April through Oct. daily; Nov. through Dec. and Feb. through March Tues.-Sun. www.henryclay.org

🆂 🚹 🍴 🅿 🏛

The Hermitage

HERMITAGE, TENNESSEE

General
Jackson's
Greek Revival
Retreat

Andrew Jackson's impressive home, The Hermitage, belies the popular image of Jackson as a rough-hewn man of the frontier. He built an elegant house, one that had an important impact on American architecture; its Greek Revival facade won many admirers, inspiring the spread of the columnar style through the upper South and the West.

The house seen today is the third Hermitage. Jackson and his wife, Rachel, were living in a plastered, clapboard-covered log cabin when they began building the first Hermitage in 1819. The two-story, federal-style, brick house, five bays wide, was adorned only by a simple arched fanlight over the door. Although the federal

The gracefully curving stairway at The Hermitage offers a close-up look at the dramatic 1830s, hand-blocked scenic wallpaper.

style was passing from fashion, its dignity and solidity appealed to Jackson. In 1831 he hired architect David Morison to enlarge the house, constructing wings for a library and dining room. Morison also added a handsome but modest Greek Revival facade, with one-story columns and a central portico somewhat reminiscent of Jefferson's Monticello (see p. 126). In 1834, just after Jackson left The Hermitage to return to the White House after a brief vacation, a chimney fire all but gutted the house. The President's son, Andrew Jr., managed to save some furniture and personal papers from the flames and was rewarded by his father's pledge, "I will have it rebuilt."

Reconstruction soon began at the hands of Nashville builders Joseph Reiff and William Hume under the supervision of Jackson's son and several of the President's friends. It is unclear who—a builder or one of the informal advisors—had the idea of erecting a grand Greek Revival facade with six, two-story Corinthian columns and a double gallery. Grafting this large colonnade onto the house created a conflict with the old window arrangement. The resolution, to increase the height of the rooms, greatly enhanced the interior. The builders also removed the old arched fanlight over the front door, installing a Greek Revival doorway topped by a horizontal cornice. To complete the renovation, the facade was painted off-white, and the columns and trim were sand-painted to resemble stone.

The furnishings are all Jackson family pieces, with nearly 90 percent dating from the period of Jackson's retirement from the Presidency, 1837 to 1845. Many items have important historical associations, such as the unusual wood-frame leather chair which was a gift from Chief Justice of the United States Roger B. Taney. The dining room contains a set of eight silver serving dishes, with covers topped by stags, once owned by the naval hero Stephen Decatur. (Jackson purchased the set from Decatur's widow when she was in need of funds.)

A ten-year restoration completed in 1996 revealed the original vibrant color scheme and restored six rooms of original wallpaper. In addition, window treatments, upholstery, and bedding have been meticulously reproduced. Particularly spectacular is the scenic wallpaper in the entrance hall depicting the mythical voyage of the Greek hero Telemachus in search of his father, Odysseus. Jackson had a particular fondness for this wallpaper, ordering it not once but three times, as the architectural critic and historian Kenneth Severens noted. Severens speculated that the story of Telemachus—a son's quest to find his father—appealed deeply to Jackson because he never knew his own father, who died before Jackson was born.

Jackson himself died at The Hermitage in 1845, and visitors can see the room where he died almost exactly as he saw it, complete with the Bible, eyeglasses, and teacup he had at his side in his last hours. He was buried in the garden alongside his wife, Rachel, in an exquisitely designed Greek Revival tomb. Jackson has long been revered in Tennessee. The Hermitage became the second Presidential home (George Washington's Mount Vernon was the first) to be administered by a preservation-minded group of women. The Ladies' Hermitage Association has managed the estate since 1889.

16 *The Hermitage: Home of President Andrew Jackson* 4580 RACHEL'S LANE (OFF I-40), HERMITAGE, TENN. 37076. (615) 889-2941. OPEN DAILY EXCEPT THIRD WEEK OF JAN. WWW.THEHERMITAGE.COM

🔲🔲🔲🔲🔲🔲🔲

NEARBY: **Belmont** *(1900 Belmont Boulevard, on the campus of Belmont University, Nashville, Tenn. 615-460-5459)* Belmont is an elaborate, 32-room mansion built in the Italianate style in 1850 for a wealthy cotton-planting family.

$\mathcal{B}$*elle Meade*

NASHVILLE, TENNESSEE

A Horseman's Columned Splendor

Known locally as the Queen of Tennessee Plantations, Belle Meade is a spectacular example of how a house's architectural history can closely reflect its owner's fortunes. The first version of the residence, built in the early 1820s, was much smaller and in the simpler federal style. (Before that, William Harding and his family had lived in a log cabin which still stands on the property.) Like The Hermitage estate, Belle Meade's growth neatly documents the financial rise of a Middle Tennessee family in the antebellum days. In the early 1850s, William Harding redesigned Belle Meade in the Greek Revival style, erecting a monumental, six-column portico with a decorative crown across the top. So impressive is this portico that some have thought it to be the work of the distinguished architect William Strickland. No evidence supports Strickland's role, however, and it is also possible that Harding modeled the house after a South Carolina mansion called Milford, which he admired.

An array of equestrian portraits greets visitors to the front hallway at Belle Meade, a 19th-century plantation famed for its horse-breeding operation.

The estate was the site of a skirmish in the Civil War, and if you look closely you can see the nicks made by musket balls in 1864 on the columns. After the war, William Harding and his son-in-law Gen. William Jackson regained for Belle Meade the fame it had previously enjoyed as a breeding ground of great Thoroughbred racehorses. Iroquois, the first American racer to win the English Derby, in 1881, stood at stud here from 1886 until his death in 1899. Another famous Belle Meade horse, Bonnie Scotland, sired more winners of the Kentucky Derby than any other horse.

Currently a property of the Association for the Preservation of Tennessee Antiquities, Belle Meade has been beautifully restored as a museum of plantation life and horse-racing history. About a third of the furnishings are original, including family portraits; the bed where President Grover Cleveland slept during a visit in 1887; silver racing trophies; equestrian portraits by such notable artists as Henry Stull, Edward Troy, and Henri DeLattre; and a pair of silver-topped inkwells fashioned from the hooves of Iroquois after the fabled stallion died.

17 *Belle Meade Plantation* 5025 HARDING ROAD (US 70S), NASHVILLE, TENN. 37205. (615) 356-0501 OR (800) 270-3991. OPEN DAILY. WWW.CITYSEARCH.COM/NAS/PLANTATION 🅢 🚶 ♿ 🍴 🅿 🏛

*H*unt-Phelan House

MEMPHIS, TENNESSEE

Headquarters for North and South

One of the oldest residences in Memphis, Hunt-Phelan House was built between 1828 and 1832 for George Hubbard Wyatt, a one-legged Virginia land speculator. He outfitted his home with gas lights—generating the gas himself by burning cottonseed and resin—and installed what was probably the first indoor bathroom in the city. Pressed by creditors, Wyatt departed for the West, leaving his federal-style brick house in the ownership of a bank. A more prosperous owner, William Richardson Hunt, added the house's beautiful Greek Revival portico in the 1850s and constructed new outbuildings, including a kitchen, a laundry, a repair shop, slave quarters, and a redbrick schoolhouse to educate the children of local white families. He also furnished the interior with imported Heppelwhite and Chippendale furniture and marble mantels. The gardens, designed by a New Orleans landscape architect, include a lily pool and a greenhouse. The Hunts entertained frequently, and counted Jefferson Davis and his wife among their guests.

During the Civil War combatants from both sides made use of the house. Confederate Gen. Leonidas Polk had his headquarters here and appointed Hunt a captain. The house switched sides after Memphis fell to Federal forces—Gen. Ulysses S. Grant and his staff used it as their headquarters in June and July 1862, though Grant, preferring to share the privations of his troops, slept in a tent in the yard. Subsequently, the Federal Army used the house as a hospital and recreation center for Union soldiers. The soldiers tore down the brick schoolhouse, but after the war a wooden one was built for the purpose of educating freed blacks. This structure, slated for restoration, was one of the first Freedmen's Bureau schools in Tennessee.

After the war the Hunt family returned to the house, bringing with them the furniture they had removed during the fighting. Their daughter Julia married into the Phelan family. A descendant, Stephen Phelan, occupied the house until his death in 1993, living as a recluse and keeping a close watch over the old family heirlooms. Three years after his death the house officially opened as a museum, with original furniture, silver, and documents.

 **18** *Hunt-Phelan House* 533 BEALE STREET, MEMPHIS, TENN. 38103. (901) 525-8225. OPEN DAILY MEMORIAL DAY THROUGH LABOR DAY; THURS.-MON. REST OF YEAR.

*M*allory-Neely House

MEMPHIS, TENNESSEE

A Victorian Gem, Lovingly Preserved

Home to one of Memphis' leading merchant families, the Mallory-Neely House preserves a festive, sumptuous, Victorian interior that ranks as one of the finest in the region, and perhaps in the country. The Italianate house was built in 1852 by the first owner of the property, Isaac Kirtland.

When James Columbus Neely purchased it in 1883, he expanded the house to three stories encompassing 25 rooms, while preserving the Italianate facade. A four-story tower presides over the entrance, which is flanked by an arcaded porch. The light brown stucco exterior imparts a warmth and charm to the facade.

The two stained-glass windows Neely purchased at the 1893 Chicago World's Fair may be seen in the front door and on the landing of the main stair—together creating a spectacular scene of color and light. Pause as you enter the house and notice how craftsmen painted the walls a delicate dark green, texturing the wet paint using grainer's combs. They then stenciled gold fleurs-de-lis along the green walls and elaborate and colorful designs onto the entrance hall's expansive ceiling. But it is the double parlor that showcases the house's high-Victorian spirit at its most exuberant. Here the ceiling features bold, star-shaped medallions and a marvelous cornice, thickly encrusted with plaster embellishments. A marble copy of "The Kiss," a sculpture by Auguste Rodin, lends the room a note of romance. Furnishings include an 1850s rococo revival mirror that hangs over a French marble-topped commode made of fruitwood and purchased in Paris. In a corner of the room stands a lovely Chinese screen, fashioned of embroidered silk in a hand-carved teak frame, purchased at the 1904 St. Louis World's Fair.

In 1900 the Neelys' youngest daughter, Frances, known as Daisy to the family, was married at home to Barton Lee Mallory. She lived here until her death in 1969 at the age of 98, preserving many of the decorations and furnishings.

19 *Mallory-Neely House* 652 Adams Avenue, Memphis, Tenn. 38105. (901) 523-1484. Open March through Dec. Tues.-Sun. www.memphismuseums.org 🟦🔼♿🏛

NEARBY: **Graceland** *(Elvis Presley Boulevard, Memphis, Tenn. 901-332-3322 or 800-238-2000)* Individual headsets tour the way through Elvis Presley's 14-acre estate, including the main house, Elvis' racquetball building, and his original business office. A trophy building houses a collection of gold records and awards, along with an extensive display of Elvis mementos. Separate museums on the property feature his automobiles and airplanes.

The social center of the Mallory-Neely House, the formal Victorian double parlor was the scene of parties, weddings, and even funerals.

Biltmore

ASHEVILLE, NORTH CAROLINA

A Vanderbilt Château in the North Carolina Mountains   The largest private residence in America—an immense mansion, in the style and on the scale of the châteaus of the French nobility—Biltmore occupies a spectacular site in the Blue Ridge mountains of western North Carolina. Completed in 1895 at the height of the Gilded Age, it was an outpost of New York's Vanderbilt family, and remains in the ownership of the builder's descendants. The founder of the family fortune was Cornelius "Commodore" Vanderbilt. One of his grandsons, George, commissioned one of the country's most prominent architects, Richard Morris Hunt, to design the house. Hunt had trained in France, where Vanderbilt had traveled frequently. Both admired the majestic architecture of the Renaissance, in particular the Château de Blois in France's Loire Valley. Hunt constructed this American interpretation out of Indiana limestone, and Vanderbilt filled it with a princely collection of art, antiques, and specially crafted furniture.

A massive entrance tower looms over the front door, which opens to a series of colossal ground floor rooms. The Tapestry Gallery, 90 feet long, displays three tapestries made about 1530 as part of an allegorical series, "The Triumph of the Seven Virtues." The gallery also displays three Vanderbilt portraits painted by two of the most eminent painters of the 19th century—John Singer Sargent, who painted George Vanderbilt and his mother, and James Abbott McNeill Whistler, who painted George's wife, Edith. The gallery serves as the passageway to Biltmore's sumptuous library. George read eight languages and collected 23,000 books, the oldest dating from 1561. About half of his collection may be seen in the library's walnut cases. The room is centered upon a massive black marble fireplace with an even larger walnut overmantel, both the work of Karl Bitter, an Austrian artist and Hunt protégé. Large carved figures of Roman goddesses adorn the overmantel, flanking a 17th-century French tapestry. To lighten what could have been a gloomy preserve, Vanderbilt purchased an enormous painted ceiling—64 feet by 32 feet, on 13 canvases—which once hung in the Pisani Palace in Venice. The ceiling depicts a mythological scene, "The Chariot of Aurora," in which the goddess Aurora and her cherubic attendants usher in the dawn.

Next, visit the Banquet Hall, the mansion's largest room, which measures 72 feet long by 42 feet wide with a barrel-vaulted ceiling rising 70 feet from the floor. Bitter carved a 25-foot-long limestone frieze entitled "The Return from the Chase" to decorate the enormous triple fireplace at one end of the room. The organ loft at the other end is decorated with a five-panel tableau of oak, depicting a scene from Richard Wagner's opera *Tannhauser*. In addition, five Flemish tapestries of the 16th century adorn the walls, portraying scenes from Roman mythology.

Biltmore offered its guests such diversions as a billiard room, a bowling alley, an indoor swimming pool, and a gymnasium. In keeping with the custom of European nobility, Vanderbilt maintained a game preserve on the estate, as well as a stable for 25 horses. Designed for entertainments of baronial extravagance, Biltmore was planned as a self-sustaining estate, supported by careful timber harvesting, farming, dairying, and other enterprises. To house the workers for this operation Vanderbilt purchased a nearby town, christened it Biltmore Village, and provided it with a church, a school, a hospital, houses, and shops. Vanderbilt further engaged the services of noted landscape architect Frederick Law Olmsted to devise a

The bibliophile George Vanderbilt took refuge in his library, one of 250 rooms in Biltmore (following pages), seen at twilight amid the scenic Blue Ridge.

plan for the vast, 125,000-acre estate. Olmsted designed a 250-acre pleasure park and set aside land for farms, but advised devoting most of the land to a commercial timber forest. The operations George Vanderbilt founded still help support Biltmore, which has been open to the public since the 1930s.

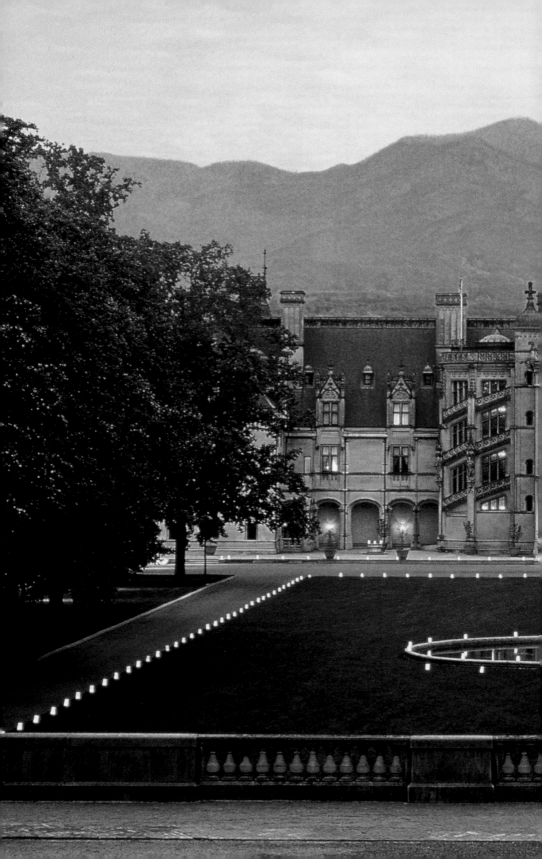

Beginning in 1870, the house served as the convent school and mother house of the Sisters of Charity of Our Lady of Mercy. In 1955 Historic Charleston Foundation acquired the property.

Although the Russell family's original furnishings have been dispersed, the house displays a superb collection of period furnishings. Many were made in Charleston itself, such as the table and sideboard in the dining room, dating from about 1800, and, in the library and dining room, chairs with backs in a Gothic arch pattern. The withdrawing room displays English armchairs once owned by the Allstons. In addition, the drawing rooms have been furnished as musical rooms with costly, imported instruments that would have been familiar to wealthy Charlestonians of Russell's day, such as a harp made in Paris about 1803, a fortepiano made in London about 1790, and a lyre-guitar dating from the 1770s.

The house is still embraced by a garden that has long been noted as one of the city's most pleasant. About 1820 an English traveler called upon Mr. Russell, whom he described as "residing in a splendid mansion, surrounded by a wilderness of flowers, and bowers of myrtles, oranges, and lemons, smothered with fruit and flowers . . . living in a nest of roses."

22 *Nathaniel Russell House* 51 MEETING STREET, CHARLESTON, S.C. 29401. (843) 724-8481. OPEN DAILY.

🔲 🔲 🔲 🔲

Heyward-Washington House

CHARLESTON, SOUTH CAROLINA

A Treasure-house of Southern Furniture

A showplace for some of the finest furniture made in Charleston, the Heyward-Washington House was home to Thomas Heyward, a wealthy planter and signer of the Declaration of Independence. He commissioned a house thoroughly in keeping with the sober Georgian style in vogue before the Revolution. In its floor plan, Heyward's residence typifies a form known as the Charleston double house—roughly square with rooms at each corner and a central stair hall. (In contrast, Charleston's single houses were only one room deep.) The severe brick facade utterly lacks adornment save for the small fanlight over the front door—the elegance is within. Scholars believe that Heyward engaged one of Charleston's most skilled cabinetmakers, Thomas Elfe, to create the woodwork adorning the interior. You can examine the fine craftsmanship in the second-floor drawing room, where the mantelpiece features an overmantel bordered with Elfe's distinctive mahogany fretwork, embodying the artist's restrained, understated style. Note, too, the two mahogany straight chairs in the drawing room that incorporate similar fretwork and may also have been made by Elfe.

The house's second name, Washington, comes not from a subsequent Charleston owner but from the President himself, who stayed here for a week in April 1791 while touring the South. Washington was charmed by the house and by Charlestonians, whom he judged to be "wealthy—Gay—& hospitable." Heyward sold the house in 1794 to John Grimké, whose two daughters Sarah and Angelina became, ironically for Charleston, leading abolitionists.

The house fell upon hard times, seeing use as a boardinghouse and bakery, until the Charleston Museum acquired it in 1929 and restored it, re-creating the rooms as Heyward

Nathaniel Russell House's magnificent "flying" staircase curves past an 18th-century portrait of Mary Rutledge Smith, a prominent early Charlestonian.

and George Washington would have seen them. Be sure not to miss the glory of the house's collection, the superlative library bookcase known as the Holmes bookcase. Fashioned by an unknown master cabinetmaker, the mahogany case stands almost 11 feet in height and features inlaid satinwood scrolls and ivory bellflowers.

23 *Heyward-Washington House* 87 Church Street, Charleston, S.C. 29403. (843) 722-0354. Open daily. www.charlestonmuseum.com 🅂 🚶

Edmondston-Alston House

CHARLESTON, SOUTH CAROLINA

A Gracious Marriage of Styles by the Battery

The stately Edmondston-Alston House is one of Charleston's most splendid dwellings. Two family names and two architectural styles coexist in this three-story, stuccoed house on the Battery with a commanding view of the harbor. Charles Edmondston, a Scottish immigrant who made a large fortune in the cotton market, built this house in the federal style in 1828, but had to sell it nine years later during an economic downturn. William Alston, a wealthy rice planter, purchased it for his son Charles, who remodeled it in the prevailing Greek Revival style and added a parapet carrying the family coat of arms. It has remained in the same family since.

Look closely at the piazza and notice how its columns reveal a change of style. The older, second story features simple Doric columns while the colonnade above features the more ornate Corinthian columns characteristic of the Greek Revival period. Gen. Pierre Beauregard, the Confederate commander in charge of the bombardment of Fort Sumter, stood on this piazza to observe the barrage that launched the Civil War.

The first two floors are open to the public, displaying furniture, paintings, silver, and other family items of the antebellum period. These include an English hunting rifle in its original carrying case, made in 1850 for Charles Alston, Jr.; a six-piece, silver tea and coffee service engraved with the Alston family crest; portraits; and books. The Alstons' library of some 2,000 volumes is displayed in the gentlemen's withdrawing room. Plates from Audubon's *Viviparous Quadrupeds of North America* decorate the ladies' withdrawing room, while a portrait of Charles Alston's grandmother Susannah Maybank looks over an English Regency furniture suite of about 1820 in the east drawing room. In the morning room, "View Along East Battery," painted in 1831, shows the house as it looked before the Greek Revival details were added.

24 *Edmondston-Alston House* 21 East Battery, Charleston, S.C. 29403. (843) 722-7171. Open daily. www.middletonplace.org 🅂 🚶

NEARBY: **Calhoun Mansion** *(16 Meeting Place, Charleston, S.C. 843-722-8205)* This 35-room mansion, built in 1876 for banker George W. Williams, displays 19th-century furnishings. **Aiken-Rhett House** *(48 Elizabeth Street, Charleston, S.C. 843-723-1159)* A massive late federal house built in 1817, it was later remodeled in Greek Revival style; five Gothic Revival outbuildings are still standing. **Boone Hall** *(S.C. 17, 8 miles W of Charleston, S.C. 843-884-4371)* This Georgian-style colonial plantation house was rebuilt in 1935 with bricks made on the plantation. The grounds feature original slave cabins. **Drayton Hall** *(S.C. 61, 9 miles W of Charleston, S.C. 843-766-0188)* This remarkable Georgian-Palladian villa, built about 1740, is shown unrestored and unfurnished to highlight its unique architectural detail. **Middleton Place** *(S.C. 61, 14 miles W of Charleston, S.C. 843-556-6020)* A Tudor-Gothic Revival guesthouse survived when Sherman's army destroyed this plantation in the Civil War. Today it spotlights original furnishings and paintings, as well as beautiful gardens.

Edmondston-Alston House's three-tiered piazza looks out onto the scenic Charleston Harbor—while capturing its refreshing sea breezes.

S wan House

ATLANTA, GEORGIA

Palladian
Perfection

Inspired by the 16th-century Italian villas of Andrea Palladio, and by the works of Palladio's followers in 17th- and 18th-century England, architect Philip Trammell Shutze brought the classic grandeur of the Renaissance to Atlanta in his design for Swan House. Gemlike in its perfection inside and out, it was completed in 1928 for Edward Hamilton and Emily Inman. They named their residence for Mrs. Inman's favorite bird, which is amply represented in the decoration and furnishings. With mathematical precision, Shutze created symmetrical facades, their perfection softened by delicately hued stucco. A massive, four-columned portico on the east facade recalls English Palladian models, while the western side evokes Italy.

The interior reflects a crucial transition in the decoration of great American houses. Its designer, Ruby Ross Wood, had worked with Elsie de Wolfe, whose influential book *The House in Good Taste* helped sweep away the last vestiges of somber Victorianism in favor of brighter, more open interiors in pastel colors, enlivened by floral prints on wallpaper and slipcovers. The result is splendid, beginning with the striking design of the entrance hall where a circular hall framed by Ionic columns opens onto a rectangular stair hall with a curving staircase—an arresting architectural combination made more dramatic by a dazzling black-and-white marble floor.

The Inmans had been purchasing furniture and decorative arts for years, and in some instances Shutze may have designed rooms around their collection. For example, Shutze may have arranged the spacing of the dining room windows to accommodate Emily Inman's beautiful pair of gilded, marble-topped, 18th-century English console tables adorned with

The perfectly symmetrical exterior of Swan House (below) opens into a light and airy interior filled with sinuous shapes and dramatic angles (opposite).

swans. And in the library, Shutze incorporated a late 17th-century overmantel, possibly by a student of the master carver Grinling Gibbons.

Upon Mrs. Inman's death in 1965, the Inman heirs sold the house, furnishings, and grounds to the Atlanta Historical Society, which today administers the property along with an adjacent museum of the city's history.

25 *Swan House* THE ATLANTA HISTORY CENTER, 130 WEST PACES FERRY ROAD NW, ATLANTA, GA. 30305. (404) 814-4000. OPEN DAILY. WWW.ATLHIST.ORG 🛈 🚶 🅿 🏛

NEARBY: **Rhodes Hall** *(1516 Peachtree Street NW, Atlanta, Ga. 404-881-9980).* Now housing the Georgia Trust for Historic Preservation, Rhodes Hall was constructed of Stone Mountain granite in the Romanesque Revival style.

Hay House

MACON, GEORGIA

Macon's Palace of the South

Proclaimed the "palace of the south" by a Macon journalist in 1860, Hay House is indeed one of the finest Italianate mansions in the region. Designed by the New York firm of T. Thomas and Son, it was built between 1855 and 1859 for local entrepreneur William Butler Johnston and his wife, Anne. Crowned by a three-story cupola 80 feet above ground, the four-story house contains 18,000 square feet of living space. The beautifully decorated entrance hall strikes a palatial note with trompe l'oeil marbleized walls, stenciled ceilings, and intricate gilded plaster cornices. The spacious dining room was designed to accommodate large banquets under a vaulted 24-foot-high ceiling. The house also featured the era's most up-to-date amenities—central heating, gas lighting, hot and cold running water, a ventilation system, and an early intercom system of speaking tubes linking 15 rooms.

W.B. Johnston, who had a flair for mechanical tinkering, apprenticed as a watchmaker in New York before opening a watchmaking and jewelry business in Macon in 1832. He prospered in the burgeoning new town, and later organized a bank, invested in railroads, and helped develop the region's public utilities. The Johnstons had barely begun decorating their house—using paintings, sculpture, china, and porcelain they had purchased on their honeymoon to Europe in the early 1850s—when the Civil War broke out. Because Johnston served as an official of the Confederate treasury, with responsibility for the safekeeping of sums as high as 1.5 million dollars, there were whispers that he kept a hoard of Confederate gold at home in a secret room. In fact the house does have a concealed chamber, but it was used as a linen closet.

After the death of the Johnstons' daughter, Mary Ellen Felton, in 1926, the house was acquired by Parks Lee Hay, an insurance executive. In 1964 Hay descendants opened the house to the public, displaying some of the original Johnston furnishings and artworks, items from the Felton period of 1888 to 1926, and furnishings from their own occupancy. As a result, Hay House reflects more than a century of southern domestic life.

26 *Hay House* 934 GEORGIA AVENUE, MACON, GA. 31201. (912) 742-8155. OPEN DAILY. 🛈 🚶 ♿ 🅿 🏛

Cà d'Zan

SARASOTA, FLORIDA

A Circus Master's Italian Fantasy

A sprawling, opulent mansion inspired by the Doge's Palace in Venice, Cà d'Zan ("house of John" in Venetian dialect) was the home of circus entrepreneur John Ringling and his wife, Mable. Designed largely by the New York architect Dwight James Baum, and completed in 1926 at the rumored cost of 1.5 million dollars, the 31-room mansion dazzles the eye outside and in. A richly decorated, 61-foot-high, Moorish-style tower, reached by a curving staircase, dominates the center of the house and looks west over Sarasota Bay. Profuse with colorful glazed terra-cotta, the exterior features balconies, tinted glass, prominent quoins, medallions, gargoyles, and a parade of windows adorned with Venetian Gothic trefoils and quatrefoils. The house's western facade overlooks a vast 200-foot-long marble terrace and a monumental marble stairway to a dock, where the Ringlings kept a genuine Venetian gondola and a 125-foot yacht.

A colonnaded loggia surrounds the garden courtyard of the Ringlings' art museum. Designed like an Italian Renaissance villa, the gallery is located on the grounds of Cà d'Zan, the Ringlings' residence.

Light floods onto the marble checkerboard-patterned floor in the Great Hall at Cà d'Zan. French doors glazed with tinted Venetian glass lead out toward Sarasota Bay.

Enormous walnut doors, 12 feet high, open onto a luxurious interior, with floors of black Belgian and white Alabama marble in checkerboard squares, walls of black Italian walnut, and painted ceilings. A two-and-a-half-story living room at the center of the house rises to a colored-glass skylight surrounded by paintings of mythological figures and heraldic shields. The room's huge crystal chandelier originally hung in the old Waldorf-Astoria Hotel in New York City. A marble staircase leads to a balcony, where a row of tapestries conceals the 1,200 pipes of an Aeolian organ, which Ringling installed at a cost of $50,000.

Near the mansion, Ringling built a separate gallery to house his large collection of European art, which focuses on the baroque period. He bequeathed the gallery, its collections, and Cà d'Zan to the state of Florida, which administers the complex as the John and Mable Ringling Museum of Art.

27 *Cà d'Zan* JOHN AND MABLE RINGLING MUSEUM OF ART, 5401 BAY SHORE ROAD, SARASOTA, FLA. 34243. (941) 359-5700. OPEN DAILY. WWW.RINGLING.ORG

𝒲hitehall

PALM BEACH, FLORIDA

The Taj Mahal of North America

In 1902 Standard Oil founding partner and Florida developer Henry M. Flagler built Whitehall as a wedding present for his wife, Mary Lily Kenan Flagler. At that time Flagler was developing Palm Beach as a resort for the ultrawealthy families of the Gilded Age. The New York architecture firm of Carrère and Hastings responded to Flagler's commission with a beaux arts-style house based on the designs made popular at the 1893 Chicago World's Columbian Exposition. (The exposition was referred to as the White City because of its monumental, classically inspired, white buildings.) Whitehall's gleaming white facade is resplendent in the Florida sun; its towering neoclassic columns and its tiled, barrel-vaulted roof evoke the days of the Spanish Empire. The mansion's size—55 rooms occupying 60,000 square feet—its sumptuous interior decoration, and the up-to-date conveniences of electricity and central heating all inspired a New York newspaper to declare it the Taj Mahal of North America.

Flagler himself took a personal hand in the design. He told his architects to moderate the Spanish influence on the exterior and to lower the ceiling of the entrance room, called Marble Hall, by 8 feet. While this decision may have reduced the grandeur of the room, it added some intimacy to the huge, 4,400-square-foot space, which is decorated with seven varieties of marble, ceiling paintings depicting Prosperity and Happiness, statuary, and furniture. The

Palm trees add to the tropical charm of Whitehall, a magnificent mansion of white stucco and marble topped by a red-tiled roof.

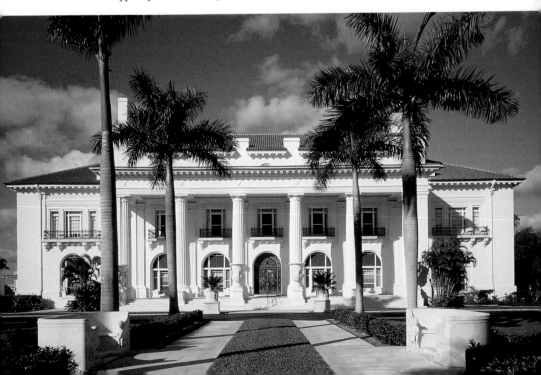

New York decorating firm of Pottier & Stymus designed the rest of the interior in keeping with the custom of the era: as a series of period rooms in styles such as Louis XIV, Louis XV, Louis XVI, and Italian Renaissance.

Some years after Flagler's death in 1913, the house was remodeled as a hotel with a 300-room tower (since removed). His granddaughter, Jean Flagler Matthews, rescued the house from demolition in 1959 and established the Flagler Museum. With many of the original furnishings returned to their rooms, Whitehall evokes the grandeur of the Gilded Age as well as the optimism and entrepreneurial spirit of Flagler himself.

28 *Whitehall* Henry Morrison Flagler Museum, 1 Whitehall Way, Palm Beach, Fla. 33480. (561) 655-2833. Open Tues.-Sun. www.flagler.org 🛈 🚶 ♿ 🅿 🏛

Vizcaya
MIAMI, FLORIDA

An Italian Villa on the Bay Fourteen years after Henry Flagler built Whitehall, Chicago industrialist James Deering vied with him in extravagance by erecting Vizcaya, a 70-room Italian Renaissance-style villa. More than a thousand workers, many brought to Florida from Europe, helped to complete the estate in 1916. Vizcaya served as a winter retreat for the sickly, cultured Deering, executive vice president of and a major stockholder in the International Harvester Company. Deering's artistic supervisor, Paul Chalfin, had studied painting under James Abbott McNeill Whistler in France, served as a museum curator at the Museum of Fine Arts in Boston, lectured at Columbia University in New York, and worked with noted interior designer Elsie de Wolfe. Chalfin selected the architect for the project, F. Burrell Hoffman, Jr., and embarked on a campaign of construction and acquisition that led Deering repeatedly to ask, "Must we be so grand?" When completed the house and its grounds required a staff of 80.

The mansion, meant to evoke a 16th-century Italian estate, achieves its goal admirably. Chalfin designed the interior in the eclectic mode so often seen in great American houses of the period. On travels with Deering, he assembled a magnificent collection of European furniture, artworks, and antique architectural elements with which to adorn Vizcaya in a four-century progression of styles, from the early Renaissance to the neoclassic. Deering would greet guests in the festive, rococo reception room; then visitors would sit down to conversation in the brooding, shadowy Renaissance hall, dominated by a massive French chimneypiece from the 1500s. Here the beamed ceiling looming overhead is framed by four antique sections of a heavy, carved, wooden cornice of the late 16th century.

A 10-acre, formal, Italian Renaissance garden extends from the southern side of the house, studded with statuary, lagoons, and grottoes. To the east Vizcaya looks over Biscayne Bay, restrained by a seawall with decorative bridges at each end. A great stone barge, a triumph of engineering, lies just offshore, built as a breakwater.

29 *Vizcaya Museum and Gardens* 3251 South Miami Avenue, Miami, Fla. 33129. (305) 250-9133. Open daily.
🛈 🚶 🍴 🅿 🏛

The grand Villa Viscaya looks out over Biscayne Bay.

aineswood

DEMOPOLIS, ALABAMA

A Greek
Revival
Treasure

One of the most fascinating Greek Revival houses in America, Gaineswood offers an imposing exterior and lavishly embellished rooms. Owner Nathan Bryan Whitfield, a wealthy planter, designed the house and spent nearly two decades constructing it, from 1843 to 1861. Whitfield enclosed the house with four colonnades of different sizes, including a severe Doric portico sheltering the porte cochere. He made extensive use of columns within the house as well, but with festive rather than monumental effect. The drawing room, which Whitfield declared "the most splendid room in Alabama," features a veritable forest of columns and pilasters topped with delicately worked Corinthian capitals. In this room Whitfield used vis-à-vis mirrors—two mirrors set across from one another—to create an infinite, playful series of reflections. Whitfield also made clever use of a mirror in the stair hall, placing it opposite the foot of the stairs so visitors seem to descend to greet themselves. The dining room and parlor express the house's theme of playful, festive monumentality as well. Both rooms contain domed ceilings with elaborate Italianate plaster ornamentation. Atop each dome a round lantern—a cupola in miniature—is accentuated by diminutive plaster columns and plaster acanthus-leaf friezes. The abundant plaster ornamentation you see throughout the house was inspired by designs from pattern books by the architect Minard Lafever. Whitfield himself designed one of the house's distinctive items, an instrument he called a flutina, which made the music of a small wind ensemble.

During the construction of Gaineswood, Whitfield had stoically endured the mishaps that plague a man who lives in a house while simultaneously building it. One night in 1848 a sudden storm sent torrents of water through the unfinished roof. As Whitfield wrote in a letter to his daughter, "I got a complete shower bath. I woke up about midnight . . . in a large puddle of water." Later that year his enthusiasm for the project wavered a bit—"I am getting quite tired of it," he wrote, "and I hope to see it completed but this I cannot hope to see under at least 12 months more." In fact it would take him another 13 years to finish the job. Nonetheless, Whitfield remained proud of his creation. When he put up a column in the hallway he tucked inside a note, discovered in the 1970s, saying that the column "was made by Gen. Nathan B. Whitfield and put together on the 9th day of August 1854."

After touring the house, wander the gardens surrounding Gaineswood and appreciate Whitfield's talent as a landscape designer. Lady banksia rosebushes flourish near the estate's Cedar Avenue entrance and the lawn features crape myrtles and cedar, oak, and redbud trees. On two sides of the house, balustrades with boxwood hedges border antebellum gardens. Whitfield again stated his Greek Revival theme near the north garden with a domed gazebo. Finally, to preside over his creation, Whitfield put up a statue of Pomona, the ancient goddess of fruit.

30 *Gaineswood* 805 SOUTH CEDAR AVENUE, DEMOPOLIS, ALA. 36732. (334) 289-4846. OPEN DAILY. WWW.DEMOPOLIS.COM/GAINESWOOD

Mirrors facing one another in Gaineswood's elaborate drawing room (opposite) create the illusion of an endless procession of columns. Moonlight illuminates the colonnaded exterior (pages 158–159), as well as a statue of the Roman goddess Pomona.

The rotunda and surrounding balconies at Waverley provided a dramatic setting for 19th-century plantation parties and dances.

Waverley

WEST POINT, MISSISSIPPI

Ingenious
Design by
an Amateur
Architect

Among the many southern mansions designed by amateurs, Waverley stands out for its cleverness, its ingeniously simple practicality, and its capacity to take you completely by surprise. Deceptively straightforward on the exterior, Waverley appears to be a two-story house topped by a large, octagonal cupola. Instead of the usual projecting portico, it features an indented veranda supported by two fluted Ionic columns. Stepping inside, you see that the builder reversed the common formula and put the architectural grandeur within. The interior hall rises four stories (65 feet) through a grand set of balconies and curving stairways, drawing your eye up. In summer the spacious hall cools the house, quite noticeably, by drawing warm air upward in an inspired and successful effort at climate control.

George Hampton Young, a cotton planter and land speculator, built Waverley in 1852 to house his family of 12. After Young's death in 1880 it passed to his son William. Although the house stood empty from 1913 to the 1960s, it survived the hiatus in good condition. The subsequent owners carefully restored the house and furnished it with an excellent collection of period pieces, including a half-tester bed from the shop of Prudent Mallard of New Orleans, and a rosewood table believed to be from the New York shop of John Henry Belter. Be sure to enter the library, which doubled as a family sitting room, and note the built-in secretary that served as an informal plantation post office, with a drop-leaf writing surface and 26 pigeon holes for incoming mail. It may have seen use in 1893 when William Young and some of his sporting associates gathered in the room to establish the National Foxhunters Association. Today Waverley is a registered national historic landmark.

31 *Old Waverley Plantation Mansion* OFF MISS. 50, E OF WEST POINT, MISS. 39773. (601) 494-1399. OPEN DAILY. 🅢 🅰 🅟 🈐

Natchez Grand Houses
Auburn, Rosalie, Melrose, Stanton Hall

Few places in the South are as rich in architectural treasures as Natchez, Mississippi, whose residents became immensely wealthy from trading in cotton raised in the surrounding lowlands. After Eli Whitney invented the cotton gin in 1793, cotton production in this area soared from 36,000 pounds to 1.2 million pounds in just four years. The city's fortunes received a further boost with the start of steamboat service in 1811.

Natchez gave the South the monumental columned portico, an architectural proclamation of wealth and pride that soon spread across the region. Resplendent rows of giant columns sprouted elsewhere, but the grandeur of Natchez remained unsurpassed. Ironically, a number of the owners and architects of the city's great houses were transplanted northerners who came to Natchez to ride the crest of the cotton wave. Occupied by Federal troops in the Civil War but largely undamaged, Natchez devotedly preserves its architectural legacy.

Auburn

NATCHEZ, MISSISSIPPI

The Birth of the Columnar Style

In the history of American architecture there are few houses more influential than Auburn—the first southern house to have a giant order, or monumental, portico. Its architect, a northerner named Levi Weeks, wrote in 1812 that Auburn would be "the first house in the Territory on which was ever attempted any of the orders of Architecture." Four Ionic columns support a triangular pediment projecting 12 feet from the brick facade. As an architectural device, the portico offers beauty as well as associations with the heroic classical epoch. Its monumentality bespeaks pride in the astounding prosperity of the southern cotton kingdom. In ensuing decades a massive row of columns, in many variations, became the hallmark of southern architecture. In his design for the rest of the house Weeks revealed a conservative taste. The interior reflects the federal style—still fashionable in 1812—with some older, Georgian elements. The fluted pilasters and heavy broken pediments of the handsome carved doorways, for example, would not be out of place in a colonial mansion. Inside, the loveliest embellishment is the graceful spiral staircase which spins a complete circle as it ascends and disappears into the second floor.

Weeks built Auburn for a fellow Yankee, Lyman Harding, a Harvard-educated lawyer from Massachusetts who arrived in Mississippi penniless, according to Weeks, and went on to become the territory's first attorney general. After his death, Dr. Stephen Duncan purchased the house in 1827 for $20,000. Duncan prospered as a cotton planter and enlarged

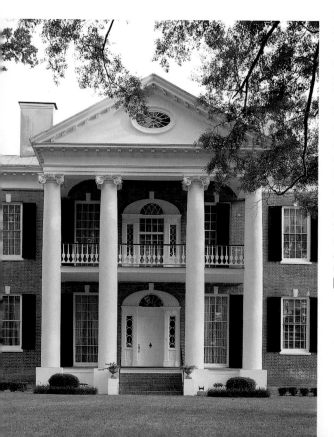

the house, adding wings at the sides and building a separate, temple-form billiard hall in the yard. Unfortunately, when Duncan's descendants gave the house and grounds to the city of Natchez in 1911, the city decided to auction the furnishings. Under the auspices of the Auburn Garden Club, the mansion has been furnished with appropriate antebellum pieces, including some items originally owned by the Duncan family.

32 *Auburn* 400 DUNCAN AVENUE, NATCHEZ, MISS. 39121. (601) 442-5981 OR (800) 647-6742. OPEN DAILY, CALL FOR HOURS AND ANNUAL SPRING AND FALL PILGRIMAGE TOUR SCHEDULE. WWW.NATCHEZPILGRIMAGE.COM

Two-story-high Ionic columns grace the grand portico at Auburn, the first house in the South to adopt the monumental architectural style that would become standard for southern plantations.

Rosalie's double parlor features John Henry Belter furniture and a pair of gilt mirrors that survived the Civil War by being wrapped in blankets and stored in caves.

Rosalie

NATCHEZ, MISSISSIPPI

A Temple of Fine Taste   The design of Rosalie, completed in 1823, continued the progression of Natchez architecture begun with Auburn. Located near the Mississippi River at the site of an old French fort, it was one of the earliest houses in the city to feature a projecting, temple-form portico. The architect, whose name is unknown, added a feature that area builders later adopted—a colonnade across the full width of the rear of the house. The architecture and furnishings of Rosalie present a mingling of time periods and styles. Rosalie is a federal-style house with Tuscan columns and a central passage flanked by double parlors on one side and a library, dining room, and side stair hall on the other. The furnishings reflect the 1850s, when the house came under new ownership after the deaths of the original owner and his wife, Peter and Eliza Little.

The next owners, Andrew and Eliza Anne Wilson, refurnished and redecorated the house in the 1850s; their period of occupancy is reflected in the furnishings on display. The Wilsons added lovely plasterwork ceiling medallions, replaced carved wooden mantels with high-style, Italianate marble mantelpieces, and installed large French gilt mirrors. Mrs. Wilson made an impressive acquisition on a shopping trip to New York—a sumptuous, 20-piece rosewood suite for the front and rear parlors, made by the renowned John Henry Belter. Its decorative pattern, which Belter incorporated in other furniture, is known as Rosalie among connoisseurs. The Wilsons also purchased wall-to-wall Brussels carpets for the parlors.

During the Civil War, Union officers used the house as a headquarters, with their troops encamped on the expansive grounds, while Mrs. Wilson and her daughter (whose beau was a Rebel captain) remained on the second floor. Gen. Ulysses S. Grant himself visited the house for a few days. The Wilsons' heirs sold the house and its furnishings in 1938 to the Mississippi State Society Daughters of the American Revolution, who maintain the house as a museum.

33 *Rosalie* 100 ORLEANS STREET, NATCHEZ, MISS. 39120. (601) 445-4555 OR (800) 647-6742. OPEN DAILY, CALL FOR ANNUAL SPRING AND FALL PILGRIMAGE TOUR SCHEDULE. WWW.NATCHEZPILGRIMAGE.COM Ⓢ 🚶 🅿 🏛

Melrose

NATCHEZ, MISSISSIPPI

Architectural
Magnificence
Preserved

Built in 1847 in a parklike setting on what was then an abandoned cottonfield on the outskirts of Natchez, Melrose set the standard for this city's architectural magnificence. Its grand Greek Revival portico thrusts out from a broad brick structure, topped by a balustrade. At the rear of the house a colonnaded gallery—fine enough to serve as the entrance of a lesser house—overlooks a courtyard flanked by two-story service buildings, each with its own colonnade. The architect, Jacob Byers of Natchez, devised an innovative floor plan for Melrose. He placed

Enormous square pillars and two-story galleries embellish the rear of Melrose and its dependencies, the kitchen and slave quarters, which form a courtyard behind the mansion.

three rooms—drawing room, parlor, and library—on the right side of the central hallway, separated by sliding doors which, when open, create a spacious, three-room salon for entertaining. The owner, prominent Natchez attorney John T. McMurran, formed an instant landscape by having mature trees uprooted and transplanted on the grounds.

Melrose was acquired after the Civil War by Elizabeth Davis, whose descendants held it until 1976. Each generation passed it almost intact to the next—the house still has no interior kitchen—with original furniture, window treatments, oil-burning chandeliers, family portraits, and other items. Many pieces can be traced back to household inventories made in 1865 and 1883, such as the 12-piece set of Gothic Revival chairs, the green and gold brocatelle draperies in the drawing room, the pair of canopied beds in the master bedroom, and the rococo revival chairs and sofa in the drawing room. The drawing room set was reupholstered early in the 20th century with fabric chosen for its similarity to the original.

Among the rarities you will see are two painted canvas floorcloths in the foyer and hall, probably made in England or Scotland, which are undergoing restoration after being obscured beneath layers of varnish. Also of note, the drawing room contains an unusual revolving sofa consisting of a pair of connected seats that swivel, and a hassock equipped with a hole to hold a small table for card games. Melrose today looks much as it did in 1856, when a young bride entered the house and declared, "all seemed like fairy land."

34 *Melrose* Natchez National Historical Park, 1 Melrose Avenue, Natchez, Miss. 39120. (601) 446-5790 or (800) 647-6742. Open daily, call for annual spring and fall pilgrimage tour schedule. www.natchezpilgrimage.com ⑤ 🚶 ♿ 🅿 🏛

Stanton Hall

NATCHEZ, MISSISSIPPI

The Natchez Style at its Peak

With its bold Greek Revival portico, elaborate cast-iron grillwork, and sumptuous interior, Stanton Hall impressed the inhabitants of Natchez from the day it was completed. The interior decoration, wrote one newspaper, "instantly arrests the attention and attracts intense admiration."

Built between 1857 and 1858 for Frederick Stanton, an Irish immigrant who amassed a fortune as a planter and trader in cotton, the house has impact in both its decor and its spaciousness. A 16-foot-wide hallway runs the length of the house—72 feet. On one side of the hall the architect, probably Thomas Rose, created a triple reception room divided by sliding doors and hanging arches, similar to that of nearby Melrose (see p. 164). This large room seems even larger in the reflection of immense pier mirrors Stanton ordered from France. Note, too, the gas lighting fixtures in the reception room and in the dining room, lavishly adorned with foliage, cherubs, and mounted Indian warriors wielding bows and arrows. Made by the Philadelphia firm of Cornelius and Baker, they may be the finest gasoliers in the country. Exquisite interior decorative appointments include carved moldings, silver hardware, and five Carrara marble mantelpieces heavily carved with flowers and fruit.

Counting the basement and the observatory on the roof—with a broad view of the city and the Mississippi River—the house boasts five levels. Six bedrooms occupy the second floor; the third story holds a billiard room, a card room, and storage space. Much of the interior plasterwork is Grecian in style, in designs taken from Minard Lafever's guide *Beauties of Modern Architecture*. The house features Italianate elements as well, such as the entrance hall's overhanging arches with paired brackets, and the arched windows in the observatory. And the cast-iron gingerbread tracery on the lovely bay porch adds a striking arabesque flavor to the east side of the house.

About a dozen original Stanton pieces have been returned to the house, which is otherwise opulently furnished with items of the period. Few southern houses match the luxuriousness of Stanton Hall, which stands as a symbol of the great wealth made possible by the cotton trade.

35 *Stanton Hall* 401 HIGH STREET, NATCHEZ, MISS. 39120. (601) 446-6631 OR (800) 647-6742. OPEN DAILY, CALL FOR ANNUAL SPRING AND FALL PILGRIMAGE TOUR SCHEDULE. WWW.NATCHEZPILGRIMAGE.COM

NEARBY IN NATCHEZ: **D'Evereux** *(160 D'Evereux Drive. 601-446-8169)* A pure expression of Greek Revival, built about 1840. **Dunleith** *(84 Homochitto Street. 601-446-8500 or 800-433-2445)* This national historic landmark, built in 1856, sits in a 40-acre park and is entirely surrounded by Tuscan columns. **Lansdowne** *(17 Marshall Road. 601-446-9401)* This 1853 Greek Revival house is owned by descendants of the builders and displays many original furnishings. **Linden** *(1 Linden Place. 601-445-5472 or 800-2-LINDEN)* This federal house, built about 1800 with a handsome gallery added later, is now operated as an inn. **Longwood** *(140 Lower Woodville Road. 601-442-6672)* A national historic landmark, this distinctive octagonal house was begun in the early 1860s and retains original furnishings. **Magnolia Hall** *(215 S. Pearl Street. 601-442-6672)* Built in 1858, the last of the city's great Greek Revival town houses now features a costume museum. **Monmouth** *(36 Melrose Avenue. 601-442-5852 or 800-828-4531)* This monumental house of Mississippi governor John Quitman, built in 1818, is now operated as an inn. Three additional grand houses in the Natchez area—**Green Leaves**, **Richmond**, and **Montaigne**—open their doors to the public twice a year during the Pilgrimage Tours; call 601-446-6631 or 800-647-6742 for more information.

New Orleans and the River Road

Gallier House, Hermann-Grima House, San Francisco, Oak Alley

The sumptuous architecture of New Orleans reflects the city's rich blending of Spanish, French, and Anglo-American cultures. High land values led to the development of town houses designed to make the best use of precious space in the old French Quarter. The southern heat made galleries and open windows a necessity, but to preserve privacy New Orleanians devised the distinctive grillwork that adorns their porches. Thus, they could enjoy air and light in privacy on an upper story while gazing down on the jostle and color of street life. Across Canal Street from the French Quarter, Anglo-Americans created the architecturally distinct Garden District, with freestanding houses enclosed by lush gardens.

The plantations along the Mississippi River brought New Orleans its wealth. While storms, floods, fire, and decay have erased many of the plantation houses that once stood on the Mississippi's shores, a surprising number have survived. Grand columned mansions can still be seen along the River Road, which follows the water's snaking path.

Gallier House

NEW ORLEANS, LOUISIANA

An Architect's French Quarter Home

One of New Orleans' most prominent architects, James Gallier, Jr., designed this town house for his family in the city's French Quarter. Like many New Orleans houses, Gallier House is festooned across its front with beautiful wrought-iron grillwork enclosing the upper level of the gallery. Cast-iron gates, flanked by Corinthian pilasters, form the entrance to the house. In some ways Gallier House, built and decorated between 1857 and 1860, typifies the New Orleans town house layout. It is a sidehall house with, as the name implies, a hall running along one wall, giving access to rooms on the right. In common Louisiana fashion (and in deference to the heat) many of the rooms open onto galleries at the front or rear of the house. Like other New Orleans town houses, Gallier House seems to guard its privacy, hiding its charms behind a demure facade. Once visitors step inside, they find a beguiling home with sumptuous appointments in the rooms designed for entertaining and cozy private chambers filled with items that evoke daily life in the 19th century.

Gallier placed a large double parlor at the front of the house, heavily decorated with plaster cornices and medallions. Fluted columns and pilasters with gilded capitals accent the room. Upstairs, Gallier modified the usual sidehall plan by expanding the hall and making it into a usable room. With four daughters to house, he needed that extra space for his library. A two-story extension at the rear includes the dining room, pantry, and kitchen on the lower floor, and servants' quarters on the upper. Amenities included hot running water in the kitchen and

Lacy, green-painted ironwork veils the second-story gallery of the stately Italianate town house designed by James Gallier, Jr., for himself and his family. The interior displays fine Victorian furnishings, including a bedroom suite (right), dating from about 1860, from the New Orleans shop of Prudent Mallard.

an iron range, an indoor water closet, built-in clothes closets, a ventilation system, and a hydrant for watering the garden.

Gallier descendants occupied the house until 1917. Although the original furnishings are dispersed, the house has been sumptuously restored and showcases a superb collection of furnishings, including a set of rosewood rococo revival chairs in the style of John Henry Belter and a complete rosewood bedroom suite from the shop of Prudent Mallard dating from 1861, with an original bill of sale. In addition, the beautiful double parlor features statuary, portraits, a gilded pier mirror, and fine chandeliers. The renovation included the kitchen, the servants' rooms, and the bathroom, with its walnut, copper-lined tub. A girls' bedroom charmingly displays dolls taking tea.

36 *Gallier House Museum* 1118-1132 Royal Street, New Orleans, La. 70118. (504) 525-5661. Open Mon.-Sat. www.gnofn.org/~hggh 🄸 🄰 🄸

Hermann-Grima House

NEW ORLEANS, LOUISIANA

Urban Elegance in Two Styles

An anomaly amid the French- and Spanish-influenced architecture of old New Orleans, the Hermann-Grima House looks out on St. Louis Street with a dignified, somewhat sober, federal facade more at home in an eastern city. William Brand designed and built the house in 1831 for a German immigrant, Samuel Hermann. Hermann came to New Orleans in 1814 with almost nothing in his pockets and prospered tremendously in trading, shipping, and finance. He wanted an American-style house, so Brand gave him a plain faux-brick facade, yielding only a little to local taste by adding a small gallery with a wrought-iron railing. Inside, however, the house is beautifully decorated with crystal chandeliers, carved marble mantels, Corinthian columns, and a boldly carved frieze separating parlor and dining room. One of the finest aspects of the decorative scheme is its use of painted trompe l'oeil effects. Fake wood grain on doors, for example, simulates the look of mahogany and maple— not because the wood was too expensive, but because fashion dictated delicate fakery.

The house displays some interesting French porcelain of the 1830s, including a set of liqueur decanters in the form of an Oriental prince and princess. An ingenious porcelain *veilleuse*, a small teapot set atop a candle stand, served as both night-light and tea warmer, and was meant for a bedside table.

Hermann had to relinquish the house when the panic of 1837 hurt him financially. In 1844 Felix Grima acquired the property. Today, the furnishings reflect two stylistic periods: the American Empire style prevalent during Hermann's occupancy, exemplified by a handsome dining room set; and the Victorian style popular in Grima's day, evidenced by Madame Grima's rococo bedroom set.

37 *Hermann-Grima House* 820 St. Louis Street, New Orleans, La. 70112. (504) 525-5661. Open Mon.-Sat. www.gnofn.org/~hggh 🄸 🄰 🄸

NEARBY: **Pitot House** *(1440 Moss Street, New Orleans, La. 504-482-0312)* A classic Louisiana house of the 18th century, similar to a West Indian bungalow, with period furnishings.

San Francisco

GARYVILLE, LOUISIANA

A Festive Riverboat Ashore on the Banks of the Mississippi

An exuberant steamboat Gothic house, San Francisco displays an upper floor and widow's walk heavily laden with grillwork and brackets, with gabled dormer windows peeking out from the roof. Plainly visible from the Mississippi River, the house brings to mind a steamboat run aground. A pair of tall cisterns, painted blue and topped by pointed domes, flank the house like sentinels. The interior, equally festive, features colorful murals and painted ceilings.

The house was originally called Saint Frusquin, a name thought to be derived from a French slang phrase meaning roughly "without a penny," in wry reference to the mansion's high cost. A later owner altered the name to San Francisco. Edmond Bozonier Marmillion built the mansion between 1853 and 1856, probably to replace a residence ruined in 1852 by floods. Marmillion's initials, EBM, were discovered on several pieces of millwork during a restoration that also revealed the original Creole-style exposed-joist and floorboard construction and handmade lead plumbing pipes. Marmillion covered the main rooms with wallpaper, but in 1860 his son and daughter-in-law extensively redecorated the house with

After harvesting a bumper sugarcane crop in 1853, Edmond Bozonier Marmillion built the flamboyant San Francisco mansion, a landmark for passing Mississippi riverboats.

Original wall panels painted in 1860 grace the gentleman's parlor in San Francisco. The entrance hall, seen through the open doorway, features a statue purchased in New Orleans at the same time.

faux marbling and graining common in many 19th-century houses. They also hired an artist, Dominique Canova, whose painted decorations, including five lavish ceilings, give the interior its unique, festive atmosphere. In a lady's bedroom, for example, you will see three cherubs framed by intricate painted latticework hover in flight, holding aloft a basket of flowers. In the drawing room, pale purple walls rise to a ceiling adorned with flowers, birds, jewels, and scrolls. The original furnishings, removed from the house in the late 1800s, were lost in a fire elsewhere, but detailed inventories of the original contents—then required under Louisiana law—aided in refurnishing the house. The restoration of San Francisco re-created the house as it looked in 1860 when the younger Marmillions, at the height of their prosperity, had just completed their redecoration.

38 *San Francisco Plantation* LA. 44, GARYVILLE, LA. 70051. (504) 535-2341 OR (888) 322-1756. OPEN DAILY.
WWW.SANFRANCISCOPLANTATION.ORG

Oak Alley

VACHERIE, LOUISIANA

A "Pleasant Sojourn" by the Riverbank

Oak Alley is a rare survivor of an architectural species once common along the lower Mississippi Valley—the large plantation house entirely surrounded by columns, a form technically known as the peripteral house. Twenty-eight colossal Doric columns ring the house and support its double gallery. Nature has provided an impressive setting for this imposing house. An alley of live oaks—28 in number, matching the house's columns—forms a majestic approach to the house, with limbs dramatically arching over a broad path. The oak alley predates the house. Sometime in the 1700s, a French settler planted the double row of trees, 80 feet apart, in a quarter-mile procession leading to the Mississippi River bank. Over the decades the trees grew to magnificent height, becoming a landmark for passing steamboat travelers.

The house was built between 1837 and 1839 for a wealthy Creole planter from New Orleans named Jacques Telesphore Roman. Roman had purchased the property with its allée of oaks as a wedding present for his wife, Celina Pilie. The design for the grand house may have been provided by her father, Joseph Pilie, who was an architect. Although Madame Roman named the house Bon Séjour (pleasant sojourn), riverboat captains had already taken to calling the spot Oak Alley, and that name stuck. The Roman family occupied the house until 1866, when their last surviving son was compelled to sell the plantation amid the financial upheaval of Reconstruction. After passing through several owners, the estate was acquired in 1925 by Andrew and Josephine Stewart, who hired architect Richard Koch to restore the house. Before her death in 1972, Mrs. Stewart created a nonprofit foundation to preserve the house and keep it open to the public. Furnished with antebellum antiques, Oak Alley has been undergoing restoration to return it to its 1830s appearance.

39 *Oak Alley Plantation* 3645 LA. 18 (RIVER ROAD), VACHERIE, LA. 70090.(504) 265-2151 OR (800) 44ALLEY. OPEN DAILY. WWW.OAKALLEY.COM

A double row of immense, gnarled, centuries-old live oak trees entwine to create a romantic—and dramatic—approach to Oak Alley mansion.

Parlange Plantation

NEW ROADS, LOUISIANA

A French House of Classic Elegance Built for a Marquis

Set amid a grove of enormous, moss-covered oaks, Parlange is perhaps the greatest surviving example of the French Colonial style of architecture in America. Constructed of heavy timbers, with a steeply pitched, four-sided roof typical of a French manor house, Parlange reveals the adaptations French builders made to the subtropical climate of Louisiana. For example, the house is built atop a raised brick basement for protection from Mississippi River floodwaters. Two levels of covered galleries wrap around the house to provide outdoor space during hot, rainy summers and to serve as protected passageways. French doors handmade from local cypress open from each room to the gallery,

lending light and air to the interior. The house was built around 1800 by a French aristocrat, Claude Vincent, Marquis de Ternant, who chose the elegantly simple French Colonial style favored by Louisianans. Originally Parlange had only four rooms interconnecting in a row—a bedroom, a parlor, a dining room, and a second bedroom. The marquis' daughter-in-law, Virginie de Ternant, added a dining room and two bedrooms to the rear of the house in the mid-1800s—the last major change to the house.

After the death of her husband, Virginie married Charles Parlange, whose name became permanently attached to the house. Parlange descendants still own the house and its surrounding farmlands. Family portraits and French antiques, some purchased by Virginie de Ternant in Paris, some dating from the original Marquis de Ternant, fill the house. A pair of octagonal brick dovecotes—once a source of squab for dinner—flank the main house.

40 *Parlange Plantation* 8211 False River Road, New Roads, La. 70760. (225) 638-8410. Open daily by appointment. 🟢 🚶 ♿ 🅿️

Rosedown

ST. FRANCISVILLE, LOUISIANA

A Rare Antebellum Survivor in a Lush Setting
Rosedown attracts thousands of knowledgeable visitors interested in viewing a Louisiana time capsule. Built by Martha and John Turnbull in 1835, Rosedown remained in the same family until 1956. Descendants of the Turnbulls sold the house and its original furnishings to a Texas couple who recognized Rosedown's inestimable value as an extraordinary relic of antebellum plantation life and preserved it intact. Today's visitors can view 16 of the house's rooms much as the Turnbulls saw them on the eve of the Civil War.

A verdant garden—famous in its own right—and a handsome allée of old oaks frame the approach to Rosedown. Constructed of cypress painted white, with a double gallery supported by Doric columns, the architecture of the main portion recalls the late 18th and early 19th centuries. Wings added in 1844 and 1859 reflect the prevailing Greek Revival style. The entrance hall presents a startling color contrast as a mahogany staircase rises along a wall decorated with pictorial wallpaper depicting the exploits of Charlemagne's knights.

The Turnbulls acquired furnishings from the New Orleans shop of Prudent Mallard—records from 1855 and 1856 show purchases of about $3,700 for furniture, a clock, rugs, wallpaper, curtains, and fabrics at Mallard's establishment. Be sure not to miss the pride of Rosedown's furniture collection, a monumental Gothic Revival bedroom suite, intended as a victory gift for Presidential candidate Henry Clay. When Clay lost the election of 1844, Turnbull acquired the set from its maker and added a wing to Rosedown to accommodate it. One of the great charms of the house is the children's bedroom, with an original child-size walnut desk, a canopy bed, a rocking horse, and a straw-hatted doll.

41 *Rosedown Plantation and Historic Gardens* 12501 La. 10, St. Francisville, La. 70775. (504) 635-3332. Open daily. 🟢 🚶 🅿️ 🏛️

The second-story gallery at Rosedown offers a breathtaking view of the canopy of live oaks leading to the house's main entrance.

Shadows-on-the-Teche

NEW IBERIA, LOUISIANA

*Gracious
Living on
the Bayou*

Shadows-on-the-Teche possesses a gracious beauty that results from a fortunate combination of architecture and setting. Built between 1831 and 1834 for planter David Weeks and his family, Shadows stands at the edge of Bayou Teche, amid extensive gardens and a grove of large live oaks that shadow the house and give it its name. Shadows rises two and a half stories, with a portico of eight giant Tuscan columns and a double veranda at the front. The wooden frieze banding the house above the second story lends a classical touch. Also of note is the unusual light hue of the house's red bricks, which help it settle into its lush surroundings. The cozy interior, three rooms wide and two rooms deep, echoes the simplicity and grace of the exterior. At the rear, the central rooms on both floors are open loggias, making the interior seem a part of the garden.

The mistress of Shadows, Mary Weeks, wrote her husband in 1834, "I never saw a more delightful airy house." At that time David Weeks was in New Haven, Connecticut, seeking treatment for an ailment that would soon take his life. Some of the furniture at Shadows was purchased by David on that trip northeast. Other items date from Mary Weeks' second marriage, to Judge John Moore. She remained a defiant occupant of the second floor during the Civil War (Union officers used the first floor as a headquarters) and lived here until her death in December 1863.

The restoration of the house reflects two periods, the mid-19th century and the period between 1922 and 1958, when Weeks Hall, a great-grandson of the builders, lived here as self-proclaimed Master of the Shadows and entertained such guests as filmmaker D. W. Griffith and author Henry Miller.

42 *Shadows-on-the-Teche* 317 EAST MAIN STREET, NEW IBERIA, LA 70560. (318) 369-6446. OPEN DAILY. WWW.NTHP.ORG

*Harriet "Pattee" Weeks, grand-daughter of the builders of Shadows-on-the-Teche, sits in the parlor's Turkish Corner at the turn of the century.
A path lined with azaleas and live oaks draped in moss leads to the columned front entrance (opposite) of the charming house.*

The Heartland

MICHIGAN • OHIO

INDIANA • ILLINOIS

WISCONSIN • MINNESOTA

IOWA • MISSOURI

ARKANSAS • OKLAHOMA

KANSAS • NEBRASKA

SOUTH DAKOTA • NORTH DAKOTA

Perhaps surprising only to those residents of the East and West Coasts, the nation's Heartland has long welcomed a diversity of cultures—an attitude reflected in the rich variety of architecture on view. From the imposing mansions of wealthy industrialists to an architect's tradition-breaking home and studio, the country's midsection offers lavish estates filled with delightful surprises.

The gracious interior of Terrace Hill, Iowa

The Heartland

NORTH DAKOTA

Fargo
Duluth
35 Medora
94 Bismarck
MINNESOTA
18
Marquette

SOUTH DAKOTA
16 St. Paul
Minneapolis
WISCONSIN
17
Green Bay
Pierre
Rapid City
34 Sioux Falls
Madison
MICHIGAN
15 Grand Rapids
Lansing
96
Detroit
1
2
NEBRASKA
Fremont
32
IOWA
Cedar Rapids
14 Prairie du Chien
Milwaukee
9
Michigan City
South Bend
11 10
12 Chicago
7
8
Cleveland
90
Akron
3
4
77
West Liberty
5
North Platte
80
Omaha
21
20 Des Moines
19
88
13
Bloomington
39 55
57
INDIANA
OHIO
Lincoln
33 Nebraska City
24
ILLINOIS
Indianapolis
71
Columbus
Cincinnati
Springfield
70
6
74
Madison
Topeka
Kansas City
Hannibal
23 55
65
KANSAS
Abilene
30
135
25
Independence
22
St. Louis
64
Ohio
Wichita
31
MISSOURI
Jefferson City
57
55
Ponca City
27
Coffeyville
44
Bartlesville
29
OKLAHOMA
Tulsa
26
ARKANSAS
55
28 Oklahoma City
Fort Smith
Little Rock
30
Red
Mississippi

Lake Superior
Lake Michigan
Lake Huron
Lake Erie

Missouri
Arkansas

0   200 mi
0   200 km

&dsel and Eleanor Ford House

GROSSE POINTE SHORES, MICHIGAN

A Home
Spanning
Jacobean
England to the
Machine Age

Edsel and Eleanor Ford's Grosse Pointe Shores home imported the charm and picturesque qualities of the English Cotswolds to the shores of Michigan's Lake St. Clair. The only child of automobile pioneer Henry Ford and his wife Clara, Edsel built the house on a 125-acre site purchased from his father in 1926. Edsel's rise to prominence in the Ford Motor Company made this impressive house possible—by 1919 he had become president of the company, after only seven years in the auto business.

While the house's exterior was not modeled after a specific Cotswold source, it combined notions that Edsel and Eleanor Ford and their architect, Albert Kahn, formulated during travels to England. Faced with Indiana limestone, the mansion recalls the homes of the Gloucestershire region with its low profile, irregular massing, and complicated roofline of gables and chimneys. The roof is made of stone shingles imported from England, laid by English artisans in the authentic Cotswold style, in which the shingles gradually decrease in size as they approach the peak of the roof.

Construction started on the house in 1926 and lasted three years. The selection of Kahn as architect was highly appropriate. Not only was the German-Jewish émigré one of the most respected architects in America, he was also experienced in the ways of Ford Motor Company, having designed Ford's Highland Park Plant in 1908 and the River Rouge Plant in 1920. Covering 30,000 square feet, many of the building's 60 rooms achieve the traditional character of an English manor house. The comfortable and inviting main entrance hall, with its low decorative-plaster ceiling, contains furnishings reflective of England from the Gothic period through the 17th century. Immediately adjacent on the south side are the library and drawing room. The paneled library, where the Ford family often had afternoon tea and informal gatherings, is filled with English period furniture and an elaborately carved chimneypiece removed from Deane Park in Northamptonshire, England. The Fords were enthusiastic art collectors and this room reveals the range of their interests, with an oil painting attributed to the Italian Renaissance artist Raphael, Persian ceramics, a carved wooden African mask, and a medieval French ivory.

The most formal room in the house, the drawing room was originally completed in an English style, but Mrs. Ford redecorated from 1955 to 1956 in a French mode to complement her collection of Impressionist and Postimpressionist paintings, including works by Paul Cézanne. Walk through the cloister leading from the drawing room to the gallery, the mansion's largest room. You will note how the space resembles an English baronial hall complete with 16th-century oak linenfold paneling, a molded, decorative-plaster ceiling, and a Gothic hooded chimneypiece brought from Wollaston Hall in Worcestershire, England. The Fords furnished the room with several pieces of Elizabethan and Jacobean furniture, notably a carved oak court cupboard made about 1615.

Off the east side of the main hall lies one of the most beautiful rooms in the house, the dining room. Paneled with dark pine from the 1740 Treaty Room of Clock House in England,

Persian rugs covering a herringbone parquet floor help define the furniture groupings in the Fords' formal drawing room. The color scheme—blue-green paneling and gold-leaf trim—was chosen to complement two works by Paul Cézanne hanging here.

It took three years to complete this 60-room house: one year to build the house itself and two years to custom-fit its many antique architectural elements. The Fords even had moss grown on the roof and English grape ivy planted about the walls in an attempt to give the home an established look.

it has no chandelier—the Fords dined by natural light, firelight, or candlelight. The gentlemen often retired after dinner to the study across the hall, which was also Edsel's personal retreat. It remains essentially as it was prior to his death in 1943, furnished with several English pieces including a late 15th-century Gothic oak cabinet, a Georgian burl-walnut pedestal from about 1800, and a Queen Anne armchair made about 1700. Edsel was an amateur photographer, and here the English oak paneling is hung with photographs of the family and their friends, including Adm. Richard Byrd, the Prince of Wales, Douglas Fairbanks, Jr., and Mary Pickford, who signed her photograph "Mary-Pick-A-Ford."

A surprise awaits at the end of the first-floor hall, the "modern room." Designed and installed in the mid-1930s by one of the country's leading industrial designers, Walter Dorwin Teague, the art moderne room represents Edsel's affection for contemporary design, and makes use of choice materials of contrasting textures such as leather, fabrics, mirrors, and rich woods including African red mahogany. Indirect light illuminates the space, and its modernity is further emphasized by the artwork, including Diego Rivera's 1931 painting, "Cactus on the Plains," and Warren Wheelock's 1924 sculpture of an abstract nude in gilt bronze. (Edsel commissioned Rivera to create the renowned "Detroit Industry" murals for the Detroit Institute of Art, which he generously supported.) This room was an early example of the progressive style in the Detroit area, a modern, machine-inspired look Ford incorporated elsewhere in his house, as well as in his company's automobile styling, perhaps best expressed in the streamlined design of the 1935 Lincoln Zephyr.

Kahn's work for Edsel and Eleanor in Grosse Pointe Shores included several auxiliary buildings as well. The Gate Lodge on Lake Shore Road, similar in appearance to the house, accommodated three generous apartments for staff members and their families. It also housed an eight-car garage, complete with a turntable to eliminate the need of backing out. Be sure to see the Tudor-style playhouse, designed at three-quarters scale by Robert Derrick in 1930 as a seventh birthday present for Josephine Ford from her grandmother, Clara Ford. Other buildings on the estate include a recreation house, a powerhouse, and a modern activity center completed in the late 1980s from what was originally the gardener's implement shed.

The buildings nestle within a landscape designed by acclaimed Danish-born landscape architect, Jens Jensen. Known for his naturalistic and ecological designs, Jensen had also done work for Henry Ford's Dearborn home, Fair Lane (see p. 186). For Edsel and Eleanor, Jensen dug a lagoon between the swimming pool and the lake and used the excavated materials to create the peninsula known as Bird Island, where Edsel could bird-watch and shelter his many boats. In addition, Jensen achieved the established, lived-in feeling Edsel wanted for his house by placing moss on the roof and planting ivy on the walls. The design also called for the large meadow running from the main house to the Gate Lodge, as well as unobtrusive paths and walkways through gardens and trees. The design's most formal aspect, the Rose Garden, was specifically requested by Mrs. Ford. In 1956, another formal garden was added—the New Garden, with a modernist design featuring a stone reflecting pool.

The Ford family on the terrace steps of the Grosse Pointe Shores home in 1937 (l to r): Edsel Ford, Eleanor Clay Ford, Henry Ford II, Benson Ford, Josephine Ford, and William Clay Ford.

Following Edsel's untimely death at age 49 of stomach cancer, Eleanor lived on the estate for another 33 years, until her death in 1976. Before she died she had established an endowment to preserve the house and its collection for the public; the house museum opened in 1978.

① *Edsel and Eleanor Ford House* 1100 Lake Shore Road, Grosse Pointe Shores, Mich. 48236. (313) 884-4222. Open Tues.-Sun. www.fordhouse.org 🅢 🧍 ♿ 🍴 🅿 🏛

NEARBY: **Fisher Mansion** *(383 Lenox Avenue, Detroit, Mich. 313-823-1684)* Noted for its fanciful interiors, this waterfront residence was built in 1927 for Lawrence Fisher, president of Cadillac Motors.

Fair Lane

DEARBORN, MICHIGAN

A Country Retreat for the Founder of the Automobile Age

Seeking privacy from the procession of reporters, salesmen, job applicants, and curious citizens who regularly appeared at his door in Detroit, auto magnate Henry Ford commissioned this 56-room home in the country in 1914. Its name reflects the peace he sought—"Fair Lane" evoked the country road where Ford's grandfather had lived in Ireland. Ford commissioned William Van Tine of Pittsburgh to design the 31,000-square-foot mansion and outbuildings, and hired landscape architect Jens Jensen to design the surrounding 2,150-acre estate, which included a bird sanctuary (with 500 birdhouses) and deer park. All together, the project cost nearly two million dollars.

Built of limestone and concrete, Fair Lane blends midwestern architecture with an American interpretation of English Gothic. You will notice this mixture of styles in the battlements and stone chimneys projecting above the roofline and the low-pitched gables typical of prairie-style houses. Despite his great wealth, Ford sought simplicity—one of his favorite rooms was the mansion's rustic-style den with a massive fieldstone fireplace, half-log cypress-paneled walls, and an oak floor pegged with walnut. (A lover of folk music, Ford invited musicians from Michigan's Upper Peninsula, Appalachia, and as far away as Maine to perform in Fair Lane's den.) Other rooms in the house are more formal and luxurious. The entrance hall, for example, features an elegant, Elizabethan-style carved stairway illuminated

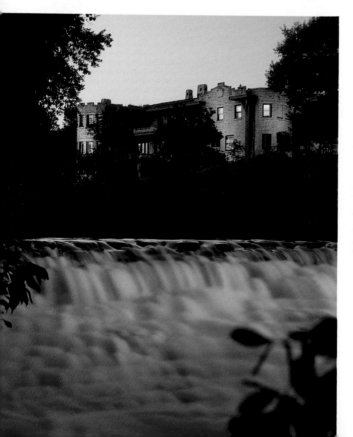

by an 18th-century chandelier and heraldic stained-glass windows. In the roseleaf mahogany-paneled dining room, Ford entertained famous guests such as President and Mrs. Hoover, the Duke of Windsor, aviator Charles Lindbergh, and baseball hero Dizzy Dean.

With the advice of his friend Thomas Edison, Ford built a four-story, hydroelectric powerhouse, connected to the mansion by a 300-foot-long tunnel. He installed a

The compound at Fair Lane was completely self-sufficient, with power coming from the river; for many years Henry Ford's powerhouse supplied enough electricity to light up the entire village of Dearborn.

steam-powered generator as a back-up system, and enjoyed tinkering with the machine after dinner. The powerhouse also contains a laboratory where Ford conducted experiments and a 20-car garage, currently housing a display of six historic vehicles owned by Ford, including his personal Model T—the car that revolutionized the American way of life.

2 *Fair Lane: The Henry Ford Estate* University of Michigan-Dearborn, 4901 Evergreen Road, Dearborn, Mich. 48128. (313) 593-5593. Open daily. Ⓢ 🚶 🍴 🅿 🏛

Stan Hywet Hall
AKRON, OHIO

A Tire Baron's American Country Estate

Stan Hywet Hall is a Tudor Revival manor custom-built in the early 20th century for extravagant living and entertaining. The builder, Frank A. Seiberling, had ample means at his disposal. He was a cofounder of Akron's Goodyear Tire and Rubber Company, which saw success manufacturing bicycle tires in the 1890s, and generated enormous fortunes when Henry Ford's 1907 Model T created a huge demand for automobile tires. Seiberling also arranged to provide Goodyear tires for every General Motors car.

Like many wealthy families of the era, Frank and his wife, Gertrude, dreamed of a stately country home for themselves and their six children. In 1912, Seiberling held a small design

Stan Hywet Hall was built with lavish entertainment in mind. The estate's motto, Non Nobis Solum—*Not For Us Alone—is carved over the entryway to the house.*

competition between eight architectural firms, each submitting their vision of the perfect rural retreat. He selected a Tudor Revival design by the New York firm of George B. Post and Sons, and began working with their top Cleveland architect, Charles Schneider. For her part, Gertrude Seiberling enrolled in classes at Buchtel College (today the University of Akron), studying architecture, interior decoration, horticulture, and gardening.

Schneider soon found himself in England and France on an exploratory mission with the couple and their daughter Irene, in April 1912. (Ironically, Seiberling had initially booked their passage to England on the *Titanic,* but changed his mind.) The group visited many English Tudor mansions, the family collecting picture postcards of interiors and facades they admired, and the architect making detailed drawings of design motifs and architectural details. Eventually, all agreed on a unique residential design combining characteristics from three English manors, dating from 1450 to 1550, with 20th-century comforts. The house was completed in 1915.

Stan Hywet Hall closely follows its English models, adapted to accommodate life in modern America. A sweeping entrance drive meandering through an apple orchard (recently restored) brings visitors to a country house overlooking the expansive Cuyahoga Valley. The house, constructed of handmade red brick laid in the English bond style, is accented by sandstone quoins and window surrounds. A slate shingle roof flows over the steeply pitched gable roof, sheltering 65,000 square feet of living space inside—a total of 65 rooms, including 18 bedrooms and 14 bathrooms set in an irregular plan with wings projecting from a central axis. The main entry is guarded by a four-story square tower capped by battlements and chimney flues. Within the tower rises the grand stairway, illuminated by delicate leaded-glass windows. These small-pane windows are found throughout the house—a total of 21,000 panes of glass set into 469 windows. Next to the tower, the entrance portico projects out from the body of the house, its design inspired by Compton-Wyngates, a castle once owned by Henry VIII. A Tudor-style arch leads to the front door, centered beneath a carved-stone heraldic crest and brick half-timbered gable.

The interiors, by New York decorator Hugo F. Huber, required more than two years to complete—an understandable time frame given the quality of the design and details. The 23 fireplaces, one for every major room of the house, are mostly decorative. F.A. Seiberling insisted on equipping the home with the latest technology, including central heating; steam radiators are hidden behind walls, windows seats, or shelving so as not to disturb the medieval atmosphere. A modern elevator and private telephone room are also hidden behind panels in the first-floor Linenfold Hallway, named for its custom-designed linenfold wood paneling, hand-carved to resemble delicate folds of fabric. In other areas of the home, oak, sandalwood, and black walnut paneling cover the walls.

The cavernous, two-story Great Hall is the largest room in the house, soaring up an extra story to a gabled, beamed ceiling. Decorated in the style of old hunting lodges, and modeled on Haddon Hall in Derbyshire, England, the room features a massive stone mantel, nearly 12 feet high, and displays rare 16th-century Flemish tapestries, 18th-century English portraits, and a collection of taxidermy. An oversize, exquisite Oriental rug runs the entire length of the room.

The Tudor Revival theme continues throughout the elaborately finished home. The reception room adjacent to the entry was also inspired by a similar space at Haddon Hall.

The Great Hall's beamed ceiling rises three stories; its carved stone mantel alone is nearly 12 feet high. The Seiberling family frequently gathered in this room to read before dinner.

The paneled master bedroom contains a handsomely carved Elizabethan-style bed, and characters from Chaucer's *Canterbury Tales* parade around the dining room in a continuous allegorical frieze painted by American muralist Robert Sewell. The music room is outfitted with many instruments, including a Steinway concert piano and a 2,000-pipe Aeolian organ. The antique harpsichord here was made in London in 1773 and, according to legend, was used by the composer Franz Joseph Haydn. Gertrude Seiberling, an accomplished vocalist, particularly enjoyed the music room. Here she entertained many guests, including four U.S. Presidents—Taft, Harding, Coolidge, and Hoover—as well as Will Rogers, Thomas Edison, Helen Keller, and the Von Trapp family singers. From the music room, you can step into an enclosed porch with an extraordinary Arts and Crafts-era tile fountain designed by Mary Chase Stratton, founder of Pewabie Pottery in Detroit.

The name Stan Hywet is old English for "stone quarry," referring to the many exhausted and abandoned pits on the property. The quarry was put to good use in the landscape plan, being filled with water and turned into scenic lagoons surrounded by naturalistic plantings, with beautiful vistas overlooking the Cuyahoga Valley. The landscape was designed between 1911 and 1914 by Warren Manning, a founding father of American landscape design and one-time chief specialist for native plant material for Frederick Law Olmsted. At Stan Hywet, Manning followed the growth of the vegetation for 14 years after the first planting, to ensure proper development of the garden landscape. The remaining gardens, measuring 70 acres, retain singular integrity as one of the few intact Manning designs open to the public.

His plantings have matured well. Note the dramatic, fully grown allées that radiate from the house and through the grounds. If time allows, be sure to stroll along the paved walk between the white trunks of birch trees forming a romantic, 550-foot-long allée leading south from the mansion to a pair of matching stone teahouse pavilions. The pavilions, with accommodations for bathers, look over the lagoon used by the family for swimming, boating, fishing, and ice-skating. In 1929, noted designer Ellen Biddle Shipman redesigned the perennial plantings of a walled English Garden close to the house, today the only one of her gardens in the United States restored and open to the public. Other unique gardens complete the landscape, including the Great Meadow, a Japanese garden, and a rose garden featuring All-American Rose selections.

The Seiberlings enjoyed entertaining, and their magnificent house provided a natural theme for its grand opening in 1916—a Shakespearean costume ball. Another memorable event, in 1928, was an unusual open house for everyone in Akron who had lived in the city more than 50 years. Some 4,000 guests accepted the Seiberling's invitation for the day-long affair of dining and dancing.

Frank Seiberling, who managed to hold on to the mansion through the economic downturn of the Depression, died there in 1955, at the age of 95. His heirs donated the estate to a newly formed nonprofit organization to ensure its continuance as a gracious host.

❸ *Stan Hywet Hall and Gardens* 714 North Portage Path, Akron, Ohio 44303. (330) 836-5533. April through Oct. daily; Feb. through March Tues.-Sun. www.stanhywet.org

ⓈⒶⒼⒾⓅⒾ

NEARBY: **Hower House** *(60 Fir Hill, Akron, Ohio. 330-972-6909)* This Second Empire-Italianate mansion was built by Akron industrialist John Henry Hower in 1870 and contains original furnishings. **Simon Perkins Mansion** *(550 Copley Road, Akron, Ohio. 330-535-1120)* Built in 1835 by Simon Perkins, Jr., the son of Akron's founder, this stone Greek Revival mansion features Victorian furnishings.

 Hay-McKinney House

CLEVELAND, OHIO

Designed by a President's Son

On a city lot in a fashionable neighborhood overlooking Wade Park, a prominent Cleveland social figure built a handsome Italian Renaissance mansion which, ironically, she never occupied. Constructed of stuccoed masonry, the mansion features a bold arched entryway that contrasts with the rectangular second-story windows that open onto iron balconies. The rear of the U-shaped house faces a magnificent courtyard with formal Italian-style gardens. The house's simplicity and dignity is a credit to both its architect, Abram Garfield, son of the slain President, and its owner, Clara Hay, who collaborated with him on construction details.

Clara was the widow of John Hay, Secretary of State under Presidents William McKinley and Theodore Roosevelt, who had died in 1905. Mrs. Hay dreamed of returning to her native Cleveland and building a home to be near her sister Flora. For this new house she salvaged elements from other buildings, including an older structure she owned in town, as well as from her father's residence, both of which were being razed. Although the mantel in the foyer came from France, many of the marble mantels were mementoes from her family's other houses. Be sure to note the grand walnut staircase carved by master crafts-man John Herkomer in 1875, embellished by stylized leaves, berries, and blossoms, under a vaulted, Renaissance-style ceiling. It once formed the centerpiece of her old home.

By the time the house was completed in 1911, Flora had died, and heartbroken Clara never moved into the house. In 1916 steel magnate Price McKinney and his wife pur-chased the mansion. Among the McKinney furnishings that remain are a pair of Italian Renaissance Revival armchairs from the late 18th or early 19th century, and a walnut drop-leaf table with a curule base and paw feet dating from the early 1900s. Today owned by

Laurel-wreath wallpaper and Greek Revival furniture dominate the formal parlor in the Hay-McKinney House.

the Cleveland Historical Society, the Hay-McKinney House is a superb example of the classic revival trend that took hold in the early 20th century, and of the upper-class life at that time.

4 *Hay-McKinney House* 10825 EAST BOULEVARD, CLEVELAND, OHIO 44106. (216) 721-5722. OPEN MON.-SAT. WWW.WRHS.ORG

NEARBY: **Bingham-Hanna Mansion** *(10825 East Boulevard, Cleveland, Ohio. 216-721-5722)* Also owned by the Cleveland Historical Society, this historic home next to the Hay-McKinney House features a restored living room and parlor.

The Piatt Castles

WEST LIBERTY, OHIO

Castles
Side by Side
in the
Smiling Valley

In the mid-19th century a pair of brothers built two elaborate stone castles in a lush wooded area the Shawnee Indians had called Mac-O-Cheek, or "smiling valley." The two brothers—along with an older sister and 11 foster siblings—had grown up on a prosperous farm here, and built their grand European-style houses of local limestone and hardwoods. Politics was a mainstay in their household—father Benjamin served as a federal circuit judge as their abolitionist mother, Elizabeth, harbored runaway slaves in a secret room tucked between false walls in the family's log house.

The youngest son, Abram Sanders Piatt, served as a brigadier general during the Civil War. After the war he took over the family farm and became a gentleman farmer, politician, animal breeder, poet, and editor of the local newspaper. In 1864 he began to build Mac-A-Cheek, a Norman-French-style château with two-foot-thick limestone walls, a slate roof, and wrought-iron balconies. Completed in 1871, the interior was updated in the 1880s by Swiss-born artist Oliver Frey, who oversaw the painting of the decorative ceilings. Be sure to note the 1790 upright clock that belonged to Abram's grandfather, which still keeps time in the front hall. Upstairs, a sitting room displays firearms collected by five generations of the Piatts, including a pair of 1800-vintage flintlock pistols carried by Abram's father to protect himself while traveling as a circuit judge. In Abram's bedroom, keep a lookout for more of his personal effects, including the sword that he used during the Civil War, a snakeskin sent by one of his sons from Florida, and a silver-topped cane given to him by his brother Donn.

Col. Donn Piatt—a noted writer, politician, social critic, and diplomat—began building his own castle, Mac-O-Chee, on a nearby hillside in 1864. It was originally designed as a modest Gothic-style retreat for his wife, who was seriously ill with consumption. Although she helped design the house, she died before it was completed. In 1879-1881 Mac-O-Chee underwent extensive remodeling and enlarging under the direction of John Smithmeyer, who later earned fame as one of the architects of the Library of Congress. A Flemish-inspired limestone front was wrapped around the original structure and towers were added to the east and west. Oliver Frey oversaw the interior wall and ceiling decoration. Donn Piatt was a writer and editor, and his ornate library is of particular interest. A painted ceiling depicts writers he knew and admired, and decorative tiles around the fireplace represent the history of literature. The imposing stairway and elaborate wood carvings on the doorways and fireplaces were executed by Ohio craftsman George Hauer.

Devout Catholics, both brothers included chapels in their castles, as the nearest large parish was two to three hours away. Far removed from urban life, the brothers created their own dream houses in the idyllic forest of their youth.

5 *The Piatt Castles: Mac-A-Cheek and Mac-O-Chee* 10051 COUNTY ROAD 47, WEST LIBERTY, OHIO 43357. (937) 465-2821. OPEN DAILY APRIL TO MID-OCT. 🅢 🏃 ♿ 🅿 🏛

Donn Piatt and his second wife enlarged Mac-O-Chee (opposite) about 15 years after it was built, adding the Flemish-inspired limestone front and towers. The couple used the castle as a retirement home.

Lanier Mansion

MADISON, INDIANA

*Home of the
Financier Who
Saved Indiana
for the Union*

One of the first Greek Revival houses in Indiana—and one of the finest in the country—Lanier Mansion was the home of the state's most influential financier, James Franklin Doughty Lanier. When Lanier built the house in 1844, Madison was the state's economic center, bustling and prosperous from processing pork, flour, and lumber, which Madison's entrepreneurs sold across the country. The son of a bankrupt storekeeper, Lanier became immensely rich from financing local industries, railroads, and from banking—he held the controlling interest in and was president of the Madison branch of the Second State Bank of Indiana, the most stable financial institution in the West. When envisioning his mansion, Lanier chose the Greek Revival style as an expression of his personal financial solidity and his confidence in Indiana's economy.

Lanier's architect, Francis Costigan, had emigrated to Madison from Baltimore. Little is known about Costigan's professional training, but judging by his work for Lanier, he possessed extraordinary talent and a sophisticated eye. He designed Lanier Mansion as a cube, with four 30-foot-tall fluted Corinthian columns supporting a portico, and oriented it toward the Ohio River, presenting its columned facade as a landmark to passing vessels and proclaiming the wealth of the town. A handsome, octagonal cupola decorated with diamond panels tops the house—and serves to ventilate the interior. Inside, you will see how an extraordinary spiral staircase, set in a large alcove at the side of the entrance hall, winds up to the cupola. The bottom of the stairway sweeps into the hall under a canopy, the total effect being one of restrained luxury. Proud of his work, Francis Costigan had his signature engraved on two silver buttons inserted into each newel-post. The hall opens onto twin parlors, furnished with Grecian sofas and magnificent gilded mantel mirrors. In the north parlor is a grand piano dating from 1850 by Lindeman & Sons and an 18th-century French harp. About a third of the furnishings in the house are original Lanier items.

The mansion's sophisticated gardens, which date from the 1850s, had a dual purpose—to provide difficult-to-acquire vegetables such as asparagus and French beans for the household's dinner table, and to create a peaceful Eden that Lanier could share with the people of Madison. Surrounded by a board fence, the garden was open to the public every morning and closed at sunset. Inside, weaving walkways of coal cinders edged in brick wandered through elaborate and colorful flowerbeds, a welcome respite from the hectic industrialized atmosphere of the 19th-century town.

Lanier and his family resided in the house for only seven years. He traveled to Europe on behalf of the state of Indiana to raise investment funds, and eventually moved to New York. Lanier continued to increase his fortune to the extent that he was able to pledge his credit and later, to lend an enormous sum, to the state of Indiana in times of great crisis during the Civil War. He guaranteed $400,000 in credit to equip six regiments of Indiana infantry, and

*Four soaring Corinthian columns support Lanier's portico (opposite). The decorative bands around
the roofline feature carvings of a Greek honeysuckle motif, as well as evenly spaced circular windows
outlined with wreaths.*

The den at Copshaholm still features Joseph Oliver's mission-style partners desk. The room is paneled in oak with hammer beams supporting the plaster ceiling.

then paid the interest on the state's debt—$640,000 in cash—when secessionists were trying to force the state into default, bankruptcy, and, ultimately, into the Confederacy.

During Lanier's time in New York, the mansion was occupied by his oldest son, Alexander, who purchased the property for one dollar in 1861. After Alexander's death, the house passed through the hands of several relatives before being donated to the state in 1925. Unlike many great houses, the Lanier Mansion never saw a period of disrepair. It continues to be carefully maintained by the state as a memorial to the man whose farsighted generosity saved Indiana for the Union.

6 *Lanier Mansion State Historic Site* 511 WEST FIRST STREET, MADISON, IND. 47250. (812) 265-3526. OPEN TUES.-SUN. 🚶 🅿 🏛

*C*opshaholm
SOUTH BEND, INDIANA

A Lovely Stone Mansion Made by a Plow   Copshaholm is an inviting Victorian house featuring original furnishings collected by three generations of one family over a span of a hundred years. The house was built for Joseph Doty Oliver, the son of James Oliver, inventor of the chilled plow. As president of the Oliver Chilled Plow Works, Joseph oversaw the manufacture of their featured product, a superior cast-iron implement, as well as other farm equipment. In 1895, he hired architect Charles Alonzo Rich of New York City to design a lovely Queen Anne-style house in the Richardsonian Romanesque fashion. The 38-room mansion was sturdily constructed of native Indiana fieldstone granite, cut by European masons on-site, and supporting a wide-gabled roof covered with distinctive red Akron Spanish tiles.

Oliver's success in industry is evident throughout the stately home, with fine furnishings and architectural flourishes in every room. Particularly impressive is the lofty three-story entrance hall surrounded by a continuous oak stairway. A tall fireplace in the hall, one of 14 in the house, is flanked by carved Ionic capitals above rope-twisted columns. From this grand area, guests could enter the formal music room, ringed by a large-scale plaster frieze inspired by a similar piece at the Duomo in Florence, Italy. Be sure to visit the library and dining room, two of the mansion's most elegant spaces. The Oliver family used the curved library as a living room, surrounded by the rich tones of the mahogany bookcases, ceiling beams, and an elaborate overmantel with paired mythological figures flanking a green marble hearth. The dining room is similarly appointed, with carved mahogany beams and window moldings, whose dark wood highlights the delicate features of the antique porcelains displayed in the built-in china cabinet. Original furnishings and family items remain in place throughout the house, including Joseph's mission-style partners desk, a 1905 mahogany Brunswick billiard table, and a collection of luggage plastered with labels obtained during the family's many travels. Connected to the house by a shady pergola, the formal Italian sunken garden, designed by Alice Neale in 1907, is currently being restored to its 1920s appearance.

7 *Copshaholm: The Oliver Mansion* 808 WEST WASHINGTON STREET, SOUTH BEND, IND. 46601. (219) 235-9664. OPEN MID-FEB. TO MID-JAN. TUES.-SUN. 💲 🚶 🅿 🏛

*B*arker Mansion

MICHIGAN CITY, INDIANA

*The House
that Freight
Cars Built*

Known locally as "the house that freight cars built," the Barker Mansion is a meticulously restored and furnished late Victorian home that represents two generations of railroad wealth. In 1857, John H. Barker, Sr., constructed a ten-room house one block from his freight-car-building works near Lake Michigan. Barker left the house and his company in the hands of his son, John Jr., who expanded the Haskell and Barker Car Company into the largest manufacturer of its type in the world. In 1900, the younger Barker and his wife commissioned Frederick Perkins to redesign the house, incorporating the original structure as a rear wing attached to a new 38-room mansion. Perkins created an unusual example of Victorian architecture, characterized by picturesque Flemish gables with finials and a two-story projecting entrance pavilion. Beautifully laid brickwork forms textures and designs on the exterior walls. Light-colored stone window surrounds, balustrades, and chimney stacks contrast pleasantly with the redbrick walls and tile roof.

Behind the ornate ironwork gates at the entrance, the interior of the home features original furnishings, tapestries, and artworks owned by the family. The hallway, dominated by a dramatic white-limestone fireplace, opens to rooms with 10-foot ceilings, decorative plasterwork, carved-wood paneling, and stately Oriental rugs. On the third floor John Jr. and his wife built a mirrored ballroom for evening dances and a schoolroom for their only child, Catherine.

The couple died after only five years in residency, leaving Catherine, age 14, as guardian of the house. In 1948 she offered the mansion to Purdue University as a study center, and in 1968 gave it to Michigan City as a cultural center and as a memorial to her father. The property includes a walled, Italian-style, sunken garden with a central fountain, marble sculpture, and a teahouse.

8 *Barker Mansion* 631 Washington Street, Michigan City, Ind. 46360. (219) 873-1520. Open daily.

*G*lessner House

CHICAGO, ILLINOIS

*A Renowned
Architect's
Fortresslike
Masterpiece*

The handsomely restored Glessner House was one of the last buildings completed by the acclaimed architect Henry Hobson Richardson before his death in 1886. One of the few private residences designed by Richardson that still survives, Glessner House represents the architect at the peak of his creative powers.

When John Glessner, an executive at a farming equipment company (later part of International Harvester), commissioned Richardson to design his residence in 1885, the architect conceived an unusual house in striking contrast with the neighboring brick Victorian mansions. He created a U-shaped plan enclosing a secluded interior courtyard. The orientation is deceptive, the house being much larger than it appears from the entrance, with

The fortresslike exterior of Glessner House raised a few eyebrows in its conventional Victorian neighborhood. One neighbor complained, "I do not know what I have ever done to have that thing staring me in the face every time I go out of my door."

the short sides of the U forming the front and rear of the house, which is three times deeper than it is wide.

When you visit this fascinating masterpiece, you will immediately note its difference from the neighboring Queen Anne and Second Empire-style houses—Glessner House's massive granite walls front the street with no projecting bays, towers, or porches. The fortresslike exterior, composed of rough-faced stones cut and laid precisely according to Richardson's own direction, artfully conceals the private spaces of the courtyard and interior rooms. Despite the facade's generally forbidding appearance, you will be able to see Richardson's sophisticated use of material and decorative details, subtly evident. Beneath the impressive round arch over the entry, for example, note how Richardson inserted a fanlight carved into naturalistic, fragile tendrils. And while most of the exterior windows are featureless openings in the solid masonry, the central set of windows above the main door are emphasized with colonnettes, topped with decorative capitals set against a patterned sill.

Dramatically different from the solid stone exterior, the brick-faced courtyard facade could belong to another house entirely. A profusion of windows, varied in shape and size, allow abundant light into the living areas and bedrooms. Semicircular bays containing a hall and dining room project into the courtyard, while dormers poking through the steeply pitched roof add architectural interest to the building. A carriageway on the far side of the courtyard extends the length of the house, from a porte cochere opening in the facade to an exit door at the rear.

The gracious interiors at Glessner House are a contrast to its severe facade. In the informal entry hall, for example, visitors are welcomed by a fireplace and raised paneling in warm quartersawn oak. The carpet is by William Morris.

Richardson and his staff worked closely with John and Frances Glessner on the arrangement and decoration of the interior spaces, which present another contrast to the exterior. Today, guests still arrive at the welcoming entrance hall paneled entirely in oak with a beamed ceiling. The parlor and library are appointed in shades of yellow and dark green against polished wood moldings. Richardson and the Glessners shared an interest in the British Arts and Crafts movement and especially in the distinctive work of renowned designer William Morris. As you tour the house, take special note of the patterned wallpapers, floral textiles, and handwoven carpets—one of the largest collections of Morris' domestic designs in the country. Richardson modeled the Glessner's library after his own study in Massachusetts, even reproducing his enormous double desk for the couple. The desk has remained in this room for more than a century. Many pieces displayed in the home, including bookcases, cupboards, tables, and bedsteads, were handcrafted by Isaac Elwood Scott, an influential Chicago designer who produced Gothic-inspired furniture in the manner of English designer A.W.N. Pugin. Over the years, the house was transferred to a number of different owners, suffering somewhat from the passage of time. Now undergoing restoration, the mansion is again a stunning showpiece of Richardson's work and his collaboration with the Glessners.

9 *Glessner House Museum* 1800 South Prairie Avenue, Chicago, Ill. 60616. (312) 326-1480. Open Wed.-Sun.

Frank Lloyd Wright Home and Studio

OAK PARK, ILLINOIS

The Master Architect's Workshop

Designed in 1889 and expanded over a period of 20 years, Frank Lloyd Wright's Home and Studio demonstrates the development of the master architect's groundbreaking ideas for American residences. Wright was a fledgling designer just 21 years old when he began to create this home for himself and his wife, Catherine.

The residence began as a modest, shingle-style, six-room house, outfitted and furnished in a manner consistent with the Victorian and Arts and Crafts styles. Experimenting with new concepts in design and their application, Wright continued to add to the house and work spaces, gradually creating a structure more than twice the size of the original, one displaying a dramatically different architectural aesthetic. Several of the house's features became noted characteristics of Wright's later residential commissions, such as the use of a circular veranda as outdoor living space, and siting a central fireplace at the "heart" of the home. Wright completed three major building phases at the house, adding a large playroom

The entryway spotlights Frank Lloyd Wright's love of the decorative arts. Limestone urns filled with flowers loom above the steps, while two "Boulder" sculptures by Richard Bock serve as bookends for the upper entry wall.

Inspired by a tale from the Arabian Nights, *the fireplace mural of the fisherman and the genie was designed by Frank Lloyd Wright and painted by Orlando Giannini for the children's playroom.*

wing to the east side and a new dining room to the south side in 1895, the studio addition in 1898, and finally in 1911 converting the home and studio into two separate residences after his departure to new working quarters in Wisconsin.

Wright's developing gift for architectural and interior design is evident throughout. In touring the house, note how its tasteful decoration with natural woods and other unfinished materials includes exposed brick, painter's flax, and hearth tiles. In certain areas, Wright installed more extravagant finishes, such as quartersawn oak paneling in the bathroom just off the majestic master bedroom, and custom-designed, leaded art-glass windows with Egyptian and floral motifs in the dining room and children's playroom. Be sure to note how the dining room windows, set in a continuous row around a three-sided bay, complement the unusual high-backed chairs, one of Wright's first furniture designs. Within the living room, the central hearth and comforting inglenook create a warm focus, while two projecting window bays extend the interior outwards, connected at the corner of the house by an early version of the cantilevered window. The plaster ceiling panels in this room replicate designs created by Wright's mentor, Louis Sullivan, for his famous Auditorium Building in Chicago.

On the second floor, above the kitchen and maid's quarters, the architect constructed an astonishing playroom for his six children—a dramatic barrel-vaulted space 18 feet long and 15 feet high, with painted murals and built-in toy benches. The short walls below the vault are laid in exposed Roman brick, a thin brick used often by Wright in his prairie-style homes for a horizontal emphasis. A large opening in the vault, softened by a decorative wood grill, was one of Wright's first uses of overhead natural light in his work, an essential element in his later designs.

In 1898, Wright decided to move his studio from Chicago to Oak Park. The brick and shingle-covered studio building holds an octagonal library with high clerestory windows, an office for Wright, a reception area, and an enormous drafting room, square on the first floor and topped by an octagonal drum. A brightly lit second-floor balcony encircles the drum, offering a view of the studio spaces and draftsmen below. As in the main house, a central hearth, open to the office and work space, provided heat as well as focus.

Along with the National Trust for Historic Preservation, the Frank Lloyd Wright Home and Studio Foundation restored the structure to its 1909 appearance. As some of Wright's most significant designs were completed here, it remains an important landmark in American architecture.

10 *Frank Lloyd Wright Home and Studio* 951 CHICAGO AVENUE, OAK PARK, ILL. 60302. (708) 848-1976. OPEN DAILY. WWW.WRIGHTPLUS.COM ⬤ 🚶 ♿ 🅿 🏛

NEARBY: **Robie House** *(5757 South Woodlawn Avenue, Chicago, Ill. 773-834-1847)* Wright's Robie House marks the first residential use of steel beams, allowing for the dramatic cantilevers; the roof extends 20 feet beyond the walls at each end of the house. The house is also noted for its many exquisite art-glass windows and doors—174 throughout the entire structure.

Charles Gates Dawes House
EVANSTON, ILLINOIS

Tudor
Paneling
and a Tiffany
Daffodil

A pair of imposing round towers stand like sturdy sentinels at the sides of this châteauesque mansion, built between 1894 and 1896 on the shore of Lake Michigan. Constructed of orange and tan bricks, with a steeply pitched, red-tile roof, the house was designed by New York City architect Henry Edwards-Ficken for Robert Sheppard, treasurer and business manager for Northwestern University. Sheppard sold the property in 1909 to Charles Gates Dawes, a lawyer, financier, philanthropist, and future politician. While Dawes added bathrooms and renovated the kitchen, he kept the house essentially as it had been built.

The Dawes House was designed for large-scale entertaining. From the main entrance you will first reach a small vestibule before entering the impressive Great Hall, appointed with oak beams and large oak arches. Dominating the space is a grand staircase that curves so deeply over the hall as to form a gallery on the second floor. Your tour of the first floor will include the beautifully paneled, Tudor-style dining room with a musicians' gallery and vaulted ceiling of molded plaster in a cornucopia motif. Be sure to notice the ceiling light, with a daffodil pattern, one of six Tiffany & Company fixtures in the mansion. Equally handsome and impressive, the library was designed in Renaissance style, with exposed beams and cherry-wood paneling with a mahogany glaze. Both library and dining room remain as they were in the 1920s.

Despite the comforts he enjoyed within these walls, Dawes had a deep concern for the poor. In 1907 he operated a bread wagon in Chicago to distribute food to the needy; and after the untimely death of his son in 1912, Dawes established, in the memory of his child, two transient hotels where the destitute could obtain inexpensive lodging. He won the Nobel Peace Prize in 1925 for his work on planning Germany's reparation payments after World War I, went on to serve as Calvin Coolidge's Vice President from 1925 to 1929, and later as ambassador to England. He returned to the United States to head up the Reconstruction Finance Corp. under Herbert Hoover. The Dawes family occupied the house until 1957.

⑪ *Charles Gates Dawes House* 225 Greenwood Street, Evanston, Ill. 60201. (847) 475-3410. Open Wed.-Sun. 🄢 🏃 ♿ 🏛

Cantigny
WHEATON, ILLINOIS

A Yankee Colonel's Southern-style Mansion

A gracious and comfortable residence built in the style of the grand southern mansions, Cantigny was the home of Col. Robert R. McCormick, owner and publisher of the *Chicago Tribune.* In the 1930s, McCormick commissioned Willis Irvin, an architect from Georgia, to enlarge and redesign a 16-room white frame house once owned by his maternal grandfather. Irvin expanded the original house by adding library and bedroom wings to each end, then enclosed the entire structure in Georgian pink brick. In the southern tradition, the final touch was a dramatic, full-height Greek Revival portico supported by four columns, creating a suitably grand entrance.

The 35-room mansion is elegantly appointed. The library, with a 20-foot-high ceiling, is paneled entirely in carved Brazilian butternut. Here you will see how the pedimented, Renaissance Revival mantelpiece frames a portrait of Colonel McCormick, who earned his rank as an artillery officer during World War I. An avid hunter, he decorated the Prints Room with lively foxhunting scenes dating from 1827.

Adjacent is the south porch, a tranquil veranda modeled on the portico of President James Madison's home at Montpelier, Virginia. The sunny second-floor sitting room and bedroom of McCormick's first wife, Amy, contains her collection of European antiques. In addition, several pieces acquired in the course of the colonel's extensive travels remain in the home, including a hand-painted mural purchased during a trip to China in 1947, now hanging in the dining room. If you look closely at the hunting scene depicted in the painting, you will see that no two figures in the intricate composition are alike.

McCormick died in 1955, leaving the estate "for the recreation, instruction, and welfare of the people of the state of Illinois." Today, the 500-acre property supports not only the mansion and gardens, but also the First Division Museum, a research center, and the Cantigny Golf Course. The colonel and his first wife are buried on the grounds, their graves marked by a large white marble exedra, a semicircular sitting area in the ancient Greek tradition.

12 *Robert R. McCormick Museum at Cantigny* 151 WINFIELD ROAD, WHEATON, ILL. 60187. (630) 668-5332. OPEN MARCH THROUGH DEC. TUES.-SUN.; FEB. FRI.-SUN. WWW.XNET.COM/~CANTIGNY

Colonel McCormick used his estate as a farm, raising horses, hogs, chickens, and cows. The mansion is now the cornerstone of 500 acres of open and wooded land, composed of gardens, museums, and a golf course.

David Davis Mansion

BLOOMINGTON, ILLINOIS

A Proper Home for a Famous Judge

The essence of propriety, the David Davis Mansion represents the sober side of Victorian architecture and design. The house was built in 1872 for David Davis, a justice on the U.S. Supreme Court, and his wife, Sarah. As Justice Davis was compelled to spend much of his time in Washington, many decisions about the house and its furnishings were made by Sarah, and her paramount directive was that the house be "comfortable and convenient."

The Davises hired a French-born architect, Alfred Piquenard, who worked for the Chicago firm of Cochrane and Gurnsey. Piquenard developed the designs for the Davises' house while supervising the construction of Illinois' new state capitol at Springfield. For the Davises' mansion he combined elements of Italian villa and French Second Empire styles,

The grand entry to the David Davis Mansion invites exploration of the first-floor rooms.

the latter most evident in the mansard roof, topped with ornamental ironwork. Constructed of yellow bricks, the house charms the eye with its irregular massing and artful combination of shapes—arched windows, prominent quoins, triangular pediment over the doorway, and delicate ornamental ironwork on the porch. The Davises budgeted $30,000 for construction, unaware that Piquenard had gained a reputation for spending well beyond his estimates. The final cost was about $75,000.

The interior typifies genteel, upper-class Victorian taste. Whereas dark walnut woodwork sets the tone for many of the rooms, the formal parlor's pink-glazed woodwork reflects a lighter and more feminine character. This is where Sarah Davis received female guests on days when she was "at home." The ten-piece Renaissance Revival set of chairs, sofa, and center table was purchased by Sarah in New York while the window treatments and carpet are reproductions typical of 1870s taste.

The house served as an appropriate social setting for a man of Davis' prominence. A friend of Abraham Lincoln, Davis served as his campaign manager in the tumultuous 1860 presidential election. Two years later in 1862, President Lincoln nominated him for the Supreme Court. Davis died at home from the complications of diabetes in 1886.

The house survived a fire in 1902 that ravaged the tower and the attic, causing extensive smoke and water damage. Davis family descendants lived here until 1959, when they deeded the house, many of its 19th-century furnishings, and 4 acres of grounds to the state of Illinois. A 1992 restoration returned the house to its original appearance.

13 *David Davis Mansion State Historic Site* 1000 East Monroe, Bloomington, Ill. 61701. (309) 828-1084. Open Thurs.-Mon.

Villa Louis

PRAIRIE DU CHIEN, WISCONSIN

A Dazzling Display of Victorian Design

Meticulous restoration has brought back the Victorian decor of this house, which epitomizes the era's love affair with color and bold patterns. In 1870, Louis Dousman, the only child of a pioneering fur trader, demolished his father's house and commissioned E. Townsend Mix of Milwaukee to build a new, more fashionable residence. Mix designed a cream-colored, Italianate brick house with a low gable at the center of the roof. One oddity of the design is the large porch that wraps around the first story, providing a comfortable sitting area but obscuring the architecture. The Italianate-style second floor seems to emerge from a plain box.

Exterior design, however, takes a backseat to interior decor. Major remodeling and redecoration began in 1885 and continued after Louis' death in January 1886 under the direction of his wife, Nina. (In memory of her late husband, Nina christened the house Villa Louis.) She hired designer John J. McGrath, the Chicago agent of London-based William Morris & Company, to design room after room of dazzling wallpaper and painted decoration. While the front hallway offers a rich expanse of wallpaper showing intricate floral patterns, the dining room walls are partly sheathed in burgundy Lincrusta, an embossed material produced from linseed oil that has the appearance of leather.

Wallpapers, paint, and Lincrusta all form a fitting background for Nina Dousman's ample collection of furnishings and art objects. Wonderfully detailed photographs of the house from the 1890s aided in contemporary restoration, and show a virtual museum of Victorian excess. Mirrors, statuettes, candles, clocks, and porcelain cover every available space and surface. The

The influence of the British Arts and Crafts movement is evident in the richly patterned wallpaper, carpeting, and upholstery in the entry hall at Villa Louis. Almost all of the furnishings and decorative arts are original to the house.

furniture ranges from a classic empire sofa to curved Victorian chairs, upholstered in richly colored fabrics. Mrs. Dousman left the house in 1913, but in the 1930s her daughter Virginia Dousman Bigelow, then a New York decorator, began restoring the residence. Another restoration in the 1990s has brought back the 1890s design in its full, colorful glory.

⑭ *Villa Louis* 521 NORTH VILLA LOUIS ROAD, PRAIRIE DU CHIEN, WIS. 53821. (608) 326-2721. OPEN DAILY MAY THROUGH OCT. 🅢 🅰 ♿ 🅿 🏛

*P*abst Mansion

MILWAUKEE, WISCONSIN

A Beer Baron's Milwaukee Mansion

Completed in 1892, this unusual Flemish Renaissance Revival mansion has been described as "a house of great dignity and repose." Designed by Milwaukee architect George Bowman Ferry, the three-story residence is constructed of tan pressed brick with stone quoins and carved terra-cotta ornamentation. Arcaded porticoes with ornamented pilasters jut out from the main facade and the west side of the building. The house was built as a retirement home for Frederick Pabst, the renowned beer baron, hotel and restaurant magnate, real estate tycoon, philanthropist, and patron of the arts. A German immigrant, Pabst rose from the ranks of cabin boy on a Great Lakes steamship to become captain and owner. After marrying Maria Best, daughter of a successful brewer, he went into the family beer business that eventually bore his name.

The opulence of the 37-room mansion reflects Pabst's status as Milwaukee's leading citizen. Both the ladies' parlour and the dining room reflect the French rococo revival style. In the former, scene of Mrs. Pabst's afternoon teas and evening salons, note the recurring shell motif as well as the white-enameled woodwork and moldings with gold-leaf highlights. In the dining room the rose is the key decorative element. Note the bouquets of the bloom on the original wall covering, and the gold-leaf rosettes within the cove of the Renaissance-style ceiling. The Matthews Brothers, the finest craftsmen in Milwaukee, custom-made all of the dining room's woodwork and furnishings. Louis XV table and chairs, fashioned out of birch, sit beneath an original gilded bronze chandelier designed to use gas, electricity, or kerosene.

The house abounds with interesting details. The finials on the grand staircase's newel-posts are carved in the shape of hops, the key ingredient in brewing beer. A nook where musicians played during parties holds one of Pabst's prized possessions—an 18th-century wood-and-leather chair bearing the crest of Prussia's ruling family and the saying "God be with us" in German. Other didactic mottoes reveal the secrets of Pabst's success: "Good attitude is half the work," reads one stained-glass panel in the servants' dining room; another near the vendors' entrance warns, "Buy with your eyes open."

⑮ *Captain Frederick Pabst Mansion* 2000 WEST WISCONSIN AVENUE, MILWAUKEE, WIS. 53233. (414) 931-0808. OPEN TUES.-SUN. 🅢 🅰 ♿ 🅿 🏛

Frederick Pabst's stately mansion reflected his position as Milwaukee's foremost citizen. Inside, his photo keeps watch over his study (pages 210–211), where the cabinetry contains 14 hidden compartments and a large cigar humidor.

 Turnblad Mansion

MINNEAPOLIS, MINNESOTA

*A Fairy-tale
Palace for a
Swedish
Millionaire*

In an affluent Minneapolis neighborhood of opulent mansions owned by Americans of British and German origin, Swan Turnblad sought to claim a place for Swedish Americans by erecting an equally grand architectural proclamation of success. A self-made millionaire and the owner of *Svenska Amerikanska Posten,* the largest Swedish-language newspaper in the United States, Turnblad was the son of a poor farmer. Yet with the income from his newspaper, he was able to build a mansion considered to be one of the most luxurious in the old Northwest. In 1904 he hired architects Christopher A. Boehme and Victor Cordella, who produced a largely French châteauesque design, recalling the architecture of Biltmore, George Vanderbilt's mansion in North Carolina (see p. 138). As Cordella was a native of Poland, the Turnblad Mansion also shows the influence of the Gothic 16th-century manor houses of Poland and the Baltic region. Turnblad directed some of the interior design himself, working from models found in Swedish architectural pattern books. This mingling of styles led to the creation of a fairy-tale castle, with numerous chimneys, gables, and pinnacles arranged around a steeply pitched roof. At the front of the mansion, a round turret topped by battlements culminates in a tall pointed tower, with a corbeled balcony clinging to its side—just the sort of place from which Rapunzel would have let down her long golden hair.

A broad archway supported by squat columns leads to a sumptuous interior of 33 rooms, lavishly decorated with carved woodwork. Craftsmen worked for more than two years to hand-carve the ornamentation in the grand entrance hall, paneled in African mahogany. Here you will see a two-story mahogany fireplace, carved by Polish artist Albin Polasek, flanked by two "barbarians" wearing animal skins and supporting pedestals on their heads. Two female figures, representing Night and Day, lean on a clock above. The hall's staircase is illuminated by a stained-glass window copied from a painting in a Swedish museum and depicting a historical scene of the sacking of the city of Visby on the island of Gotland. Note the pair of mahogany griffins, mythological animals, guarding the stairway—the handrails of the balustrade emerge from their backs. In Greek mythology, the fearsome griffin protected the gold of the Scythians. Griffin iconography appears throughout the house, from stone gargoyles on the roof to the decorative plaster ceilings, and even on a settee, where griffins form the armrests and legs.

The music room presents more handsome carving in exotic Honduran mahogany. Here, 52 carved cherubs, each with different kinds of wings—butterfly, bird, dragonfly, and angel among them—take flight. (The carver, Ulrich Steiner, reportedly vowed that he would never carve another cherub in his life.) In the dining room, an intricate bas-relief carving above the mantel depicts a Swedish legend in which two trolls spirit a maiden away from her earthly home to their enchanted world. Two formal figures known as caryatids appear on either side of the fireplace, supporting candelabra pedestals.

*For the elaborate woodcarving in the entrance hall, which took craftsmen
more than two years to perfect, Swan Turnblad imported such exotic woods
as African and Honduran mahogany grown in virgin forests.*

Swan Turnblad's architects used smooth-faced Indiana limestone and asymmetrical design elements such as turrets and steep roofs to achieve the castlelike effect.

Turnblad and his family lived in the mansion from 1908 to 1915, when they moved into an elegant third-floor apartment in their newly constructed newspaper building. In 1929, Turnblad gave the mansion to the American Institute for Swedish Arts, Literature, and Science (later the American Swedish Institute), which he had founded. The institute maintains the house as a museum and Swedish cultural center and strives to tell the story of Swedish immigrants in America through artworks and artifacts, of which the house itself is the most compelling. Also of interest is the institute's unrivaled collection of decorative *kakelugnar*, traditional Swedish porcelainized tile stoves. A combination of fireplace and heating stove, a kakelugnar will heat an entire room for some 30 hours on one load of wood.

16 *Turnblad Mansion: The American Swedish Institute* 2600 PARK AVENUE, MINNEAPOLIS, MINN. 55407. (612) 871-4907. OPEN TUES.-SUN. WWW.AMERICANSWEDISHINST.ORG

James J. Hill House

ST. PAUL, MINNESOTA

From Great Wealth, Simplicity of Design

The enormous stone mansion James J. Hill built on the heights of Summit Avenue accurately captures his character: rugged, overpowering, massive, and disdainful of luxurious display. One of the great railroad builders of the 19th century, Hill orchestrated the development of the northern tier of the American West, accumulating a vast fortune in the process. Between 1888 and 1891, he spent more than $900,000 constructing his mansion— a time when laborers earned less than two dollars a day. His house was the largest and most costly home in the state. Four stories high in the front, and five in the rear, the house could be seen plainly, as a contemporary account in the St. Paul *Pioneer Press* noted, "from almost every point in the business portion of the city."

Hill engaged the Boston firm of Peabody and Sterns, experienced at designing large houses in the Romanesque manner of famed architect Henry Hobson Richardson. They used massive stone blocks to shape the tall chimney stacks, shadowy cloisters, and broad arches, creating a formidable yet forthright house far different from the opulent palaces being constructed in Newport, Rhode Island, and along New York's Hudson River. As the exterior was being completed, the architects incurred Hill's wrath by twice countermanding his personal instructions to the stone carvers, so Hill fired them and engaged another Boston firm, Irving and Casson, to complete the interior.

The mansion's 36,000 square feet of living space comprise 42 rooms, including a 100-foot-long reception hall, a two-story skylit art gallery, and 13 bathrooms. Warmed by 22 fireplaces and lit by 16 crystal chandeliers, the house also features central heat, gas and electric lighting, and a ventilation system. Tiffany & Company, which designed stained glass for the house, also felt the sting of Hill's temper when he bluntly rejected some of their work as "*anything but* what I want."

After Hill's death in 1916 and his wife, Mary's, in 1921, their heirs gave the house to the Roman Catholic archdiocese for use as a residence, school, and offices. In 1978 the Minnesota Historical Society acquired the mansion. Restored but largely unfurnished, it retains the atmosphere the *Pioneer Press* described over a century ago—"impressive, fine, even grand in the simplicity of design," but evincing no desire "to flaunt an advertisement of wealth in the eyes of the world."

Hefty stonework and towering chimneys dominate the Hill mansion. Heavy Syrian arches distinguish the porte cochere in front.

⑰ *James J. Hill House* 240 SUMMIT AVENUE, ST. PAUL, MINN. 55102. (651) 297-2555. OPEN WED.-SAT. WWW.MNHS.ORG

*G*lensheen

DULUTH, MINNESOTA

*The House
of Two
Phi Beta
Kappas*

In 1904 St. Paul architect Clarence H. Johnston designed this 39-room mansion in the Jacobean Revival style, which emulated the great country houses of 17th-century England. The tall chimney stacks and three prominent gables on the front facade represent hallmarks of the style. Two are steep, triangular gables that flank a third formed of curving sides with a half circle on top. The St. Paul design firm William A. French and Company continued the Jacobean theme inside with wood-work ornamented with strapwork, so-called because the carving resembles flat leather straps. You will sense how the massive main stairway, fully ornamented with strapwork panels, sets a baronial tone for the main rooms of the house.

Completed in 1908, Glensheen symbolizes the remarkable rise of its owner, Chester Congdon, who arrived in Minnesota in 1879 with a law degree and little else. His fiancée, Clara Bannister, waited patiently during a six-year engagement for Chester to find his professional footing. (Clara was no Victorian wallflower—one of the first female graduates of Syracuse University, she earned a Phi Beta Kappa key, as did Chester, her classmate.) After a dreary year in Minnesota, he toted up his net worth at $9.67 in cash. After four years as assistant to the U.S. district attorney, he returned to private practice, moving to Duluth in 1892. Then, at a chance meeting, Chester so impressed a mining executive that he was hired as counsel for the Oliver Iron Mining Company. His knowledge of the industry led to several large acquisitions of iron-rich land that he eventually sold to U.S. Steel.

Beyond its impressive main rooms, the house contains private spaces of great charm and sophistication. The breakfast

Two brick retaining walls create a terraced effect for Glensheen's formal gardens.

room, surrounded by glass and tile, offers a cozy and relaxed setting for informal meals and conversation. The third floor contains a superb collection of Minnesota Arts and Crafts, or mission-style, furniture, custom-made for Glensheen. In addition to four boys' bedrooms, this floor also holds a large guest room, an infirmary, a darkroom, a trunk room, a study lounge, and a 21-foot, walk-in closet.

Donated by the family to the University of Minnesota in 1968, Glensheen has been restored as an example of the prosperity the mining industry brought to Duluth around the turn of the century, and the talents of the state's architects and designers.

18 *Glensheen: The Historic Congdon Estate* 3300 London Road, Duluth, Minn. 55804. (218) 724-8864 or (888) 454-4536. Open May through Oct. daily; Fri.-Sun. rest of year. www.d.umn.edu/glen/

rucemore

CEDAR RAPIDS, IOWA

Queen Anne Elegance and Roller-skating in the Halls
A stately, 21-room mansion, Brucemore features the steep gables, turrets, contrasting colors, and decorative brickwork that are hallmarks of the Queen Anne style. Caroline Sinclair, a 31-year-old widow with six children, built the house between 1884 and 1886 at a cost of about $55,000. Her husband, who had amassed a comfortable fortune in the meatpacking business, had died in a factory accident. When her children were grown, Caroline looked for a smaller house, exchanging properties in 1906 with George and Irene Douglas, whose renovations gave Brucemore the appearance it has today. They imparted a warm but imposing atmosphere to the grand entrance hall by installing butternut wood

George and Irene Douglas added the distinctive butternut paneling to Brucemore's grand oak staircase, which rises the full three stories of the house.

paneling, ceiling beams, and a mural depicting scenes from Richard Wagner's *Ring* cycle of operas. The Douglases also installed a 678-pipe Skinner player organ on the third floor, and a sleeping porch designed by the local artist Grant Wood before he gained national fame for his paintings. Irene Douglas encouraged the artistic interests of her three daughters—who showed talent for sculpture, writing, and music—and she did not mind when the girls roller-skated in the entrance hall or played Ping-Pong on the mahogany dining room table. Irene expressed her creativity through gardening and book binding, and had her own bindery on the estate.

Tragedy touched the family in April 1912, when the news reached Cedar Rapids that the White Star liner *Titanic* had struck an iceberg. George's brother Walter and his wife, Mahala, were passengers on the voyage. George and Irene left immediately for New York, where they found Mahala alive; but Walter, like many other male passengers, had refused a place on the lifeboats and lost his life. His body was recovered from the Atlantic and brought to Cedar Rapids for burial.

Brucemore remained in the Douglas family until 1981, when Margaret Douglas Hall died at the age of 84, bequeathing the house where she had roller-skated as a child to the National Trust for Historic Preservation.

19 *Brucemore* 2160 LINDEN DRIVE SE, CEDAR RAPIDS, IOWA 52403. (319) 362-7375. OPEN FEB. THROUGH DEC. TUES.-SAT. WWW.BRUCEMORE.ORG ⑤ 🚶 ♿ 🅿 🏛

*T*errace Hill

DES MOINES, IOWA

Victorian Surroundings for the Iowa Governor

With its two towers—one rising 90 feet above the front door—mansard roofs, dormers, and chimneys, Terrace Hill is a dramatic example of Second Empire architecture. The redbrick mansion's situation atop a steep hill further accentuates its vertical design. In addition, an English landscape designer was hired to sculpt the 30-acre site and judiciously cut down trees to provide dramatic views of the house and enhance its size and grandeur.

Benjamin Franklin Allen, a Des Moines financier and one of Iowa's first millionaires, commissioned William Boyington, a well-known Chicago architect, to design the 20-room mansion. Completed in 1869, it was one of the most luxurious houses in the state and a prominent symbol of the owner's great wealth. Six years later, Allen's fortune was gone. Forced into bankruptcy, he eventually sold Terrace Hill to a Des Moines businessman, Frederick Hubbell, for $55,000—a fraction of what it cost to build.

The interior features spacious rooms, with ceilings reaching more than 14 feet high and massive doors, some weighing 400 pounds. A 9-by-13-foot stained-glass window on the stair landing has been carefully restored. As you tour the mansion, note the Pier mirrors designed by a New York craftsman that hang above the eight Spanish and Italian marble fireplaces. The music room features a tête-à-tête love seat and a Steinway grand piano, while in the drawing room a silver-and-crystal chandelier glitters with more than 1,500 prisms, casting its light on a John Henry Belter set of sofa and chairs and an 18th-century Aubusson silk tapestry. This room witnessed a momentous family event in 1899, when Hubbell's daughter Beulah was married to a Swedish count in a lavish ceremony.

The pale limestone quoining, windows headers, and bracketed cornice provide a rich contrast to Terrace Hill's redbrick walls. The house now serves as Iowa's governor's mansion.

The Hubbell family owned Terrace Hill until 1971, when they turned the grand mansion over to the state of Iowa to be used as the governor's residence. While the governor's family occupies the third floor, the two lower floors are open to the public and provide a view of opulent life in the Victorian era.

20 *Terrace Hill Historic Site* 2300 Grand Avenue, Des Moines, Iowa 50312. (515) 281-3604. Open Tues.-Sat.

$\mathcal{S}$alisbury House
DES MOINES, IOWA

A Medieval Palace Filled with Eclectic Art

Of the many wealthy Americans who have tried to house themselves in the grand style of England, few succeeded as magnificently as Carl and Edith Weeks. Between 1923 and 1928 the Weekses constructed their version of English splendor, called Salisbury House, with 42 rooms in 22,500 square feet of living space. They decided to build a house modeled on the medieval King's House, which they had seen in Salisbury, England. The Weekses attempted to copy every detail of the structure, an effort that eventually cost them and their company, Armand Cosmetics, some three million dollars. A pharmacist, Weeks made his fortune on a mixture of face powder and cold cream, creating a foundation cosmetic that became extremely popular in the 1920s.

Although the couple utilized the talents of a local architecture firm, Boyd and Moore, and later the New York partnership of Rasmussen and Wayland, they decided upon many of the details themselves. Carl's brother-in-law, Paul van Slyke, served as construction manager and liaison between the owners, the architects, and the craftsmen. The process did not prove to be a smooth one. As Carl Weeks, van Slyke, and the architects continued to make and remake decisions, entire walls and foundations were torn down and rebuilt. As accuracy was paramount, Weeks insisted that the designers copy each of the three periods of the King's House architecture—a Tudor portion, an older Gothic porch, and an addition from the Charles I period—while adding modern conveniences. Thus, amid the aura of the English medieval past, Salisbury House boasted electricity, an elevator, and such appliances as washing machines, dishwashers, and dryers.

Weeks and his team were particular about their materials. Although much of the house is constructed of Indiana limestone, Weeks also obtained flint from the chalky deposits of the famous white cliffs of Dover. Surprisingly, he did not have to travel to England to acquire it, since transatlantic ships were using the stone as ballast. In addition, not wishing to spoil his antique design with new bricks, Weeks purchased old paving bricks from a street in downtown Des Moines that was being torn up. For the interiors, Weeks agreed to remodel an English boys' home in exchange for the building's 16th-century oak paneling, which was carefully removed, shipped to Iowa, and installed in the common room, library, and dining room. Timbering for the Great Hall was salvaged from the White Hart Inn in Salisbury, which was being demolished. Dating back to the time of Shakespeare, the timbered ceiling fit Salisbury House perfectly, a testament to the accuracy of the plans.

Edith and Carl Weeks traveled extensively, collecting art and furniture for the house. While their architectural taste was firmly rooted in medieval England, their art acquisitions were broad and eclectic. In addition to the couple's medieval antiques (such as a 700-year-old trestle table), the house displays a vase from Cyprus dating back to 1500 B.C.; a series of Navajo rugs; statues from six different Chinese dynasties; and works of art by Van Dyck, Sir Thomas Lawrence, Joseph Stella, and George Romney. The Weekses considered buying art from both Grant Wood and Thomas Hart Benton, hiring a plane to transport the artists and their work to Des Moines. Also of note is the couple's rare-book library and extensive manuscript collection, which includes letters from many important figures in American history. In addition, Louis Armstrong, Cab Calloway, and other jazz musicians were invited to perform on the

The elegant library at Salisbury House contains numerous rare books and letters. The oak paneling, dated 1580, was originally wainscoting in an English home. Also from the 16th century is the Ming Dynasty statue of a fish vendor, at left.

family's custom-designed Steinway piano. The couple's passionate commitment to the arts is conveyed in the writings of Carl Weeks, who penned in 1953, "When you speak to most persons of art, music, drama and sculpture, you get a turned-up nose or contemptuous or superior look. Yet if you were to take those four away, out of our lives, you and I would live a life lower than that of any animal. Every house and home, dress or drape, is better because of art."

21 *Salisbury House* 4025 TONAWANDA DRIVE, DES MOINES, IOWA 50312. (515) 274-1777. OPEN BY APPOINTMENT, CALL FOR TOUR TIMES AND RESERVATIONS. WWW.SALISBURYHOUSE.ORG 🔲🔲🔲🔲🔲

NEARBY: **Hoyt Sherman Place** *(1501 Woodland Avenue, Des Moines, Iowa. 515-244-0507)* Completed in 1877 for pioneer businessman Hoyt Sherman, this house contains period rooms, hand-carved woodwork, marble fireplaces, and a collection of 19th-century paintings.

Samuel Cupples House
ST. LOUIS, MISSOURI

Gargoyles, English Oak, and a Zodiac by Tiffany

Samuel Cupples, who reaped a fortune selling broom handles, ax handles, and other wooden implements, hired Thomas Annan to design a mansion befitting his financial success. For inspiration Annan turned to the imposing Romanesque style of Henry Hobson Richardson, and designed a castlelike mansion of rough-hewn purple Colorado sandstone with limestone gargoyles, soaring round turrets, a steep gable, and elaborate architectural details. Four arches on stout Tuscan pillars loom over the entrance. Given carte blanche, Annan brought stone carvers from England to execute the most demanding and detailed work, such as the numerous gargoyles that hold the downspouts at the roofline. Completed in 1890, the 42-room mansion cost $500,000.

Annan decorated much of the interior with imported English oak paneling, which he used to great effect in the large main hall, measuring 1,300 square feet. Here you can appreciate how the straight lines of the oak panels and beams form a pleasing contrast to the parquet floor and curved musicians' gallery overlooking the space. For the gallery level Annan commissioned Tiffany & Company to create a beautiful four-paned, stained-glass scene depicting pagan gods and the signs of the Zodiac. The scene, derived from a painting by the English Pre-Raphaelite artist Burne-Jones, is inscribed with verses written by the St. Louis poet Eugene Field.

More English oak, finely carved, adorns Cupples' library. Carved arches and pilasters flank a fireplace of Italian marble mosaic, fitted with a locally made, wrought-iron firebox. Note the carved motto over the fireplace which reads, *Vita hominis sine literis mors est*—the life of man without literature is death.

When St. Louis University acquired the house in 1946 the building had never been significantly altered. The university installed an art gallery in the basement, but restored the rest of the residence to its original appearance, recognizing its importance as a rare surviving example of Richardsonian Romanesque architecture in St. Louis.

22 *Samuel Cupples House* ST. LOUIS UNIVERSITY, 221 NORTH GRAND BOULEVARD, ST. LOUIS, MO. 63103. (314) 977-3025. OPEN FEB. THROUGH DEC. WED.-SUN. WWW.SLU.EDU/THE_ARTS/CUPPLES 🔲🔲🔲

Campbell House

ST. LOUIS, MISSOURI

The
Mountain
Man's House
in the City

An elegant town house in St. Louis' most fashionable district seems an incongruous home for a mountain man, but Campbell House was exactly that. Robert Campbell, an Irish immigrant, spent more than a decade in the West trapping and trading in furs, fighting Indians, and sharing danger with some of the most famous figures of the frontier—Jedediah Smith, Kit Carson, and Jim Bridger. In one of his Western sketches, writer Washington Irving said of Campbell, "His exploits partake of the wildest spirit of romance. No danger nor difficulty can appall him."

Exhausted and sick from his exploits, Campbell decided to settle down in St. Louis. He started a business providing supplies to trappers and settlers, married, and rose to become president of a bank. In 1854 he purchased a town house on Lucas Place, the city's finest residential area. He and his wife, Virginia, furnished it in high-Victorian style, indulging

The informal sitting room in the Campbell House reflects the cluttered look that characterizes late Victorian decorating style. The sofa nestled in the window bay displays the classic curvilinear outline of the rococo revival style.

themselves on shopping trips to the East and Europe. Despite their prosperity, the Campbells did not find complete happiness in their home. Virginia gave birth to 13 children, 10 of whom died before the age of seven. The surviving three sons never married, and lived as recluses in the house until their deaths in the 1930s. Although the sons made some alterations to the residence, visitors today see the house largely as it was in the 19th century.

The drawing room—the social hub of any Victorian house—retains its mid-1850s rococo revival furniture, including sofas, a center table, an étagère, mirrors, and a set of chairs. The Campbells purchased these items in Philadelphia, along with a grand piano and gilded gasoliers. The dining room table includes nine leaves, suggesting that the mountain man enjoyed large-scale entertaining.

23 *Campbell House Museum* 1508 LOCUST STREET, ST. LOUIS, MO. 63103. (314)421-0325. OPEN DAILY.

🔵 🚶 🏛

NEARBY: **Chatillon-DeMenil Mansion** *(3352 DeMenil Place, St. Louis, Mo. 314-771-5828)* A Creole farmhouse that was transformed into a Greek Revival mansion in the 1860s, this house was rescued from highway planners in the 1960s and thoroughly restored.

Rockcliffe
HANNIBAL, MISSOURI

Site of
Mark Twain's
Swan Song

The hometown of Samuel L. Clemens, renowned as Mark Twain, boasts a number of mansions constructed with fortunes made in shipping and timber. One Greek Revival house was built by lumber baron John Cruikshank, which he named Rockcliffe for its location—a rocky promontory overlooking the Mississippi River. It was completed in 1900.

The interior presents a variety of styles. Be sure not to miss the spectacular Moorish room, painted in intricately patterned bright colors and rising to a vaulted ceiling supported by gilded Corinthian columns. The Green Room, site of Mrs. Cruikshank's afternoon teas, reflects the style of Louis XIV through its elegant gold-leaf furnishings and white onyx fireplace. Throughout the house you will see many of the original Tiffany fixtures commissioned by the Cruikshanks, including chandeliers, wall fixtures, and windows.

After the death of John Cruikshank, Rockcliffe's doors were closed in 1924. The house remained empty for 43 years, earning a reputation as Hannibal's own haunted house. Two weeks before its scheduled demolition, Rockcliffe was purchased by three families committed to its preservation. Through their efforts, the original decorations were recovered and the furnishings preserved by the family were brought out of storage and returned to the mansion.

With the help of the restoration, today it is easy to visualize a legendary literary event. On a memorable evening in 1902, Samuel Clemens, a close friend of the Cruikshanks, stood on the great staircase in the reception room and regaled a large group of guests with stories. This turned out to be his last visit to Hannibal, his farewell to the midwestern town that had proved so inspirational.

24 *Rockcliffe Mansion* 1000 BIRD STREET, HANNIBAL, MO. 63401. (573) 221-4140. OPEN DAILY. 🔵 🚶 🅿 🏛

Vaile Mansion was constructed of hand-pressed red brick, kilned on the property from local clay. The estate also included a wine cellar reported to have a capacity of 48,000 gallons, some made from grapes grown in Colonel Vaile's own extensive vineyards.

Vaile Mansion

INDEPENDENCE, MISSOURI

Heartland
House of Gold

A festive example of the Second Empire style of architecture, the Vaile Mansion revels in a profusion of wooden brackets, moldings, stick braces, and pendants. Above the entrance, a four-story tower rises 80 feet, sporting two balconies, dormer windows, and a crown of iron filigree. The house boasts no fewer than 112 windows. Harvey Vaile amassed a fortune from land investments, ranching, and a government contract to deliver mail to rural "star" routes in the West. He and his wife, Sophia, built the 31-room mansion in 1881 and 1882 at a cost as high as $150,000. Vaile spent freely on such furnishings as the Carrara marble mantel in the main parlor, and on such up-to-date conveniences as a speaking-tube communication system, hot and cold running water, flush toilets, and marble washbasins. The house impressed the townspeople, who began to call it Maison d'Or, "house of gold." Vaile also sparked gossip with the painting that adorned the master bedroom ceiling, which originally depicted a reclining woman, nude above the waist. Rumor swirled that the model was Sophia, who found herself snubbed by polite society. A lacy bodice was later painted over the most suggestive part of the picture. Restored with period furnishings, the house fully captures the exuberance of the late Victorian era.

25 *Vaile Mansion* 1500 North Liberty, Independence, Mo. 64050. (816) 325-7430. Open daily April through Dec. 🛇 🚶 🅿 🏛

Clayton House

FORT SMITH, ARKANSAS

Meticulous
Restoration
of a
Prosecutor's
Home

Born in 1840 and named for the popular presidential candidate of the period, William Henry Harrison Clayton moved to this 1850s house in 1882. Here he lived with his wife, Florence—together raising two sons and six daughters—while he served as U.S. District Attorney of the Western District of Arkansas in the famous court of the "hanging judge," Isaac Parker. Of the some 10,000 cases Clayton prosecuted in Judge Parker's court, 80 men were convicted of murder—a record unparalleled in the American justice system.

The Clayton House, extensively remodeled in the 1880s, is notable for its hand-carved woodwork and elegant black walnut staircase. Today open to the public, it is home to the Fort Smith Heritage Foundation and stands as a testament to meticulous restoration. An enormous effort was made to keep the structural integrity of the house by using such original construction methods and materials as mortise for the floor joints; mortise and tenon for the framework; and square nails handmade of iron. Thanks to detailed drawings, impressions, and color checks, the geometric frescoes on the music room ceiling are precise reproductions of the originals, of necessity destroyed while repairing the underpinnings of the second floor. The house is filled with period furnishings and complemented by an herbal garden.

26 *W.H.H. Clayton House* 514 North Sixth Street, Fort Smith, Ark. 72901. (501) 783-3000. Open Wed.-Sun. and by appointment. 🛇 🚶 🅿

Frank Phillips Home

BARTLESVILLE, OKLAHOMA

An Oil
Magnate's
Graceful
Residence

The 26-room neoclassic mansion constructed for Frank Phillips—who began life as the son of a dirt-poor farmer and ended up a millionaire oilman—is a reflection of the spectacular fortunes made in Oklahoma in the first decade of the 20th century. After striking oil in 81 consecutive wells, Phillips built this substantial house in 1908-09. The exterior walls are made of mottled pinkish brick, trimmed with blocks of white sandstone and topped with a red-tile roof. Over the years the house has been remodeled twice, but it retains its original grace.

The four-level house contains a grand paneled entrance hall and a music room complete with a portrait by John Singer Sargent. More than 2,000 volumes line the white-oak paneled library beneath an elaborate plasterwork ceiling. Note the library bench, covered with needlepoint worked by Frank's wife, Jane. The couple entertained frequently, and their dining room features a matching suite made of solid Philippine mahogany taken from forests owned by Jane's well-to-do banker father. Their dinner parties hosted a wide array of Oklahoma society—businessmen, ranchers, cowboys, and Native Americans. The first white man adopted into the Osage tribe, Phillips occasionally wore their ceremonial clothing but was usually seen in cowboy boots, jeans, and ten-gallon hat, the stereotypical wildcat oilman. The second-floor bathrooms reflect Frank and Jane's different tastes—hers is outfitted with gold fixtures and ceiling mirrors, while his features a barber's chair, recalling his early days when he worked at that profession. Like many houses of the period, the third floor holds a large formal ballroom and, with an eye toward Oklahoma's tornadoes, the basement contains a storm shelter.

In 1917 Frank and his brother joined forces and created Phillips Petroleum Company, an international giant. At his death in 1950, Frank left 600 million dollars to charity—a true tribute to the state's early wildcatters.

27 *Frank Phillips Home* 1107 S.E. CHEROKEE AVENUE, BARTLESVILLE, OKLA. 74003. (918) 336-2491. OPEN DAILY. WWW.BARTLESVILLE.COM

Overholser Mansion

OKLAHOMA CITY, OKLAHOMA

A Château
Rising from
a Cornfield

In 1903 a three-story, French château-style mansion rose up amid the cornfields on the outskirts of Oklahoma City. Designed by W.S. Matthews, a London-trained architect, the gabled Overholser Mansion brought a touch of elegance and high style to a rough-and-tumble town that had been settled overnight by land-rush settlers 14 years earlier.

Henry Overholser was among the first pioneers, arriving with eight prefabricated buildings that he immediately rented out. Confident in the future of the city, he built a number of important structures, including the Grand Avenue Hotel and the Overholser Opera House. For himself and his wife, Overholser constructed a fashionable European-style residence.

After its official opening reception in 1904, one observer described the interior decoration as a combination of "French antique, flamboyant Oriental and the finest furnishings of the era." Today, most of the original furnishings remain, and they reflect the art deco style popular in Europe at the turn of the century, rather than American taste. For example, English hand-loomed carpets cover polished hardwood floors; French stained-glass windows and Antwerp oak and mahogany woodwork embellish the interior spaces; silk brocade draperies and Brussels lace curtains hang on windows; and doors and hand-painted canvases cover walls and ceilings.

The house includes two formal entrances—one on the east side through enormous double doors; the other to the south, under a porte cochere. The main stairway, which rises without any visible support, features a landing with two stained-glass windows, each decorated with a life-size female musician. In the smoking room you will see hand-carved teakwood chairs, while the drawing room, dubbed the gold room by Mrs. Overholser, offers Louis XIV and Louis XV furniture, with a baroque canvas painting on the high, arched ceiling. In the dramatic red room, a corner fireplace and chimneypiece display a Sevres porcelain clock set. This sumptuous setting, a center of Oklahoma City society for many years, survives as a monument to the energetic entrepreneurial spirit of the Oklahomans, who made mansions rise from cornfields.

28 *Overholser Mansion* 405 N.W. FIFTEENTH STREET, OKLAHOMA CITY, OKLA. 73103. (405) 528-8485. OPEN TUES.-SUN. 🅢 🛗 🏛

The man known as the Father of Oklahoma City built a mansion befitting his position. The residence retains many of its original furnishings and the third-floor ballroom displays period clothing.

Marland Mansion

PONCA CITY, OKLAHOMA

A Florentine Palace on the Oklahoma Prairie

On a trip to Italy in the 1920s, Oklahoma oil magnate Ernest Whitworth Marland gazed on the Palazzo Davanzati in Florence and decided he had to have a house just like it, a "palace on the prairie" for the petroleum royalty of America. Marland hired architect John Duncan Forsyth to bring the dream to fruition. Forsyth sketched plans for a mansion of 55 rooms— including 12 bathrooms and 3 kitchens—clad in rough stone, with square windows and rounded arches, all under a red-tile roof. Though inspired by the Old World, the Florentine architecture looks perfectly at home under the Oklahoma sun. Construction, completed in 1928 at a cost of 5.5 million dollars, took three years, during which time Marland's wife, Virginia, died. He quickly found another, much younger bride in a manner that might seem scandalous in another era, marrying his late wife's niece Lydie, whom he had earlier adopted as a daughter. E.W. and Lydie had the adoption annulled, and the nuptials duly took place.

In keeping with Marland's wish for sumptuousness, Forsyth decorated the interior in royal style, with a gold-leaf ceiling and two Waterford crystal chandeliers for the ballroom, and an elevator lined in leather. The formal dining room has a royal accoutrement—a hand-carved mantel and woodwork of very rare Pollard oak, cut with special permission from the

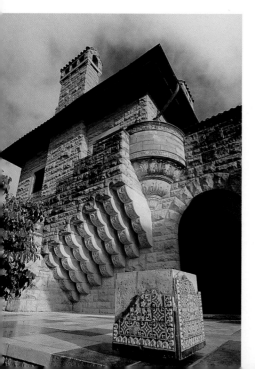

A series of corbels made on-site by a Swedish stonecarver support a private balcony on Marland Mansion's north terrace.

royal forests of England. Tapestries and artwork decorate many of the rooms. The Florentine mural painter, Vincent Margliotti, was brought in to paint several of the ceilings, including a gold-domed ceiling above the landing, and others with themes such as dragons and angels. Another Italian craftsman carved decorative stonework, such as a pair of owls that peek out at visitors from niches in the main stairway.

The spectacular sprawling gardens and surrounding landscape constituted an important aspect of life for the Marlands. The gardens were terraced and filled with perhaps the finest collection of flowers, plants, and bushes west of the Mississippi. Nearby fields carved from the 37 acres of property provided a venue for Marland's favorite sports, foxhunting and polo. (His love of horses and dogs can also be seen in certain decorative motifs in the house, particularly in wall sconces and stained-glass windows.) Marland imported foxes from Pennsylvania and is credited with introducing foxhunting to Oklahoma society.

By the time Marland built his mansion, he had already made and lost one fortune. The son of an Englishman, E.W. grew up in Pittsburgh, took a

The vaulted ceiling in the loggia features canvas painted with a chinoiserie design (sometimes called Chinese Chippendale). Although the canvas was painted on a flat surface and then applied to the curved ceiling, there is no distortion in the figures.

degree in law, and then studied geology to learn to identify rich coal and oil lands. Indeed, he did strike oil, but lost his fortune in a financial panic in 1907. Undeterred, he moved to Oklahoma, leased a tract from a Ponca Indian, and again struck it rich in 1911. His company, Marland Oil, grew so rapidly that it controlled one-tenth of the world's oil supply by 1922.

Marland used his fortune generously, supporting the arts in Ponca City, building 400 homes for his workers, and granting his employees health care, a bonus system, and stock options. Despite his success, Marland was ousted from his own company in a takeover by J.P. Morgan & Co. in 1928. Unable to pay the utility bills, he was forced out of his mansion two years later, though he retained ownership. He and his wife moved into a comfortable, but hardly comparable, artist's studio on the property. Marland had lived in the mansion for a shorter time than it took to build it, but where another man might have shrunk from the public eye in humiliation, Marland successfully ran for Congress, and then for governor. In 1941 his finances compelled him to sell the mansion, for the trifling sum of $66,000, to the Carmelite Fathers. He died six months later. Ponca City, which acquired the property in 1975, is restoring the mansion to its original grandeur.

㉙ *Marland Mansion* 901 MONUMENT ROAD, PONCA CITY, OKLA. 74604. (580) 767-0420 OR (800) 422-8340. OPEN DAILY. WWW.MARLANDMANSION.COM 🛇🚶🅿🏛

Seelye Mansion

ABILENE, KANSAS

The House
Concoctions
Built

One of the finest houses between Kansas City and Denver, and certainly the grandest in turn-of-the-century Abilene, the Seelye Mansion was built in 1905 as home to pharmaceutical entrepreneur Alfred Barnes Seelye. His wealth came from more than 100 different products, including spices and perfumes, and from concocting such medicines as Wasa-tusa, Ner-vana, and Fro-zana—cures for both man and beast. In the 1890s, a corps of itinerant peddlers driving wagons loaded with Seelye's goods fanned out across the Midwest. Their success prompted him to expand into the mail-order business and publish the *Seelye Almanac: Health Guide and Cookbook*. After a visit to the 1904 St. Louis World's Fair, Seelye and his wife decided to build a mansion equipped with the modern conveniences on view at the exposition. Plans for the 25-room Georgian Revival mansion were drawn up by an unknown New York architect and executed by a master carpenter under Seelye's close supervision. Seelye, who wanted plenty of light and fresh air, specified first- and second-story porches across the

Four large, fluted Ionic columns support the Seelye Mansion's massive pedimented portico. Just inside, the center hall features a Tiffany-designed fireplace with ceramic tiles from Venice.

full width of the front, and a captain's walk on the roof. He also specified a steel-reinforced storm cellar in the basement as a refuge from the twisters that periodically sweep Kansas.

Seelye made liberal use of Thomas Edison's new electric lights, which he had seen at the exposition, as well as telephones, placing six in the house and two more in outbuildings. The lines for all of this technology were buried underground in the front yard, allowing the two-story Ionic portico to be viewed unobstructed. The house was also equipped with an elevator and a pump to carry water to the second floor. For entertainment Seelye bought a 1905 Edison cylinder phonograph, installed a bowling alley in the basement, and built a ballroom on the third floor.

The Seelyes' two daughters sold the house in 1982 to two brothers, Terry and Jerry Tietjens, who had long admired the house and its family (they allowed the sisters to continue to live in the house until their deaths). The Tietjens built a new structure on the grounds to house artifacts from Seelye's laboratory and samples of the products that cured the ills of the farm belt and built Abilene's finest house. Both structures are open to the public

30 *Seelye Mansion* 1105 NORTH BUCKEYE, ABILENE, KANS. 67410. (785) 263-1084. OPEN DAILY. Ⓢ ⚐ Ⓟ

NEARBY: **Lebold Vahsholtz Mansion** *(106 North Vine Street, Abilene, Kans. 785-263-4356)* C.H. Lebold, an early Abilene banker and entrepreneur, built this striking 23-room Victorian mansion in 1880.

ℬrown Mansion

COFFEYVILLE, KANSAS

Jeffersonian Architecture Tames the Wild West

When W.P. Brown built his 16-room, neoclassic mansion in 1904, he brought gentility and sophistication to a town barely out of its Wild West days. Just 12 years earlier, Coffeyville had been the scene of a ferocious gunfight that killed four citizens and four members of the bank-robbing Dalton Gang.

With a fortune accumulated from natural gas, lumber, and agricultural interests, Brown commissioned the architectural firm of Wilder & Wight of Kansas City, Missouri, to design his showplace. Built at a wholesale cost of $125,000, the house was one of the largest residences in the region and perhaps the most up-to-date. Interestingly, the modernity of the house's conveniences contrasts with the classicism of its exterior. In designing the west and south facades—with matching, full-length, two-story verandas fronted by sturdy Tuscan columns—the architects looked back to Virginia houses designed by Thomas Jefferson. The second-story overhanging balcony, for example, is decorated with chinoiserie-patterned railings, one of Jefferson's favorite design motifs and prominent at his residence, Monticello (see p. 126).

Inside, you will see original furnishings, polished dark-wood moldings, comfortably worn Oriental rugs, and nine fireplaces of nine different designs. (In a nod to Brown's business interests, the architects designed only one of the fireplaces to burn wood; the rest were plumbed for natural gas.) A Tiffany & Company chandelier graces the dining room, and a Tiffany leaded-glass panel, featuring fleur-de-lis shapes, is inset in the front door. The main

A signed Tiffany chandelier is the centerpiece of the dining room at the Brown Mansion. The house, built near the turn of the 20th century for the substantial sum of $125,000, has survived with few changes.

floor includes a living room, parlor, music room, library, conservatory, dining room, billiard room, kitchen, and maid's quarters. Brown's daughter, Violet, occupied the house until 1973, happily keeping the interior virtually unchanged. She sold the property and its contents to the Coffeyville Historical Society to be maintained as a museum.

31 *Brown Mansion* ELDRIDGE AND WALNUT STREETS, COFFEYVILLE, KANS. 67337. (316) 251-0431. OPEN MAY THROUGH NOV. DAILY; MARCH, APRIL, AND DEC. SAT.-SUN. Ⓢ 🚶 🅿 🏛

Louis E. May Museum
FREMONT, NEBRASKA

Georgian Revival on the Nebraska Plain

Named for the local philanthropist whose trust fund saved it from the wrecking ball, the Louis E. May Museum preserves a house that tells the story of a family's rise to wealth on the frontier. When Theron Nye arrived in Fremont in 1861, he started a business shipping grain to Denver by ox-drawn wagons. He then expanded into the lumber and farm-equipment business, helped start a bank and a hotel, and was elected Fremont's first mayor. In 1874 he built an elegant two-story, brick house, later expanded into a much larger, grander, and more fashionable mansion by his son Ray in 1901. Ray Nye hired the Milwaukee architectural firm of Ferry & Clas, who had gained attention with their design for the Palace of Fine Arts at the 1893 World's Columbian Exposition in Chicago (now the Museum of Science and Industry). They redesigned the house in the Georgian Revival style then popular among Nebraskans proud of the wealth and sophistication they had brought to the plains. While preserving some interior elements of the old house, Ferry & Clas created an imposing new facade with a columned entrance, a balustrade around the roof, and formal gardens.

When the house was in danger of demolition in 1969, officials of the May Trust, a fund established by Fremont businessman Louis E. May, bought the property and donated it to the county as a museum. The mansion's original Nye pieces and other furnishings reflect middle- and upper-class domestic life in the West. For example, since electricity was unavailable after 11 p.m., the house contains both electric and gas lighting fixtures. Also note how the finely woven lace curtains in the sitting room appear exceptionally long—weights at the bottom hold the fabric flush against the windows, in place of window screens. Don't miss the second-floor Fremont Room, which contains a set of unusually fine furniture from the New York home of western explorer and adventurer John C. Frémont, for whom this Nebraska town was named.

32 Louis E. May Museum 1643 North Nye Avenue, Fremont, Nebr. 68025. (402) 721-4515. Open April through Dec. Wed.-Sun.

Sturdy front columns and a unifying balustrade dominate this Georgian Revival residence. In the 1960s, the house was saved from the wrecking ball and donated to Dodge County as a historical museum.

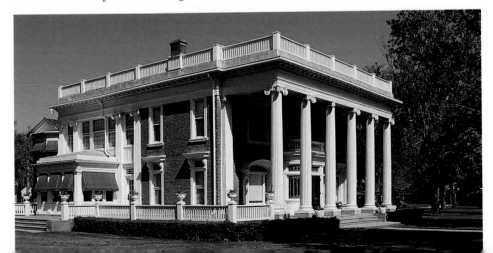

Arbor Lodge is flanked—appropriately—by towering trees. The grounds now feature more than 200 species of trees covering 65 acres of wooded land. Joy Morton added the terraced Italian garden in 1903.

Arbor Lodge
NEBRASKA CITY, NEBRASKA

A Monument to Trees, on the Treeless Plain

Between 1902 and 1905, Joy Morton, founder of the Morton Salt Company, enlarged his parent's modest home in Nebraska City into a stunning, 52-room neocolonial mansion. Distinguished by two-story semicircular porticoes with Corinthian columns that project from the sides of the house, the exterior shelters a reception hall rising 30 feet, with more Corinthian columns supporting the ceiling beams. A sun porch showcases a Tiffany skylight that can be raised or lowered to adjust ventilation, and the basement holds a bowling alley. Incongruously, these splendid surroundings contain some older, simpler, 19th-century furnishings. These Joy Morton kept despite his wealth, as reminders of his parents, who had been pioneers in Nebraska. Indeed, he wished his mansion to become a memorial to his father, who had not known the financial success that came to Joy Morton, but had given his country a lasting gift.

The wooden house that Morton enclosed in his mansion had been built by his parents, Julius Sterling and Caroline Morton, who had moved here from Detroit as newlyweds in 1855. Their original four-room house was reputedly the only frame structure between the Missouri River and the Rocky Mountains. Sterling Morton tirelessly planted trees on the treeless Nebraska plain and campaigned to make tree-planting a general custom. As the editor of Nebraska's first newspaper, he pointed out the benefits of trees as fuel, as a source of building materials, and as windbreaks against fierce prairie storms. His efforts led to the creation of Arbor Day. In 1885, the Nebraska legislature made this a legal holiday in the state and set Sterling's birthday of April 22 as the date. Delighted that his long campaign had borne fruit, Morton declared, "Other holidays repose upon the past. Arbor Day proposes for the future." Before his death in 1902, Sterling expanded the house three times into a two-story structure with a double gallery. Joy further added 18 rooms, stuccoed the walls, and put up the columns seen today.

Joy named his mansion Arbor Lodge to honor his father and in 1923 he donated house and 60 acres to the state of Nebraska as a living monument to his father's ideals. The arboretum includes Osage Orange trees planted as a fencerow by Sterling Morton in the 1850s.

33 *Arbor Lodge State Historical Park and Mansion* SECOND AVENUE AT TWENTY-THIRD STREET, NEBRASKA CITY, NEBR. 68410. (402) 873-7222. OPEN DAILY MARCH THROUGH DEC. 🛆 ♿ 🅿 🏛

Pettigrew Home and Museum
SIOUX FALLS, SOUTH DAKOTA

Petrified Wood and Carrara Marble

Completed in 1889—the same year that South Dakota became a state—the Queen Anne-style Pettigrew Home reflects the buoyant optimism of a newly established society on the American frontier. Wallace Leroy Dow, an eminent regional architect known as "the builder on the Prairie," designed the house for local attorney Thomas McMartin and his bride. The exterior is made of contrasting red brick and native Sioux quartzite, while the interior features an asymmetrical

Characteristic of Victorian architecture, the exterior of the Pettigrew Home blends contrasting materials—in this case, red brick and quartzite. Opposite: Marble busts of R.F. Pettigrew (right) and his brother, Frederick, stand guard over the ceramic tile fireplace in the entrance hall.

arrangement of rooms. Lincrusta, an embossed wall covering that looks like leather, adorns the walls and ceilings of the foyer as well as the second-floor landing of the grand staircase. The house also boasts five polished ceramic tile fireplaces designed by Dow, and stained glass and glass jewels that enliven the windows.

In 1911, 62-year old Richard Pettigrew and his wife, Bessie, purchased the residence for $12,000. As a young man, Pettigrew had helped survey the prairie of eastern Dakota Territory, and had seen the potential of Sioux Falls. He made his fortune in real estate, railroads, and local industry, before turning his attention to government. Actively involved in territorial and state politics for 30 years, he served as South Dakota's first full-term U.S. Senator.

A world traveler and amateur archaeologist, Pettigrew collected so many artifacts that he eventually tore down the back porch of the house and built a two-story museum, which he opened to the public in 1925. Dedicated to the memory of Pettigrew's brother Frederick, who had shared his passion for archaeology, the addition incorporates slabs of petrified wood from Arizona on the brick and quartzite exterior. Among the museum's artifacts you will see Native American objects, walking sticks, and natural curiosities acquired by the Pettigrew brothers. Note, too, the Carrara marble busts of the adventurous twosome which flank the fireplace in the residence's entrance hall. In 1926 Senator Pettigrew suffered a stroke and died, but not before arranging to donate his house and museum to the people of Sioux Falls.

34 *Pettigrew Home and Museum* 131 NORTH DULUTH AVENUE, SIOUX FALLS, S. DAK. 57104. (605) 367-7097. OPEN TUES.-SUN.

Château de Mores

MEDORA, NORTH DAKOTA

A Rough-Hewn Palace in the Badlands

On a bluff overlooking the Little Missouri River, in the midst of the rugged North Dakota badlands, the Marquis de Mores, a French nobleman, constructed a two-story, 26-room hunting lodge in 1883. Though plain by Gilded Age standards, the rambling wooden structure, staffed with servants, was a marvel of elegance to the local ranchers and cowboys. The exterior maintains the original color scheme—French gray walls offset by red shutters and a red-shingle roof. A wide, covered veranda wraps partway around the house. Inside, all of the rooms have plastered walls, an oddity on the Dakota frontier.

The marquis built his home with a distant view of Medora, the town he had founded and named after his wife. Medora von Hoffman, the daughter of a highly successful Wall Street banker, was accustomed to comfort, so in short order railroad cars filled with luxuries began pulling into town—a seashell-shaped tin bathtub, fine French champagne, plover's eggs and truffles, silver pieces from Tiffany, furniture from Lord & Taylor, art supplies from Knoedler's Galleries, and a box grand piano. The marquise spent her days painting, playing Beethoven, and hunting with gusto in a custom-made hunting wagon preserved at the château. The

aristocratic couple added a hunting room to the house, to display their big game trophies. Many original furnishings remain, including the marquis' morris chair, a chaise lounge, and wicker chairs. The dining room displays elegant Minton china in the de Mores' own blue-and-white pattern, used when serving such dinner guests as their neighbor Theodore Roosevelt. Also of interest, the marquise's bedroom features a mahogany bed with an elaborate lace canopy, while the nursery offers an Eastlake crib, child-size chairs, and toys for the two de Mores children, each of whom had their own nanny.

The idyll did not last long. By the end of 1886, the marquis' plans for a meat-processing empire collapsed, and thereafter the château was visited only infrequently by the family. Opened as a museum in 1941, the romantic outpost remains a poignant symbol of the dreams inspired by the vast western wilderness.

35 *De Mores State Historic Site* US 10 OFF I-94, MEDORA, N. DAK. 58645. (701) 623-4355. DAILY MID-MAY TO MID-SEPT., AND BY APPOINTMENT. 🟢 🚶 ♿ 🅿️ 🏛️

The Château de Mores (below) stood as a symbol of capitalism and culture on the frontier, overlooking the dramatic bluffs of North Dakota's badlands. The Marquis de Mores (right) took his western wear with him when he returned to Paris in 1889.

The West

TEXAS • NEW MEXICO

ARIZONA • COLORADO

UTAH • WYOMING

MONTANA • IDAHO

WASHINGTON • OREGON

NEVADA • CALIFORNIA

HAWAII • ALASKA

⤳

For Americans, the very words "The West"
conjure up images of cattle barons and
gold miners amid spectacular scenery.
While not every settler struck it rich,
enough of those who did decided to build
magnificent houses to celebrate their wealth.
Many such grand estates, in a
surprising variety of styles, have been
preserved and opened to the public.
In wood, stone, and brick, these houses
express the driving energy and optimism
of the western spirit.

Neptune Pool, Hearst Castle, California

The West

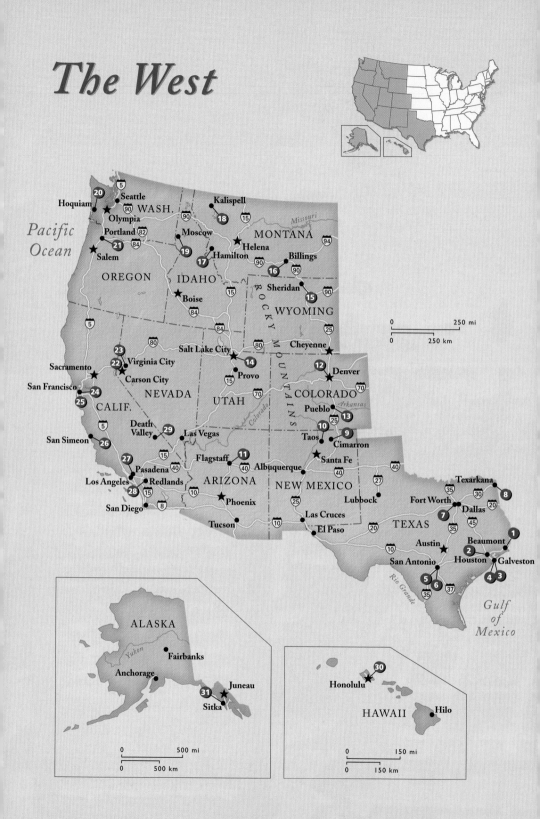

Pacific
Ocean

WASH.

Hoquiam
Seattle
Olympia
Portland
Salem

OREGON

Kalispell

MONTANA

Moscow
Helena
Hamilton
Billings

IDAHO

Boise

Sheridan

WYOMING

Cheyenne

Missouri

Salt Lake City
Virginia City
Carson City
Provo

Sacramento
San Francisco

NEVADA

UTAH

Denver

COLORADO

Pueblo

CALIF.

San Simeon

Death
Valley

Las Vegas

Taos
Cimarron
Santa Fe

Colorado

Arkansas

Pasadena
Redlands
Los Angeles
San Diego

Flagstaff

Albuquerque

Lubbock

Texarkana

ARIZONA

NEW MEXICO

Fort Worth
Dallas

Phoenix

Tucson

Las Cruces
El Paso

TEXAS

Austin
San Antonio

Beaumont
Houston
Galveston

Rio Grande

*Gulf
of
Mexico*

0   250 mi
0   250 km

ALASKA

Yukon

Fairbanks
Anchorage
Juneau
Sitka

0   500 mi
0   500 km

Honolulu

HAWAII

Hilo

0   150 mi
0   150 km

$\mathcal{M}$cFaddin-Ward House

BEAUMONT, TEXAS

*From
Victorian
Silver to
Mousetraps*

In January 1901, when a great geyser of oil erupted from the ground at Spindletop, just outside of Beaumont, William Perry Herring McFaddin was one of the Texans who suddenly became a lot richer. W.P.H., as he was known, had already succeeded in real estate, rice farming, cattle raising, and meatpacking. Accustomed to prosperity, McFaddin did not use his new oil wealth to build himself a palace; rather, he bought from his sister a house she and her husband had just finished building on McFaddin Avenue.

The McFaddin House was designed in 1906 by Henry Conrad Mauer, a Texas-born architect who had graduated from the Pratt Institute in Brooklyn, New York. After the oil strike at Spindletop, Mauer moved to Beaumont and set up an architectural firm. In his design for the McFaddin House, Mauer looked to the past for an architecture of permanence, stability, and tradition. His overall design combines beaux arts principles with the colonial revival, an artistic movement that had gained popularity after the 1876 Centennial Exhibition. As you approach the house, you will see four two-story Ionic columns that are more Greek than colonial, but when you step inside you find a floor plan, with a central hall flanked by four rooms, that harkens back to 18th-century Georgian design.

The interior of the house reflects the McFaddin family's taste. Visitors entering the main hall basked in the glow from the two large lamps atop the newel-posts of the stairway, and from the medieval-style fireplace Mauer ordered from Boston. Note how the McFaddins added an exotic flavor to their decor by displaying such items as a Japanese Satsuma vase adorned with monkeys in bas-relief, and a French statue, almost 3 feet high, of an African bedouin astride a horse made by the Parisian sculptor Émile Guillemin circa 1890. The large crystal chandelier dates from the 1920s; originally the hall was lit by copper fixtures more in keeping with the historical revival decor. The dining room features two large candelabra made in 1842 by Robert Garrard of London, silversmith to Queen Victoria. Garrard delicately mingled a naturalistic leaf and grape motif with scrollwork in this fine example of rococo revival silver. As in many houses of the upper classes, the McFaddins followed Imperial Russian dining etiquette—a butler served food to each person, trays were never passed from one diner to another, and food was never placed on the table.

Perhaps the most impressive room in the house is the parlor, done in French style. For this room Ida McFaddin purchased a three-piece set of Louis XV-style gilt chairs from the Robert Mitchell Company of Cincinnati, and hung pink damask draperies. The walls and ceiling, covered in canvas framed with gold-and-white rococo moldings, are painted with trailing vines of roses. An itinerant artist did the work while the McFaddin children watched in fascination. One of those children, Mamie McFaddin, celebrated her wedding in this room in 1919. A formal room used on very important family occasions, the parlor remained almost completely unchanged for 75 years.

Indeed, the house remains largely as it was early this century because after Mamie married Carroll Ward, the couple moved into the house with her parents and never left. One item on

With its imposing Ionic columns, the McFaddin-Ward House served as a perfect backdrop to Ida's opulent entertaining. Ida's daughter Mamie later followed her mother's lead as a lavish hostess.

The breakfast room and adjoining conservatory, adorned with art-glass windows, were added in 1907. Records indicate that such features as the columns, paneling, and oak flooring were ordered through the mail.

the third floor could not have been discarded even if the Wards had wished to be rid of it— the billiard room holds a table so large that curators are not certain how it got there in the first place. According to family oral history, the house originally included a shaft, later closed off, through which the table was hoisted. One of the pleasures of visiting this house comes from strolling through the rooms and finding so many reminders of daily life in decades gone by. Be on the alert for small, charming surprises. Because the McFaddins and the Wards hardly ever threw anything away, the house's collections include a variety of silver, glassware, and textiles (including the silk underwear worn by W.P.H. McFaddin on his wedding day), and everyday items right down to pots, pans, handkerchiefs, and mousetraps. It was opened as a museum in 1986.

1 *McFaddin-Ward House* 1906 McFaddin Avenue, Beaumont, Tex. 77701. (409) 832-2134. Open Tues.-Sun. Tours leave from Visitor Center, Calder Avenue and Third Street.

NEARBY: **Pompeiian Villa** *(1935 Lakeshore Drive, Port Arthur, Tex. 409-983-5977)* This unusual U-shaped house, outfitted in pink stucco, was built in 1900 for Isaac Ellwood, who helped invent barbed wire.

ayou Bend

HOUSTON, TEXAS

Miss Ima's
Cultural
Bridge to
the Nation's
Heritage

Bayou Bend houses the superlative collections of American furniture, art, and decorative arts amassed by Texas philanthropist Ima Hogg. More than 4,800 items are displayed in 28 room settings, reflecting American tastes from 1620 to 1870, and indirectly telling the personal story of one of the nation's great collectors. In 1920 Miss Ima, as she was called by virtually everyone, was sitting for a portrait at the studio of New York painter Wayman Adams when an antique chair caught her eye. Intrigued to discover that it had been made in colonial times, Hogg decided to look for something similar, and soon acquired an 18th-century Queen Anne-style chair from New England. The purchase launched her on a lifetime vocation of collecting Americana.

Her brother Will, himself a noted collector, had acquired one of the earliest collections of the Western paintings of Frederick Remington. He encouraged her interest in American antiques and loaned his sister a copy of Luke Vincent Lockwood's book, *Colonial Furniture in America*. It became one of Miss Ima's early guides to the field. In 1927 Ima and her brothers Will and Mike hired architect John F. Staub to build a residence in Houston to house Miss Ima's growing collection of 17th-, 18th-, and 19th-century American furnishings.

Staub's pink stucco house combines classic revival elements with a strong southern flavor. In its layout—a five-part plan with a central block joined by two one-story hyphens to a pair of two-story units—the house recalls the Palladian villas of Italy and England. Its rear facade, however, is pure southern plantation, with a row of four, two-story, Ionic columns supporting a large entablature. To adorn this plantation facade Staub obtained wrought-iron grillwork from a New Orleans house that was being demolished.

Ima Hogg and her siblings had spent part of their childhood in a Greek Revival house in Austin—the Governor's Mansion. Their father, James Hogg, was the first governor of Texas born in the state, serving from 1891 to 1895. A fiery speaker, regarded warily by some as a demagogue, Hogg championed the interests of the state's small farmers against outside business interests, particularly the railroads, whose rates for hauling agricultural goods often determined whether farmers made a profit or went bust. In 1901, the governor purchased a ranch that he felt certain contained oil. Though repeated drilling yielded no results, Hogg made his heirs promise not to sell the land for at least 15 years after his death. Sure enough, in 1917, 11 years after the governor died, the Hogg children struck oil. Despite her new wealth, Ima was deeply depressed by the loss of her father; collecting antiques became one of her major solaces, along with music.

The cornerstones of her impressive collection are furniture, portraits, silver, and ceramics. She acquired important works by such great American painters as Gilbert Stuart, John Singleton Copley, Charles Willson Peale, and Samuel F.B. Morse. The extent that Miss Ima treasured the atmosphere of the past can be seen in her bedroom and sitting room suite, where she had Staub install floorboards and paneling from two colonial-era Massachusetts houses. In 1954 Hogg brought several renowned collectors to Bayou Bend, including Henry Francis du Pont, who shared her passion for collecting and had transformed his family home, Winterthur, into a museum (see p. 81). For decades Hogg and du Pont had been friendly rivals in their collecting; on his visit du Pont noticed a piece that Hogg had beat him to in an auction in the 1920s, and jokingly proclaimed it "my settee." In 1957, Hogg decided to follow du Pont's lead—while remaining in residence at Bayou Bend, she donated it to the Museum of Fine Arts, Houston, and began to arrange her collection in a series of period rooms. For her first project she re-created a colonial common room of the 17th and early 18th centuries, with an oak floor painted in a checkerboard pattern, a Connecticut "great chair," a cupboard from Massachusetts, and a table set with English and American pewter

Although Bayou Bend's architecture is eclectic, its southern plantation influences are clear on the north facade. The home's interiors borrow more heavily from the traditions of the North; the music room (opposite) reflects the prosperity of federal New England.

and earthenware. In her Newport Room, Hogg displayed a beautiful collection of silver, including a sugar dish made by Boston silversmith and patriot Paul Revere, a large soup tureen presented by the citizens of Baltimore to naval hero Stephen Decatur after the War of 1812, and an unusual silver toy for a wellborn toddler, consisting of a whistle, bells, and a bit of coral believed to be good for teething and for warding off evil.

The furnishings of Miss Ima's sitting room are indicative of 18th-century leisure pursuits. A card table made in Boston between 1730 and 1760, with circular recesses at each corner to accommodate round-bottomed candlesticks, evokes an evening of card playing by candlelight, a pastime enjoyed by both men and women. Nearby, a Rhode Island tea table, dating from between 1740 and 1775, holds a tea set—pot, sugar bowl, cream pitcher, waste bowl, tea caddy, and spoon tray—suggesting the complexity of this social ritual.

American interior decoration experienced a change in focus between the end of the Revolutionary War and the beginning of the Civil War, a shift apparent in three rooms at Bayou Bend. The Federal Parlor captures the restraint and delicacy of the classical taste, with wallpaper reproduced from an original at a 1790s Connecticut house, inspired by ancient Roman wall paintings unearthed at Pompeii. Note the lovely gilt bronze clock on the mantel which pays tribute to George Washington, depicted holding a scroll and resting his arm next to an American eagle. Next move to the Chillman Parlor, showcasing the Greek-inspired Empire style, which gained popularity in the early decades of the 19th century. The furniture here includes a superb pair of chairs designed by architect Benjamin Henry Latrobe for a house in Philadelphia around 1808, with beautiful inlays depicting mythological creatures.

Finally, the Belter Parlor luxuriates in the elaborate curves, vivid colors, and the glitter of gilt that the rococo revival brought to the Victorian age. Hogg acquired a sumptuous ten-piece parlor set made in 1855 by John Henry Belter and initially purchased for $1,300 by a wealthy Georgian. This is the only known complete set of Belter's furniture with its original receipt. Belter's rococo revival creations appeared in many southern plantation homes in the mid-19th century, but by the 20th century many collectors considered the style excessively florid and not worthy of the attention of furniture connoisseurs, preferring instead the more restrained, classic lines of 18th- and early 19th-century furniture. Ima Hogg, however, had a fondness for Belter's work, perhaps because of its associations with the South—one of her early purchases was a laminated rosewood Belter chair. Hogg once defended her taste before a skeptical critic, maintaining that the profuse accumulation of curved ornament on a Belter work was "every bit as good as Chippendale."

Ima Hogg quite deliberately chose to concentrate on collecting items that reflected the upper-class customs and tastes of the East and the older parts of the South. She was well aware that Texas seemed to many Americans, including many Texans, a cultural backwater and place apart. As Hogg herself said, "Texas, an empire in itself, geographically and historically seems to be regarded as remote or alien to the rest of our nation." She viewed her collecting—and her philanthropy toward many of the state's cultural and historical institutions—as a means to bring cultivation to her part of the West, and as a way of forging a cultural link to the rest of the nation. In 1966, nine years before her death, she moved out of Bayou Bend, having completed the transformation of her home into a museum. At that time Miss Ima declared, "I hope in a modest way Bayou Bend may serve as a bridge to bring us closer to the heart of an American heritage which unites us."

2 *Bayou Bend Collection and Gardens* 1 Westcott Street, Houston, Tex. 77007. (713) 639-7750. Open Tues.-Sun. 🆂 🚶 ♿ 🅿

Galveston Residences
Ashton Villa, Moody Mansion

After its early days as a pirate lair—the den of the notorious Jean Lafitte in the 1810s—
Galveston transformed itself into a sophisticated city, the Queen of the Gulf. Situated on a
low-lying, sand barrier island 27 miles long, Galveston possessed a protected anchorage on
its leeward side. Briefly the capital of the Republic of Texas in 1836, Galveston was organized as a city in 1838 and grew to become one of the most important seaports in the entire
West. The Queen of the Gulf shipped cotton from the interior and received manufactured
goods, and immigrants, from around the world. Galveston saw the first telegraph in Texas,
the first electric lights, the first banks, and the first golf course. The city's commercial street,
The Strand, earned the nickname Wall Street of the Southwest for its numerous financial
firms and trading companies, which erected the handsome brick-and-stone offices still
standing today. In the second half of the 19th century, the island's upper-class families began
to build their residences along Broadway, which retains Galveston's largest concentration of
mansions, though many Greek Revival and Victorian houses can be found on quiet streets on
the eastern half of the island.

At the turn of the century, Galveston endured the worst natural disaster in U.S. history
when the great hurricane of September 8, 1900, struck the island with devastating force,
destroying about a third of the city. The precise total is unknown, but estimates place the
death toll in Galveston at 6,000. To prevent a recurrence of the flooding, Galveston raised its
grade level several feet and constructed a seawall along the Gulf shore. Galveston recovered
from the hurricane, but the city of Houston garnered the lion's share of the region's ship traffic
after dredging a deepwater channel. As in many other old American cities whose fortunes had
ebbed, Galveston became too poor to build new commercial districts and mansions, so it kept
what it had. Today The Strand has new vitality as a tourist destination, and the mansions
along Broadway testify to the sophistication that once again graces the Queen of the Gulf.

Ashton Villa

GALVESTON, TEXAS

*Refuge from
the Storm
of the Century*

In 1859 James Moreau Brown built himself the largest and finest residence
Galveston had yet seen—a three-story Italianate brick house with a handsome veranda of wrought iron—and started a trend. Ashton Villa was the
first expensive house to rise on Broadway, in an unfashionable part of
town; but soon other wealthy Galveston families were following Brown's
lead, and Broadway became the finest address in the city. It also turned out to be one of the
safest, occupying some of the highest ground on Galveston Island. Broadway and its great
houses survived the terrible devastation wrought by the hurricane of 1900.

Brown had come to Galveston in the 1840s as a bricklayer, prospered as a hardware
merchant, and became president of a regional railroad. The family's wealth allowed Brown's
daughter Rebecca, known as Bettie, to develop her talent in painting, which women of the
19th and early 20th centuries were allowed to take up as a hobby but not as a serious pursuit.

The large painting keeping watch over Ashton Villa's entry hall was painted by James Moreau Brown's daughter, Bettie. The family's great wealth afforded her the opportunity to study art in Vienna.

Ashton Villa displays many of Bettie Brown's works, including a demure painting of cupids kissing considered so scandalous her father covered it with drapery, which could be closed when guests arrived.

Many original furnishings remain on display at the house, including gilded pier mirrors and cornices that Bettie ordered for the double parlor in the 1890s. Inspired by the decoration of a Stanford White mansion across the street, she transformed the parlor from a dark, Renaissance Revival preserve into the festive Gold Room. On the landing in the stair hall you can see a large secretary bookcase containing some of the mementos Bettie collected on travels, including an enamel box with sand from the Sahara Desert, a Bedouin wedding cap, and shoes from Constantinople.

On the awful night of September 8, 1900, as the hurricane shrieked overhead, tearing at Ashton Villa's roof and uprooting trees in the yard, Bettie, her mother, her sisters, and a newborn niece huddled terrified inside. The house survived the storm—its bricks had been sturdily laid four decades earlier by the Brown family's slave named Alek. Ashton Villa also weathered later use as a Shriners' hall, and has been restored to the period when polite society could still be scandalized by a painting of a kiss.

③ *1859 Ashton Villa* 2328 Broadway, Galveston, Tex. 77550. (409) 762-3933. Open daily. www.galvestonhistory.org 🅢 🚶 ♿ 🅿

Moody Mansion

GALVESTON, TEXAS

Childhood Home of the First Lady of Texas Finance In the aftermath of the catastrophic Galveston hurricane of September 1900, when many survivors left the city for good, prominent businessman W.L. Moody, Jr., declared his faith in Galveston's future by acquiring this handsome mansion on fashionable Broadway. Built between 1893 and 1895 for Narcissa Willis, whose daughter had placed the house on the market before the disaster struck, the stone-and-brick mansion survived the hurricane in good condition. Moreover, it suited Moody's position in Galveston society. Its architecture—an eclectic combination derived largely from Henry Hobson Richardson's Romanesque Revival style—bespoke solidity and wealth. (When Moody was negotiating the purchase, he wrote to his wife, "well . . . we may live and die in a palace yet.") A bold arcade of stone arches spreads across the front facade, which boasts three towers, one conical, one

Libbie Moody took this photograph of her four children on their porch circa 1904. Shown from left to right are Shearn, Mary, Libbie, and William Lewis Moody III. Mary would take the reins of her father's fortune.

hexagonal, and the other in the shape of a pyramid. An English-born architect named William Tyndall had designed the house for Willis.

The mansion included many mechanical features that offered such modern comforts and conveniences as a one-passenger elevator, a dumbwaiter, speaking tubes for calling servants, a laundry with drying racks, combination gas-and-electric lighting fixtures, and electrical and heating systems. When Tyndall designed the house, fresh drinking water was perennially scarce in Galveston. His clever system of drains and pipes collected rainwater and directed it into cisterns; gravity and pumps circulated the water to bathrooms and the kitchen. By the time Moody acquired the house, the city had completed a waterline from the mainland.

The interior was decorated by the well-known New York firm Pottier & Stymus, which had handled commissions for many wealthy clients, including William Rockefeller, George Westinghouse, Jr., Henry M. Flagler, and Leland Stanford. Here, Pottier & Stymus created an oak-paneled entrance hall with a beamed ceiling, pilasters flanking the doorways, and an oak parquet floor. Be sure to climb the stairs and answer the greeting of the classically garbed family depicted in the large stained-glass window on the landing. The motto, "Welcome Ever Smiles," is still appropriate.

To the left of the hall lies the formal parlor, decorated in 18th-century French style with blue, gray-green, and gold silk wall coverings enhanced by delicate rococo revival decorations and furnishings. A ceiling painting depicts a frolicking group of putti, one on a leaf-form chariot in a cloud-filled sky. The painting was probably executed by Virgilio Tojetti, an Italian-born painter who had studied in Paris and emigrated to New York in 1870.

The adjacent library harkens back to the Empire Revival, a style popular in the early 19th century. Note how the plaster cornice surrounding the ceiling features a gilded flower motif and the moldings are painted to simulate the mahogany wood trim of the casework. In addition, Ionic columns, palmettes, laurel wreaths, and classically garbed figures adorn the room.

In 1911, the house was the scene of what a Galveston newspaper described as "a very smart gathering of fashionable people," when 200 guests gathered for the social debut of Mary Moody, oldest daughter of W. L. Moody, Jr. An orchestra, seated in the conservatory, played for guests dancing in the three rooms cleared for the party. The Moody family had prospered in the cotton trade after the Civil War, but W.L. Moody, Jr., brought the family fortunes to great heights through private banking and investments in insurance, real estate, ranches, and hotels. In 1905 he founded the American National Insurance Company, which became one of the largest insurance companies in the country. After Moody's son Shearn, his heir apparent, died suddenly in 1936 at age 40, the financier turned to his daughter, Mary Moody Northen, to take the reins. The former debutante eventually became president or chairwoman of some 50 companies, and she devoted much of her time later in life to philanthropy. Before her death in 1986, Northen envisioned turning her family home into a museum, a project that was completed in 1991.

4 *Moody Mansion* 2618 BROADWAY, GALVESTON, TEX. 77550. (409) 762-7668. OPEN DAILY. 🄱 🚶 ♿ 🅿 🏛

NEARBY: **The Bishop's Palace** *(1402 Broadway, Galveston, Tex. 409-762-2475)* This high-Victorian house was built in the late 1800s for a Civil War colonel using native Texas limestone, pink and gray granite, and red sandstone, all cut in a workshop built on the construction site.

A recent restoration of the exterior of Moody Mansion (opposite) included replacing many of the limestone windowsills and lintels. The arcaded porch was the architect's answer to Galveston's sultry summers.

S teves Homestead

SAN ANTONIO, TEXAS

An Immigrant's Mansion in "Sauerkraut Bend"   This handsome three-story Victorian house presents an eclectic architectural mix—arched windows and porches in the Italianate style, a French Second Empire mansard roof with cast-iron cresting, and Gothic touches in the decorative trim and room arrangement. Though built in 1876 for a lumber merchant, the house was constructed of locally quarried ashlar limestone. The front of the house faces towering pecan trees, a formal garden, and a working circular fountain of cast iron and zinc alloy that was originally painted to simulate marble. The owner, Edward Steves, purchased the fountain after seeing it at the Philadelphia Centennial Exhibition in 1876.

Edward Steves was among the German immigrants who flocked to the San Antonio area in the mid-19th century. Starting out as a farmer, Steves owned the first threshing machine in the area and made a fortune selling grain in Mexico. By the late 1860s he had started a successful lumber company, invested in real estate, and become active in local politics. Eventually he wanted a residence that would reflect his economic and social success. He decided to build his home, at a cost of $12,000, on the east bank of the San Antonio River, an exclusive German enclave nicknamed the "Sauerkraut Bend." Steves added ingenious touches of his own to the house. Running water was brought into the bedrooms and upstairs bathroom via a system that he devised. A windmill pumped artesian well water into a rooftop reservoir; making use of gravity, pipes then delivered water to various rooms.

The 14-foot ceilings in the first-floor rooms feature hand-painted stenciling. Note the original family furnishings, including a walnut marble-topped table with an inscription

San Antonio's Steves Homestead is fronted by formal gardens, towering pecan trees, and an original stake fence. The elegant Victorian features a concave mansard roof with iron cresting.

written in pencil on the underside of the marble, "purchased for our new home, Edward Steves, 1877." The formal parlor has a seven-piece set of rococo revival furniture and a Bavarian tea set that belonged to Mrs. Steves. In the family room you can admire a rosewood melodian, a pier mirror in the French Empire style, and bas-relief plaques of Mr. and Mrs. Steves, made in Florence, Italy, where the couple celebrated their 25th wedding anniversary.

The house displays Texas craftsmanship as well—a cottonwood pie safe made by local German immigrants, and a pedestal table inlaid with 26 different woods that was made in nearby Fredericksburg and given to Steves by his children. Located in what is now known as the King William Historic District, the Steves Homestead is one of a number of grand houses built in a 30-year period that reflects the ascendancy of the local German population.

5 *Steves Homestead* 509 KING WILLIAM STREET, SAN ANTONIO, TEX. 78204. (210) 227-9160. OPEN DAILY. WWW.SACONSERVATION.ORG ⑤ 🚶 ♿ 🅿 🏛

Spanish Governor's Palace
SAN ANTONIO, TEXAS

An Architectural Relic of Spanish Rule

The Spanish Governor's Palace, an adobe-and-white-stucco home, is one of the few surviving 18th-century Spanish houses in the United States. The Commandancia, or "commander's quarters," was erected in the 1740s as part of the Presidio de San Antonio de Bejar, intended to protect the nearby mission. Begun about 1722, the palace was completed in 1749, a date the visitor will see inscribed in the keystone over the front door. By the 1780s, the house had been transferred to private ownership. In 1804, José Ignacio Pérez, a wealthy businessman and one-time acting interim governor, purchased the property for 800 pesos. The Perez family owned the building for the next 125 years, eventually converting the residence to shops, a restaurant, and a schoolhouse. When the state of Texas acquired the structure in 1929, it began the lengthy process of restoring this important example of Spanish Colonial architecture.

The reserved white stucco facade of the one-story, flat-roofed house is embellished with projecting roof timbers, large windows, and two massive hand-carved walnut doors. Above the central doorway is a sculptural keystone, decorated with carved filigree and a double-headed eagle, the coat of arms for King Ferdinand VI, ruler of Spain in the 1700s. Inside, the nine main rooms are stacked three deep, interconnected by aligned doorways and differentiated by floor types, laid in dark-hued tile or stone. Rough, hand-hewn timbers support the heavy earth-covered roof. The dining room is one of the most impressive spaces in the house, marked by a narrow refectory table at the center and a series of 18th-century Spanish chairs against the walls. A wide hood over the fireplace, an early form of the chimney flue, funneled smoke from the room. Near the front of the residence, a small chapel features a 17th-century sculpture of the Virgin and Child placed protectively within a wall niche.

An outdoor walled terrace behind the home leads to a large plaza paved with a unique pebble mosaic, created in the 1930s restoration. It also features an original octagonal garden fountain and well used for centuries by the house's many residents.

6 *Spanish Governor's Palace* 105 PLAZA DE ARMAS, SAN ANTONIO, TEX. 78205. (210) 224-0601. OPEN DAILY. ⑤ 🏛

*T*histle Hill

FORT WORTH, TEXAS

A Cattle Heiress' Mansion, Texas Style

This stately mansion was done Texas style—everything executed on a slightly larger scale than usual. Set on a bluff overlooking the Trinity River, it was originally built in 1903-1904 as a colonial revival house, then extensively remodeled in 1911-1912 into a more formal Georgian Revival design. Six enormous limestone columns grace the entryway and emphasize the grand height of this two-and-a-half story structure. The Palladian doorway's fanlight and sidelights of zinced-and-leaded glass portray a wedding-ring pattern, repeated on the upper window panels in the front of the house.

In the reception hall you will find an impressive horseshoe staircase and landing, as well as columns, wainscoting, and decorative exposed beams crafted out of white oak. The billiard room is also a study in oak, although in this room the coffered ceiling and wainscoting are made of bog oak probably imported from Great Britain. Dominating the game room is a massive, 3,000-pound billiard table once used in a Fort Worth men's club. Heraldic shields and mottoes written in Old English calligraphy grace the walls and set a convivial tone proclaiming "Drink Down All Unkindness" and "Hang Sorrow, Let's Be Merry."

The newlyweds who built the house embraced those sentiments completely. Electra Waggoner, a spirited cattle heiress known as the Princess of the Panhandle by her father's cowboys, returned from a trip to Asia at the turn of the century with a tattoo and a fiancé, Albert Buckman Wharton, from an old Pennsylvania family. They promptly set about constructing Thistle Hill (named for its prairie site, where cattle and wild thistle once thrived), and establishing themselves as lavish hosts. Festivities included a Fourth of July party complete with an extravagant display of fireworks, and a Halloween costume party featuring a "phantom dance" amid candlelit pumpkins.

Thistle Hill's parlor inkstand holds Electra Waggoner Wharton's 1902 bridal portrait (above). An original stained-glass lamp highlights the Arts and Crafts library (opposite), which was used as a daytime study room for the children and an evening gentleman's room.

On Christmas 1909 Electra's father surprised the couple with a completely stocked ranch carved out of his own empire—a gift worth over two million dollars at the time (and some 20 million dollars today). Although the Whartons sold Thistle Hill two years later, stories about the flamboyant Electra lived on. She would meet a tragic end, dying in her New York apartment at age 43 of cirrhosis of the liver.

The new mistress of Thistle Hill, Elizabeth Scott, also had a fortune based on ranching, but was of a different temperament than Electra. A woman of quiet dignity, she added a tea-house, a pergola, and a formal English garden to the grounds. Sadly, her husband, Winfield, died before renovations were completed, but Elizabeth remained at Thistle Hill until her own death in 1938, enjoying her garden and playing bridge in the Stay All Day card club.

7 *Thistle Hill* 1509 PENNSYLVANIA AVENUE, FORT WORTH, TEX. 76104. (817) 336-1212. CLOSED SAT.

🔲 🔲 🔲 🔲

NEARBY: **De Golyer Estate** *(8525 Garland Road, Dallas, Tex. 214-327-8263)* Now part of the Dallas Arboretum and Botanical Center, this Spanish Colonial Revival house was built for oilman Everette Lee De Golyer to remind him of Mexico, where he made his first oil discoveries.

---

*A*ce of *Clubs House*
TEXARKANA, TEXAS

The Luck of — According to legend, the money to build this Italianate-Victorian mansion
the Draw — in 1885 came from a winning poker hand. James Draughon, a local
Builds a — lumberman and dry-goods merchant, drew an ace of clubs and won a rich
House — pot. Flush with his winnings, he supposedly decided to build a house that would resemble the ace of clubs when seen from above. Indeed, from a bird's-eye view the house's three octagonal bays and one long rectangular room, arranged around a central octagonal stair hall, do look like Draughon's lucky card. The exterior walls are three bricks thick, covered in stucco, and scored to look like stone. A dry moat surrounding the house aided with drainage in an area where the water table was very close to the surface and helped cool the house during the summer months. Cool air collected in the moat and then was drawn through the house via an updraft created by opening the windows in the cupola 46 feet above the central hallway.

In 1894 a prominent local attorney, Henry Moore, purchased the Ace of Clubs and soon added kitchen and bath wings (until that time an outhouse was used). In the 1920s the family replaced the original iron galleries in front of the house with a Moorish-Spanish Revival porch. Moore family members lived in the house until the death of Olivia Smith Moore in 1985, at which time the house was transferred to the Texas Museums System.

Olivia Moore was a devoted patron of the Neiman Marcus department store, as the visitor will observe by the more than 500 pairs of shoes on display in her 1930s dressing room—a fitting note of excess for a gambler's house. In her last years, salesmen and models would come to the Ace of Clubs to present the latest footwear fashions. Today the house is furnished in varying styles—each room representing a different time period—to convey its century of use. Note, for example, in the 1880s Draughon library a richly carved Wooten desk that retains all of its original drawers and cubbyholes. The room also includes a card table, as Draughon was a renowned—and obviously successful—gambler.

8 *Draughon–Moore Ace of Clubs House* 420 PINE STREET, TEXARKANA, TEX. 75501. (903) 793-4831. OPEN TUES.–SAT. 🔲 🔲 🔲 🔲 🔲

The Ace of Clubs House was said to be inspired by the card that won James Draughon a poker fortune. The octagonal chimneys cap this unique design.

Villa Philmonte

CIMARRON, NEW MEXICO

An Oilman's Dream of Mountainside Leisure

In a spectacular location looking west toward the Sangre de Cristo Mountains, oil multimillionaire Waite Phillips built a ranch house he named Villa Philmonte. Born in 1883 on an Iowa farm, Phillips spent three of his teenage years wandering the Rockies, working as a laborer in mining and timber camps, before going to college and taking a job as a bookkeeper. Two older brothers, who would later found Phillips Petroleum Company, got him into the oil business. In 1925 he sold his oil interests for 25 million dollars. Eager to realize his youthful dream of owning a ranch in the mountains, he acquired 300,000 acres in northeastern New Mexico and hired a Kansas City architect, Edward Delk, to design a rustic residence. Phillips, his wife, Genevieve, and Delk sailed the Mediterranean together, seeking inspiration from the villas of Spain and Italy.

The resulting design combines the spirit of Spain with elements of Spanish-American and Native American architecture. A series of ells and wings enclose three courtyards, which

The Mediterranean influence is clear in the three courtyards at Villa Philmonte, which serve as grand outdoor rooms. The arches are repeated in doorways and walls throughout the house.

Villa Philmonte's rustic Trophy Room is dominated by its rough-hewn beam ceiling and a large stone fireplace. The bison at left came from the ranch herd that Phillips donated to the Boy Scouts.

function as large outdoor rooms. Balconies and portals open the house to mountain views and air. Inside, Phillips entertained guests in rooms with a southwestern theme, evocative of up-country hunting lodges. The Trophy Room features a mosaic of a cowboy on a bucking bronco, animal paintings, and mounted animal heads and skins. The adjacent trapper's closet contained hunting and fishing gear for guests. The Territorial Room celebrates the colonial New Mexican period with a Spanish architectural motif, old-fashioned tin lighting fixtures, and a wall niche traditionally set aside for a santo, a religious statue. The ranch's blacksmith, Ted Paddock, created decorative wrought iron for a number of rooms in the villa. For the solarium, for example, you can view how he fashioned a pair of iron gates fitted with cut-metal images of stallions, bison, and flowers. For a fireplace screen, he used cut-metal forms to create a vignette of the sun setting amid tall pines.

In 1941 Phillips donated the mansion and 127,000 acres to the Boy Scouts of America for use as a wilderness camping area, declaring that the ranch had "represented an ideal of my youth . . . now I want to make it available to other boys." The mansion has been preserved with many original furnishings and its atmosphere of mountainside serenity still intact.

⑨ *Villa Philmonte* PHILMONT SCOUT RANCH, N. MEX. 21, CIMARRON, N. MEX. 87714. (505) 376-2281. OPEN DAILY JUNE THROUGH AUG. 🟢 🚶 🅿️ 🏛️

$\mathcal{B}$*lumenschein Home*

TAOS, NEW MEXICO

Adobe House for a Family of Artists

This rambling adobe house, part of which dates back to 1797, served as the home and studio for a family of artists from 1919 until the 1960s. Ernest Blumenschein had spent summers in New Mexico since 1910 and had helped found the Taos Society of Artists. In 1919 his wife, Mary Shepherd Greene Blumenschein, decided to leave New York City and join Ernest in Taos, bringing their daughter, Helen, with her. Mary and Ernest purchased five rooms of the house at that time, and later bought five adjacent rooms. Over the years, they furnished their residence with their own work as well as their collection of Hispanic and Native American art, expressing the fascination Anglo artists felt in encountering the older cultures of the Southwest.

The dining room, part of the oldest section of the house, reflects this melding of cultures in its architecture and decoration. Be sure to note the ceiling, fashioned of heavy ponderosa pine beams and called vigas, covered by a layer of split cedar and juniper shakes and topped by a coating of earth, which serves as insulation. The Blumenscheins hung a selection of remarkable paintings created when Native Americans made use of European paints for the first time, in the 1920s and 1930s. The dining room also displays a Taos bed crafted by a Spanish artisan in the 1930s. The Blumenscheins remodeled other rooms in an Anglo mode. In the library, for example, Mary had the windows enlarged, raised the roof, and installed built-in bookcases. While the kitchen boasts amenities considered up-to-date in the 1930s, such as electricity and running water, it also contains a curious "California cooler" that chills food naturally via a chimney that drew air over a container of water.

After Ernest's death in 1960, Helen established the house as a museum to display the family's art in the surroundings that nurtured it. Don't miss visiting the large, sunlit studio where her father painted amid the austere beauty of adobe. Here, basked in the famed New Mexican light, you will experience how the luminance softens any straight line and makes architecture seem to spring directly from the earth.

❿ *E.L. Blumenschein Home and Museum* 222 LEDOUX STREET, TAOS, N. MEX. 87571. (505) 758-0505. OPEN DAILY. 🟢 🚶 🏛️

NEARBY: **Martinez Hacienda** *(708 Hacienda Road, Taos, N. Mex. 505-758-1000)* Also part of the Kit Carson Historic Museums (along with the Blumenschein and Kit Carson houses), this large adobe structure was built with thick, windowless exterior walls to protect against Indian raids.

iordan Mansion
FLAGSTAFF, ARIZONA

*One House
for Two
Families, in
Rustic Style*

Surrounded by a stand of ponderosa pine, the rustic mansion of the
Riordan families, built in 1904, seems to blend into its northern Arizona
landscape. Large but utterly unpretentious, the house's charm emanates
partly from its architecture and partly from the story of those who built it.
In the 1880s, Irish-Catholic brothers Timothy and Michael Riordan
migrated from Chicago to Flagstaff, where they joined an older brother in
operating a successful lumber mill. When the brothers married two sisters, Caroline and
Elizabeth Metz, the families built a single mansion with separate wings joined by a common
room in the center.

Though the Riordans engaged the services of Charles Whittlesey, company architect for
the Santa Fe Railroad, family records indicate that one of the Riordan brothers provided
many of the basic ideas for the design—its
overall rustic character, achieved through the
use of log facing, planks, stone, and shingles;
the positioning of nearly identical wings at an
angle to a central core; and the use of massive
stone arches. Whittlesey adapted some of these
features in his acclaimed design for the El
Tovar Hotel at the Grand Canyon. The
Riordans furnished the house with Arts and
Crafts chairs made by Gustave Stickley and
Harvey Ellis, Tiffany-style stained-glass panels
and lighting fixtures, Native American artworks, and natural artifacts such as petrified
wood, which both families collected.

In 1927, tragedy struck both Riordan families on the same day. Tim's beloved daughter
Anna, just 26 years old, died of polio in an
upstairs bedroom despite her father's desperate
attempts to keep her alive with artificial
respiration. Elsewhere in Flagstaff, Michael's
30-year-old son Arthur died of the same disease on the same date.

The family deeded the house to the state in
1979, with the proviso that Michael's daughter
Blanche could remain in the house for her life-

*The Riordan Mansion's two wings are joined
by a large rustic room shared by both families.*

time. Thus tourists were visiting Tim's wing of
the house while she was still in residence in the other. The wing Blanche occupied until 1985
is undergoing restoration.

11 *Riordan Mansion State Park* 1300 Riordan Ranch Street, Flagstaff, Ariz. 86001. (520) 779-4395.
Open daily. www.pr.state.az.us

Molly Brown House

DENVER, COLORADO

The Mansion of the Unsinkable Grande Dame

The stylish high-Victorian residence of Margaret Tobin Brown, who became known as the "unsinkable Molly Brown" after she survived the *Titanic* disaster in 1912, remains as testament to her many years as a prominent Denver hostess, lavish entertainer, and active philanthropist. Molly moved from Hannibal, Missouri, at the age of 19 and married a successful mine manager, J. J. Brown, within a year of her arrival. The house had been built in 1889 for the Large family, who commissioned William Lang as architect. The Browns purchased the fashionable Capitol Hill house in 1894.

The Queen Anne-style house is also known as the House of Lions for the pair of carved-stone animals guarding the entry stairs. The residence itself is built of rough-faced pink and gray rhyolite, a volcanic stone similar to granite. Carved woodwork and decorative shingles cover the wide front porch and steeply pitched gables. Inside, the house is exquisitely appointed, preserved as if at the ready for one of Molly's extravagant fund-raising parties (one notable event counted 800 people in attendance). Brown traveled extensively, toting items for her collection from the corners of the earth. She referred to the entry hall as the Turkish corner and decorated it with a full-size exotic robed statue of a figure holding an electric lamp, standing on woven rugs reminiscent of the Middle East. Note how the carved golden oak mantel in the hall complements the original gold-painted wall coverings made of intricately patterned papier-mâché. In addition a pair of vividly colored stained-glass windows in a stylized floral motif bring diffused light into the adjacent stairway, reflecting on the open squares and turned-wood knobs of the unusually carved balustrade. The dining room also features a whimsical touch, a trompe l'oeil ceiling painted in the likeness of a glass greenhouse. Upstairs, the bed-

rooms have colorful walls upholstered in green and blue silk damask. One bedroom, called the Tobin Room, reflects Molly's more humble beginnings, the simple furnishings recalling her childhood in Missouri.

After Molly's death in 1932, the house passed through various owners and saw use as apartments and as a halfway house until Historic Denver purchased the building in 1971. The group has restored the house to its appearance in 1910, the busiest period of Molly's active social life, and the decade when she survived the great disaster at sea.

12 *Molly Brown House Museum* 1340 PENNSYLVANIA STREET, DENVER, COLO. 80203. (303) 832-4092. OPEN JUNE THROUGH AUG. DAILY; SEPT. THROUGH MAY TUES.-SUN. WWW.MOLLYBROWN.ORG

A pair of lions (opposite) keeps a stoic watch over the entrance to Denver's Molly Brown House, built of local lava stone with sandstone trim. The 1912 photo above shows Molly and A.H. Rostrom, captain of the rescue ship S.S. Carpathia, who was presented with a gift of thanks from Titanic survivors.

Rosemount

PUEBLO, COLORADO

*Rooms of
Rose and
an Ancient
Mummy*

Rosemount, an opulent three-story, 24,000-square-foot mansion, stood in striking contrast to most of the other buildings in early Pueblo, a dusty frontier town of dirt roads and low-slung adobe structures. Set on a hillside, it was completed in 1893 for John A. Thatcher and his wife, Margaret, an admirer of roses who named the magnificent mansion for her favorite flower. Thatcher, an Easterner who had made his fortune in Colorado as a merchant and banker, commissioned Henry Hudson Holly, a noted New York architect of the Victorian era, to design the picturesque 37-room residence. The design is a combination of Richardsonian Romanesque and Queen Anne styles. Except for the wood

Ornate golden oak woodwork, especially visible on the staircase, highlights the main hall at Rosemount.

trim, all the materials used in the exterior are rose-hued, with rough-facade pink Colorado rhyolite volcanic stone walls, red sandstone stairs, a red Vermont slate hipped roof with cross gables, and red columns supporting a full-width veranda with semicircular end pavilions. The veranda has golden oak ceilings and can be reached from inside the house through 10-foot-high sash windows.

The interior features oak, mahogany, birch, cherry, maple, and lacewood paneling and many original furnishings custom-made to H.H. Holly's specifications to coordinate with the surrounding woodwork. A spectacular, twelve-panel, stained-glass window 13 feet high dominates the impressive main stairway. Designed by Charles Booth of New York and titled "Kingdoms of Nature," the window depicts classical figures cloaked in brightly colored robes gathered in a verdant garden beneath a huge Romanesque arch festooned with floral swags. Another unique piece of art, a hand-painted French pastoral mural, decorates the walls of the dining room above carved golden oak paneling. The oak table at the center of the room expands to seat 18 diners comfortably. Here and elsewhere you can see hanging from the ceilings Tiffany lighting fixtures of brass, silver, and gold plate that could accommodate both gas and electricity. The French-style parlor features original furniture, upholstered in silk damask. In a circular bay, under a frescoed ceiling hand painted with cherubs, a rare Steinway grand piano—one of only 200 made in its series—awaits a musician.

13 *Rosemount Museum* 419 West Fourteenth Street, Pueblo, Colo. 81003. (719) 545-5290. Open Tues.-Sun. www.rosemount.org

Thomas Kearns Mansion

SALT LAKE CITY, UTAH

The Governor's Château, Courtesy of a Mining Fortune

Restored to its former glory after a devastating fire in 1993, the Thomas Kearns Mansion is once again a proud symbol of Utah's rich mining history. Thomas Kearns, a partner in the Silver King Mining Company, built the 28-room manor on fashionable South Temple Street, a wide boulevard lined with historic homes and churches, after making his fortune on silver claims in the nearby Wasatch Range.

The three-story mansion is the most elaborate example of the châteauesque style in the state, with prominent end-towers framing a curved baroque stairway and projecting entrance portico. The carefully detailed facade features Italian Renaissance-style columns and ornament carved from native Utah limestone.

President Theodore Roosevelt once watched a local parade from the neoclassic second-floor marble balcony above the entry. On the third floor, a single lofty dormer with a Palladian window rises into the trees, centered between the conical roofs of the matching towers. Numerous windows of varied sizes and shapes march across the facade, divided by colonnettes and surrounded by bas-relief frames and floral garlands or protected by deep stone hoods.

The interior of the home has been fully restored following the fire, with the greatest efforts dedicated to the ornate woodwork, much of which was recarved. The elegant main rooms are outfitted for entertaining, centered around a formal hall and towering three-story floating staircase hand-carved by European artisans of French oak. The steps are free of visible support, twisting upward to the second-floor living spaces and the third-floor ballroom and billiard room. An elaborate plaster dome, decorated with shining Dutch metal ornament, tops the graceful stairway. The Kearns family

Restored after a 1993 fire, the Kearns Mansion serves as Utah's official governor's mansion.

resided in the house for more than 35 years. In 1937, Thomas Kearns' wife, Jennie, presented the building to the state as the governor's mansion.

⑭ *Thomas Kearns Mansion* 603 EAST SOUTH TEMPLE STREET, SALT LAKE CITY, UTAH 84102. (801) 538-1005. CALL FOR HOURS. 🚶 ♿ 🅿

NEARBY: **Beehive House** *(67 East South Temple Street, Salt Lake City, Utah. 801-240-2671)* The official residence of Brigham Young, this adobe house was named for the wooden beehive that sits atop its cupola, a Mormon symbol of industriousness.

Trail End

SHERIDAN, WYOMING

A Former Cowboy's Lavish Town Residence

Trail End, the luxurious town residence built for John B. Kendrick, a cattleman and later governor and U.S. senator, is not the typical western cowboy's quarters. The three-story brick mansion is distinguished by a unique triad of curved gables on the facade, the only example of Flemish-style Victorian architecture in the state. Construction of the house began in 1908 under the direction of Glenn C. McAlister, an architect from Montana, and D. Everett Waid, a New York interior designer.

Located on a promontory, the Trail End house overlooks the Big Goose Valley and the Bighorn Mountains beyond. A naturalistic garden surrounds the house, informally planted with trees, flowers, and hedges scenically placed with vistas onto the wide Wyoming landscape. One specimen of nearly every tree native to the state is planted here, including juniper, ponderosa pine, blue spruce, wild plum, silver poplar, chokecherry, and honeysuckle. Morell & Nichols, a Minneapolis landscape architecture firm, designed the gardens, which were the first in Wyoming to be professionally designed.

Trail End is a picturesque mansion of eclectic tastes, with a columned neoclassic portico at the main entry framed by two enormous pavilions and matching one-story porches.

Built as a cattleman's town home, this mansion speaks to the vast wealth John B. Kendrick acquired on the open range. Ironically, Kendrick began his political rise just a year after the house was completed, and Trail End became simply a summer retreat.

Kendrick insisted that the work be finished in the finest detail, evident today in the subtle corner quoins, a proud stone cornice with bold dentils, and curvaceous Flemish gables outlined with stone moldings. The interior spaces are equally well appointed, each room distinguished by a different color scheme and accented by polished woodwork. Note, for example, how the crimson entrance hall features a heavy beamed ceiling and a broad stairway to the upper floors while the library, decorated in green and gold, displays rows of books behind leaded-glass doors. Stained-glass windows illuminate the honey-colored English oak woodwork to create a Gothic character in this reading room. Portraits of John and Eula Kendrick hang in the adjacent drawing room, a comforting space warmed by French silk damask wall coverings, a handmade Kurdistan rug, and an Italian marble fireplace. As a politically active family, the Kendricks held many events at Trail End, most often in the third-floor ballroom, outfitted with a maple dance floor and musician's loft.

The house lavishly stated Kendrick's success—the rise of a man who arrived in Wyoming in 1879 as a boy on a cattle drive from Texas. Having once shivered under a blanket on the open range, Kendrick kept his 18-room mansion warm during Wyoming's harsh winters by burning a ton of coal every day.

⓯ *Trail End State Historic Site* 400 Clarendon Avenue, Sheridan, Wyo. 82801. (307) 674-4589. Open daily April to mid-Dec. 🚶 ♿ 🏛

Moss Mansion
BILLINGS, MONTANA

Hotel
Elegance on
the Frontier

Rising in the middle of wheat fields some distance from the booming city of Billings, the Moss Mansion was constructed of blocks of reddish-brown Lake Superior sandstone shipped to Montana by rail. Built between 1901 and 1903, the three-story residence was designed by Henry Janeway Hardenbergh, a New York architect famous for designing elegant hotels, including the original Waldorf-Astoria and the Plaza. Hardenbergh designed only a handful of private residences and the Moss Mansion is his only known western commission. How he was chosen to design the house remains a mystery, though some speculate that the owner responded to a newspaper advertisement in which Hardenbergh offered his services to anyone able to meet his price. Cost was of little concern for Preston Boyd Moss, one of the wealthiest men in the new state of Montana, and he sought a mansion to reflect his exalted social position. Hardenbergh's skillful design and a Chicago decorating firm's touches combined to create sophisticated and dramatic interior spaces. The mahogany entrance doors to the house lead into a Moorish hall with ornate Saracenic arches inspired by the Alhambra, the 14th-century royal palace in Granada, Spain. Rising atop mahogany columns, the hand-painted arches touched with gold leaf are set off by walls covered with painted burlap. The entryway's ceiling, a reproduction of an old Arabic dome, features a bronze light fixture with a ruby art-glass globe.

As you pass beyond the arches, which serve as a kind of opening to a stage set, you will enter the main hall, which was used as a music room, and see the mansion's grand staircase, with a landing where an orchestra would play during parties. Silk velour fabric decorates the

Two imposing Corinthian columns stand guard over Moss Mansion's Louis XVI French Parlor, where all decorative details were finished with genuine gold leaf. Preceding pages: Richly colored Oriental rugs and ornate Saracenic arches grace the Moorish Hall; the wainscoting is red birch, stained to look like mahogany.

walls and original Oriental rugs cover the hardwood maple floors.

Off the main hall extends a double parlor decorated in the Louis XVI style. Two Corinthian columns separate the 33-foot-long parlors, where seven coats of enamel paint buffed with pumice stone were employed to make the woodwork look like fine ivory porcelain. Panels of rose-colored damask silk decorate the walls and custom-made Aubusson rugs based on designs approved by Moss' wife, Mattie, cover the floors. Note how the Gobelin tapestry used to upholster the Louis XVI Revival furniture coordinates with the French carpet. In addition, the handsome fireplace is made of Algerian onyx and the ceiling includes hand-painted frescoes showing fields of flowers beneath clouds.

A more masculine spirit imbues the library, Moss' favorite haven. His leather-topped desk and set of leather furniture dominate the room, which is paneled in curly birch with a beeswax finish. Atop the built-in bookcases with leaded-glass doors you will see a collection of Indian baskets from the Northwest, where the Mosses often vacationed. Three stained-glass windows—the center one depicting Shakespeare—bring light into the room.

Hand-carved woodwork stained to look like English oak embellishes the walls and ceiling of the Empire-style dining room. An entire wall is taken up by a built-in sideboard and china cabinet and floor-to-ceiling French windows flank the fireplace, lending a view of blooming flowers in the attached glass conservatory. The domed, 15-by-25-foot conservatory has a mosaic tile floor and is heated—as is the rest of the house—by hot water.

P.B. Moss had not intended to settle in Billings. Leaving Paris, Missouri, in 1892 for Butte, Montana, he stopped in Billings and found "more activity in the middle of the night than in Paris in the middle of the day." In short order he took over the First National Bank of Billings, founded a newspaper, and started a utility company. A man with a vision, Moss also had a nose for real estate. Though most of the founding fathers lived on the south side of town, Moss chose to live on the town's undeveloped western edge. People thought he was crazy for building his grand mansion seemingly in the middle of nowhere, but Moss knew what he was doing. Soon his neighborhood became the most fashionable in town, and today his house sits in the heart of downtown Billings.

16 *Moss Mansion Historic House Museum* 914 DIVISION STREET, BILLINGS, MONT. 59101. (406) 256-5100. OPEN DAILY. 🟢 🚹 ♿ 🏛

*D*aly *Mansion*
HAMILTON, MONTANA

The Abode of the Copper King

Built as a summer home in Montana's majestic Bitterroot Valley, the 42-room Daly Mansion occupies 24,000 square feet and includes 24 bed-rooms and 14 bathrooms. The first version of the house was purchased in the late 1880s by the Irish-born "Copper King," Marcus Daly, and it underwent three remodelings from the Victorian period to the current, 1910 Georgian Revival version by A.J. Gibson.

Marcus Daly's life was the quintessential rags-to-riches immigrant story. Arriving in New York from Ireland as a 15-year-old boy with no money or friends, he delivered messages for a telegraph company until he earned enough for a cheap passage to California. Working in the mine fields of California and Nevada, he gained renown as a "miner's miner" while digging out silver in the famous Comstock Lode. Sent to Montana to scout mining possibilities, he discovered the world's greatest copper mine, the Anaconda. Daly quickly bought up all the surrounding property and set up his own empire: He developed the largest smelting operation in the world, and established the city of Anaconda, a classic company town that included a Daly-run bank, newspaper, theater, and hotel for workingmen. Daly held court at the barroom in Anaconda's showplace Montana Hotel. To decorate the bar, he hired a New York artist to reproduce the head of his favorite racehorse, Tammany, in a hardwood inlay in the floor.

Daly bred Tammany, along with many other prizewinning Thoroughbreds and trotters, at the 22,000-acre stock farm that surrounded the Daly Mansion. The grounds included a mile racetrack, as well as a half-mile covered track for winter training. In addition he maintained a man-made lake stocked with trout, and a deer park, where the family kept herds of deer, elk, and antelope.

The spacious mansion has seven fireplaces, five of Italian marble. Among the original furnishings you will see are a mahogany Adam-style dining room set with 14 chairs, two sideboards, and a china hutch. In addition, the bedroom furniture that Daly bought for his

A majestic cottonwood tree towers over the front of Daly Mansion, summer home of one of Montana's colorful "Copper Kings." After Mrs. Daly's death in 1941, the home was boarded up until 1987.

wife in the early 1880s remains in the master bedroom. Made of burled walnut with a high-backed headboard, the bed has a matching marble-topped dresser. Partially hand-painted wallpaper still covers the children's dining room, and the grounds include a three-room play-house for the Daly children.

The immigrant millionaire gladly left his Fifth Avenue residence in New York City every summer to enjoy his Montana mansion—an idyllic playground where, surrounded by his children and horses, he could ride, hike, and enjoy the mountain air while living in splendid style.

17 *Daly Mansion* 251 Eastside Highway, Hamilton, Mont. 59840. (406) 363-6004. Open daily mid-April to mid-Oct.

Conrad Mansion

KALISPELL, MONTANA

A Trader's Elegant Mansion

A sprawling 26-room residence, constructed of native cedar shingles and completed in 1895, the Conrad Mansion sits on a hilltop overlooking the spectacular mountains of Glacier National Park. Arches, bay windows, long gables, a large covered front porch, and enormous chimneys of native stone enliven the combination Arts and Crafts and shingle-style exterior. Kirtland Cutter, a well-known architect from Spokane, Washington, designed this handsome mansion.

Hardwood doors containing mullioned glass from Europe lead into the Norman-style interior. In the entrance hall, or Great Hall, the largest room in the house, you will be greeted by a golden oak staircase and paneling, an enormous sandstone fireplace, wrought-iron light fixtures, and leaded diamond-paned windows. In an archway beneath the staircase, musicians once played for guests attending the many festive dances and parties held in this room—at Christmastime revelers gathered around a two-story-tall tree emblazoned with hundreds of beeswax candles. The Great Hall was also the setting for meetings between Native American tribal leaders and the town fathers.

The dining room has its original Chippendale table that could extend to accommodate 14 chairs. Dinners prepared by Japanese cooks were served on elegant Limoges china. Note the oak barrel at the end of the room that served as a pass-through for food from the butler's pantry. Guests included some of the most famous personages in the West, including the artist Charlie Russell, the naturalist William Hornaday, the ethnologist George Bird Grinnell, and the railroad magnate James Hill.

Charles Edward Conrad was drawn to the area by his friendship with Hill. A Virginia native who arrived in Montana with less than a dollar in his pocket, he and his brother ran a prosperous business trading and freighting goods along the Missouri River. When Conrad learned that Hill's Great Northern Railway Co. would be laying track through the area, the entrepreneur quickly bought land, founded the city of Kalispell, and then succeeded in bringing the railroad directly to town—thereby profiting wildly on his original investment. Conrad's elegant mansion—with its imported marble bathroom sinks and 11 Tiffany glass window panels—was the social center of Kalispell and reflects his rise from pioneer trader to one of the state's richest and most respected citizens.

18 *Conrad Mansion National Historic Site* FOURTH STREET EAST, KALISPELL, MONT. 59901. (406) 755-2166. OPEN DAILY MID-MAY TO MID-OCT. WWW.MONTANAWEB.COM/CONRADMANSION

McConnell Mansion

MOSCOW, IDAHO

The Most Impressive House in Town

An eclectic mix of Eastlake, Victorian, Gothic, and Queen Anne styles, this two-story clapboard residence was the most impressive residence in town when it was built in 1886—partly because it possessed indoor plumbing. The owner of the mansion, William J. McConnell, was an energetic pioneer who had left his native Michigan as a young man of 21 to drive a wagon train across the country. A miner, schoolteacher, vegetable farmer, merchant, and rancher in California, Oregon, and Idaho Territory, he also served as a U.S. deputy marshall when his Idaho ranch became the target of horse thieves. Settling in Yamhill, Oregon, McConnell married Louisa Brown, opened a successful store, and got into state politics, eventually turning down an offer to run for governor.

When wanderlust took hold of him once more, McConnell set his sights on Moscow, a newly established but promising railroad town in a fertile agricultural region of Idaho Territory. Here he established a general store and invested in local grain elevators. As his business boomed, McConnell built a grand mansion to reflect his optimism in this new territory. On Christmas Eve of 1886, his wife and four children arrived by train from Oregon and were met with a hay-filled bobsled. Neighbors had prepared an elaborate dinner, and the newly finished house was decorated with two Christmas trees—one in the front parlor and one in the dining room—ablaze with tiny tallow candles.

Reentering politics, McConnell became Idaho's second senator and, in 1893, governor of the state. But even at the height of his political power, he could not stave off economic disaster. A national depression in 1893 coupled with a disastrous wet harvest season forced McConnell into personal bankruptcy. He lost his store, his grain elevators, and, eventually, his magnificent home.

The interior retains the original cedar louvered shutters and hall stair bannister that were shipped from San Francisco by steamboat and wagon, as well as a few of the McConnell original furnishings, including a Victorian majolica vase in the formal parlor, a Gothic Revival-style plant stand and Eastlake armchair in the family parlor, and a single place setting of china and initialed flatware. Period furnishings, as well as pieces from subsequent owners, fill the rest of the house, but the structure itself remains a monument to McConnell's enterprising frontier spirit.

⑲ *McConnell Mansion* 110 South Adams, Moscow, Idaho 83843. (208) 882-1004. Open Tues.-Sat.

🅢 ♿ 🏛

*H*oquiam's Castle

HOQUIAM, WASHINGTON

Rooms Full
of Rainbows

The 20-room, four-story Hoquiam's Castle sits grandly on a hillside overlooking Grays Harbor and the Pacific Ocean beyond. Built in 1897 from a Henry Hobson Richardson pattern book, it has stone archways characteristic of Romanesque architecture. The wooden frame house also features a tower on the southwest corner that opens onto an observation deck from which the owner, Robert Lytle, would have been able to oversee his booming sawmill operation. A native New Yorker, Lytle came to Washington State in 1889 and entered the grocery business with his brother. When one destitute logger could not pay his bills, he turned over his operation to the Lytles. The brothers flourished in the new business, opened one of the early lumber mills in Grays Harbor, and soon were among the most important lumbermen on the West Coast.

As befitting the mansion of a timber baron, you will notice extensive woodwork throughout the house, including a paneled and oak-columned entry hall. The woods used are primarily golden oak on the first floor and cedar on the second. The house's flooring is made from maple, pecan, and fir. In addition, the main salon has benches built into its circular corner, as well as recessed seats flanking the yellow Venetian-tiled fireplace.

The town's first private residence to have electricity, the house features elaborate light fixtures throughout: The main salon is lit by a chandelier made up of 600 pieces of crystal, the dining room has a six-foot-wide brass fixture, and the music room hosts one made of hand-blown Venetian glass. The windows throughout the first floor are made of ground crystal, with the upper portions prismatically ground so that sunshine scatters small rainbows

The bold elegance of Hoquiam's Castle offered quite a contrast to the town's turn-of-the-century sawmills and dusty bars. The third floor features a 1,200-square-foot ballroom and its own saloon.

through the rooms. The third floor, however, reflects the rough-and-tumble atmosphere of this lumber town—here Lytle built a saloon, incorporating a carved bar from New Orleans' French Quarter and a roulette table from an Alaska gambling house.

20 *Hoquiam's Castle* 515 CHENAULT AVENUE, HOQUIAM, WASH. 98550. (360) 533-2005. OPEN MEMORIAL DAY THROUGH LABOR DAY DAILY; SAT.-SUN. REST OF YEAR; CLOSED DEC.

$\mathcal{P}$ittock Mansion

PORTLAND, OREGON

French Castle
for a Leading
Oregonian

Overlooking the city of Portland, the majestic Pittock Mansion is one of the largest historic houses in Oregon, symbolizing the successes of Henry and Georgiana Pittock, hardworking and prosperous pioneers. An enthusiastic outdoorsman and self-made millionaire, Henry built his fortune operating the *Oregonian,* a daily newspaper, and through investments in real estate, banking, railroads, and other ventures. He and his wife lived in a modest home downtown until 1909, when Henry commissioned a young and busy California

City officials and Portland residents came together in 1964 to raise enough money to purchase Pittock Mansion, putting an end to a developer's plans to raze the house to make way for a new subdivision.

architect, Edward T. Foulkes, to design a new house on a scenic bluff almost a thousand feet above the city.

The four-story châteauesque beaux arts home commands striking views of Mount Hood, the snowcapped peak rising prominently across the valley. Loyal to the region, Henry Pittock insisted on hiring only northwestern craftsmen and artisans to work on the building and ordered fine woods, marbles, and other materials for construction exclusively from the western states. The wide V-shaped Pittock Mansion is reminiscent of a five-part French castle, with the central facade framed by two circular turrets, and wings projecting back from each side. Above, peaked dormer windows and four immense chimneys punctuate the steeply pitched, red terra-cotta roof. The exterior is faced with Tenino sandstone, a finely graded, light-colored stone quarried in Washington. The total effect is one of European elegance, maintained in the interior throughout the principal rooms, each decorated in a unique period style.

One-third of the interior space in the 16,000-square-foot home is dedicated to the central hallway, floored in white California marble. Its centerpiece is a regal, three-story floating staircase, outlined by a sinuously curved eucalyptus wood railing over an intricate bronze grillwork balustrade. Italian marble columns support balconies overlooking the open stairway. Next enter the nearby French salon-style drawing room, no less spectacular, with walls decorated in softly colored Italian fabric lit by sparkling crystal chandeliers. An intricately detailed plaster crown molding encircles the oval-shaped room, which still holds the Pittocks' 1880s Steinway grand piano.

The family spent a great deal of time in the library, a favorite gathering place after meals for conversation and reading. This room was designed in the English Jacobean style, paneled from floor to ceiling with warm carved oak. Don't miss the bas-relief wood carving of the Pittock crest above the fireplace, which depicts a medieval knight's helmet crowning a shield, embellished with birds and a roaring lion; it is surrounded by elaborate filigree and framed by fluted pilasters. The double pocket doors to the room feature unusual linenfold carvings, resembling soft pleats of fabric. In an early example of indirect lighting, popular in grand houses of this period, the patterned plaster ceiling is dramatically illuminated by electric lights hidden in a space above the crown molding.

The dining room is finished in the Edwardian manner, with a heavy beamed ceiling and mahogany paneling. An enormous built-in wood sideboard on one wall echoes the simple lines of the carved wood mantel alongside it. Above the fireplace hangs one of seven paintings by Thomas Hill, a noted western landscape artist, displayed in the mansion.

One of the smaller first-floor spaces, the oval smoking room, displays Moorish architecture influences and is notable for its stunning, domed plaster ceiling with brilliantly colored interwoven patterns A 1914 Otis elevator still functions (disabled visitors are invited to make use of it). When you go upstairs to see the four-room master suite, be sure to notice the unusual shower in the bathroom: Its perforated horizontal bars are designed to spray water onto the bather from every direction.

Both Henry and Georgiana Pittock were grandparents over the age of 70 when they moved into the home with nine of their family members in 1914. The senior Pittocks died within five years, leaving the opulent house to their descendants, who lived here until 1958. In 1964, the city of Portland purchased the property and began an 18-month program to restore the building. Some original Pittock pieces are on display in the house, including a bronze bust of Henry in the north entryway.

21 *Pittock Mansion* 3229 N.W. PITTOCK DRIVE, PORTLAND, OREG. 97210. (503) 823-3624. OPEN DAILY.

Bowers Mansion

CARSON CITY, NEVADA

With Money to Throw at the Birds

Perched on the eastern slope of the Sierra Nevada Mountains, this U-shaped mansion represents the overnight fortunes made—and quickly lost—in the silver mines of the Comstock Lode. Constructed out of granite quarried in the hills behind the house and sandstone shipped from San Francisco, this handsome residence combines Georgian and Italianate elements in its design.

Nevada's first silver millionaires, Sandy Bowers and his wife, Eilley, had no reason to stint on expenses in creating their dream home. With her husband boasting, "I've got money to throw at the birds," Eilley set her sight on creating the most elegant mansion in the West. A San Francisco architect designed the house, and stonecutters were imported from Eilley's native Scotland. Before the house was completed in 1864, the newly minted millionaires went on a European shopping spree, buying furniture, statuary, and paintings to fill the residence—including $3,000 mirrors from Venice. Dubbed Queen of the Comstock, Eilley tried to arrange a meeting with England's Queen Victoria while she was in London—to no avail. She did, however, return with a clipping of ivy from Westminster Abbey, which she planted next to the mansion and claimed was a personal gift from the English monarch.

Eilley hardly began life as a queen. Raised in poverty in Scotland, by the late 1850s the twice-divorced woman was running a boardinghouse for miners in Nevada. In settling up an unpaid bill, one of the miners gave her a 10-foot claim that turned out to be part of the Comstock Lode. Another boarder, her soon-to-be husband Sandy Bowers, owned the adjoining claim. In short order, their combined 20-foot claim was pumping out $50,000 a month.

But the mine ran dry in 1867, and the following year Sandy died of lung disease at age 35. More tragedy was in store when their only child, a 12-year-old girl, died suddenly in 1874, and Eilley's attempt to keep the house by turning it into a hotel and resort failed. In 1876 the mansion and furnishings were sold at auction. Before leaving her beloved home, Eilley poured lye on her English ivy, so that no one else could inherit her "gift" from Queen Victoria. Eilley—who believed she could predict the future by peering into a crystal ball that she called her "peepstone"—became a fortune-teller in Reno and San Francisco, eventually dying penniless in California in 1903.

For many years a ruin, the mansion has been completely restored and furnished with period pieces. There are a few original items left from the Bowers—including a set of initialed silver flatware forged in Europe out of silver from their own mines, and the wooden doll buggy used by their daughter—poignant reminders of the family's ill-fated history.

22 *Bowers Mansion Regional Park* 4005 US 395 NORTH, CARSON CITY, NEV. 89704. (702) 849-1825. OPEN MEMORIAL DAY THROUGH LABOR DAY DAILY; MAY, SEPT., AND OCT. SAT.-SUN.

Eilley Bowers tried to hold onto her beloved mansion (opposite) by turning it into a hotel, but she lost the property in a civil suit in 1876. She became a fortune-teller and died destitute in California 27 years later.

The Castle

VIRGINIA CITY, NEVADA

Silver Doorknobs High Above the Comstock Lode

Built in 1868 and known variously as The Castle and the House of the Silver Doorknobs, this is one of the most spectacular mansions to rise during Nevada's first mining boom. Robert N. Graves, superintendent of the Empire Mine, built this home in Virginia City, modeling it after a château in Normandy, France. He constructed his house on the side of Mount Davidson, the site of the fabulous Comstock Lode of gold and silver, discovered in 1859.

The three-story mansion retains its original furnishings, including many pieces collected in Europe and delivered thousands of miles by sea and land to this remote site. Graves lavishly decorated the house, sparing no expense in the finishing touches. The front door was carved from black walnut imported from Germany. Inset oval glass panels, etched with monograms, allow light into the foyer and illuminate paired niches where a butler and footman stood on duty. For the house's two hallways, which intersect, Graves purchased a clock from Nuremburg, Germany, made about 1852, and a bronze statue from France entitled "Goddess of Light." As you enter the parlor, note the 200-year-old cut rock crystal chandeliers from Czechoslovak, the ornate French gold-leaf mirror, and the Carrara marble mantel. Here, as in the other rooms throughout the house, Graves placed a wood stove inside the fireplace—a concession to the fierce mountain downdrafts that would blow smoke and ash back into the rooms if the hearth were completely open.

An Italian hanging staircase, with no visible support above or beneath it, leads to the upper floors. Like the massive front door, the stairway railing and balustrade are carved from

Edged by an elaborately turned railing, The Castle's front terrace is supported by sandstone blocks. It is located in Virginia City, the largest federally designated historical district in America.

black walnut that contrasts with the hand-blocked French wallpaper embellishing the walls. Displayed in the master bedroom is an extremely rare, Bohemian satin swirl lamp, one of only two known to exist in the world. All of this imported opulence brought refinement to a barren Nevada hillside, which one contemporary observer labeled the most forbidding spot on earth.

㉓ *The Castle* 70 SOUTH B STREET, VIRGINIA CITY, NEV. 89440. (702) 847-0275. OPEN DAILY LATE MAY THROUGH OCT. 🆂 🚶 🅿

NEARBY: **Mackay Mansion** *(129 South D Street, Virginia City, Nev. 702-847-0173)* Noted for its colonnaded veranda, this house was built in 1859 by the father of William Randolph Hearst.

---

*H*aas-Lilienthal House

SAN FRANCISCO, CALIFORNIA

A Tear in the Wallpaper, with a Story to Tell

Among San Francisco's superb collection of Victorian residences, only Haas-Lilienthal is open to the public as a house museum. Built in 1886, the 24-room mansion was designed by local architect Peter Schmidt for William Haas and his family. Born in Bavaria in 1849, Haas arrived in San Francisco in 1868, joining a cousin in the grocery business. Although he started as a clerk, by the time the business was incorporated in 1897 he had become its first president. When Haas built his house, San Francisco had already passed through its adolescence as a gold rush boomtown and entered its maturity as the West Coast's finest city—without, however, losing any of its architectural zest. Exuberance is clearly evident in the Haas-Lilienthal House. The three-story residence epitomizes the Queen Anne style, with its profusion of gables, projecting bays, curved windows, applied wooden ornamentation, and lofty tower. Visitors who expect a gaudy, multicolored exterior find instead a subtle palette of several hues of grays in the painting of the walls and ornaments.

Just after 5:00 a.m. on April 17, 1906, the house shook but did not fall during the devastating earthquake that struck San Francisco. In the three days that followed, fire spread through the city and destroyed some 28,000 buildings. The Haas mansion stood just east of the last line of defense against the fire—army and civil authorities dynamited houses along Van Ness Avenue to form the firebreak that finally stopped the inferno. The earthquake left only a single, very slight scar on the Haas house, a tear in the wallpaper still visible along the wall of the main staircase.

In 1909 William Haas' youngest daughter, Alice, married Samuel Lilienthal. The couple moved back to the family house after the death of her father, and she lived there until she died in 1972. Her heirs donated it to the Foundation for San Francisco's Architectural Heritage along with some original furnishings, including a dining room set fashioned of golden oak with matching built-in cabinets.

㉔ *Haas-Lilienthal House* 2007 FRANKLIN AVENUE, SAN FRANCISCO, CALIF. 94109. (415) 441-3000. OPEN WED. AND SUN. WWW.SFHERITAGE.ORG 🆂 🚶 🏛

Filoli

WOODSIDE, CALIFORNIA

An Estate named for Justice, Love, and Integrity

Located only 30 miles south of San Francisco, the tranquil country estate of Filoli is worlds away from life in the metropolis. William Bowers Bourn II, manager of the Empire Mine, president of the Spring Valley Water Company, and vineyard owner, built this dignified house and shaped the lush gardens from the scenic California landscape in 1915.

Bourn called the estate Filoli, a name created from the credo "FIght for a just cause, LOve your fellow man, LIve a good life." He commissioned architect Willis Polk to design the 36,000-square-foot Georgian Revival manor, containing 43 rooms and 17 fireplaces. Projecting wings, forming a U shape, enfold the entrance courtyard. At the center of the redbrick facade is a neoclassic entry porch of stone, covered with purple wisteria and white clematis. The west wing contains a lavish ballroom, while service rooms fill the wing opposite.

The interior of the house is exquisitely maintained and decorated with a mixture of original pieces and gifts to the estate, including a recently acquired collection of Anglo-Irish 18th-century furniture and paintings. The first-floor rooms, connected by a 175-foot-long hallway, face formal gardens to the rear. As you enter the reception room, you will find it strikingly ornamented with a 200-year-old fireplace of Italian marble and a colorful antique Chinese Coromandel palace screen 12 panels wide. Next, step into the library, paneled from floor to ceiling in American black walnut, with portraits of the Bourn family displayed amid rows of books. The centerpiece of the dining room is a fireplace mantel made of brecciated marble, its beauty emphasized by dark, stained-oak paneling and a Louis XIV-style bronze chandelier. Cross to the opposite end of the first floor to reach the study, a private space with only one entry to the main hall, unlike the interconnected formal rooms. You will sense a hushed atmosphere in this room, floored in oak gouged to create unusual patterns. Nearby, a dramatic stairway leads upstairs, the steps made of Belgian black marble complemented by a filigree design balustrade of black wrought iron. Beyond the stairs on the main floor is the entrance to the grand ballroom. Murals along the 70-foot-long walls depict idyllic scenes of Muckross, the Irish estate given by Bourn to his daughter and her husband as a wedding present. The room is overscaled, with 21-foot-high ceilings and an enormous Machiavelli marble fireplace decorated with ormolu carvings of Hercules and lions.

Gardens surrounding the home are dedicated to the efforts of Lurline B. Roth, second owner of the mansion with her husband, William. After a 38-year tenancy and careful preservation of the estate, Mrs. Roth deeded the house and 653 acres to the National Trust for Historic Preservation. Both exotic and native species flourish in the 16-acre formal gardens, designed by Bruce Porter for the Bourns and expanded by Lurline Roth. The landscape features more than 500 types of roses, stately magnolias, brilliantly colored Japanese maples, and weeping Japanese cherry trees. A splendid neoclassic white clock tower rises above the carriage house, overlooking the sunken garden and a series of shallow pools. The brick garden house, designed in the style of the Italian Renaissance, is currently used for

Filoli's paneled oak front door (opposite) can be protected, if needed, by two panels that slide into the side walls. In spring, the wisteria and clematis draping the front entrance provide a colorful welcome.

Woven in India from an Isphahan pattern, the rug in the walnut-paneled library was formerly at Osborne House on the Isle of Wight. The fireplace, one of 17 at Filoli, is surrounded by Tavernell marble.

exhibits, its wide glass doors opening up to views of the brightly planted Chartres Garden. At one end of this area, an iron gate displaying the Filoli crest leads to the yew allée, which is flanked by the Knot Gardens, rose garden, and Daffodil Meadow. If you have time to stroll throughout the grounds, you will see more than 200 Irish yews, grown from cuttings taken from the Muckross estate in Ireland, which continue to thrive and prosper in the mild California climate.

25 *Filoli House and Gardens* 86 Canada Road, Woodside, Calif. 94062. (650) 364-8300. Open mid-Feb. through Oct. Tues.-Sat. and for special Christmas programs. www.filoli.org

---

NEARBY: **Winchester Mystery House** *(525 South Winchester Boulevard, San Jose, Calif. 408-247-2000)* Sarah Winchester, heir to the Winchester rifle fortune, was told by a psychic that she would never die if she kept building on her house. Work began on this rambling Victorian mansion in 1884 and workers continued adding towers and staircases, some leading nowhere, until Winchester died in 1922.

Hearst Castle

SAN SIMEON, CALIFORNIA

*Hearst's
Storybook
Castle by
the Sea*

High in the Santa Lucia Range above the scenic California coast rise the distinctive twin bell towers of La Cuesta Encantada ("the enchanted hill"), better known as Hearst Castle. Truly enchanted, the castle was a fantasy come to life through the vision of William Randolph Hearst, one of the wealthiest American entrepreneurs of the early 20th century. Hearst's rise to fortune began at age 24, when his father, George, a millionaire mining baron and U. S. senator, gave his son the *San Francisco Examiner.* The young Hearst soon became a mogul in his own right, building an unparalleled communications empire with 30 newspapers, 14 magazines, 8 radio stations, a film company, wire services, and paper mills under his control.

Hearst began the palatial estate when he was nearly 60 years old, siting the home on high ground overlooking the Pacific Ocean on his family's 250,000-acre ranch named San Simeon. During his worldwide travels, he had amassed an impressive collection of fine and decorative arts and architectural pieces, as well as Egyptian, Greek, and Roman antiquities.

*Architect Julia Morgan answered William Randolph Hearst's desire for a "winter" pool with
a stunning, million-dollar design that called for every surface to be covered in mosaics.*

The main house, three guest mansions, and luxurious grounds are overflowing with statuary, tapestries, antiques, and paintings. Hearst Castle is today one of the few opulent estates of the era furnished with the original collections of its famous builder.

Hearst worked closely on the design with Julia Morgan, an architect schooled at the University of California, Berkeley, and at the École des Beaux-Arts in Paris—indeed, she was the first woman admitted to this exclusive program in 1898. Both Hearst and Morgan were inspired by the 1915 Panama-Pacific International Exhibition in San Francisco, featuring monumental architecture and elaborate gardens. They worked together for two decades, shaping and reshaping the dream castle according to Hearst's latest wishes.

The house is situated within a mini-kingdom of luxurious fountains, pools, and cultivated landscapes. Hearst dedicated over four million dollars of his fortune to building Casa Grande, as the main house was called, yet never finished the structure. Visitors to the estate often remarked on the scale of the imposing, churchlike facade rising 111 feet to the top of two ornate, Spanish-style cathedral towers, outfitted with carillon bells. Hearst entertained hundreds of guests here during his lifetime and became famous for his extravagant weekend parties. Guests were free to roam through the impressive residence, which contained 32 bathrooms, 26 bedrooms, two libraries, a theater, and enormous entertaining spaces. The Assembly Room, the largest of 14 sitting rooms, was often the center of socializing at the estate. Here Hearst liked to surprise his guests by suddenly appearing through a hidden door next to the towering carved French fireplace. Hanging above the antique Italian choir stalls lining the walls, a series of four woven tapestries, made circa 1550, illustrate the story of a Roman general, each panel measuring more than 300 square feet. The end walls of the 82-foot-long room are also decorated with four marble medallions by Danish sculptor Albert Bertel Thorvaldsen.

The medieval Refectory, the only dining room in the mansion, is a grand affair with colorful silk Italian banners on the walls, a stone fireplace from France, and a 400-year-old carved-wood ceiling from Italy. At the center are two 16th-century Italian tables, set end to end; they accommodated large parties of guests at sumptuous evening dinners or buffet lunches. The billiard room features a rare French millefleur tapestry from the 16th century depicting a group of men on horseback hunting a stag and a carved cabinet of the same period that illustrates mythological stories in a series of applied enamel plaques. The massive stone fireplace at one end of the room almost reaches the height of the Gothic-period wood-beamed ceiling from Spain.

One requirement of the nightly round of entertainment was attendance at the Hearst theater, featuring films produced by Hearst's company, those starring his longtime companion Marion Davies, or movies not yet released to the public. The walls of this elegant showroom are covered in red silk damask and marked by a series of gilded caryatids—female figures supporting roof brackets and holding bouquets of electric lights in their hands. Fifty comfortable red-brocade-and-gold-velvet seats face the stage and retractable movie screen. Hearst often ran two screenings, an early show for employees and a late-night presentation for guests and kitchen workers. After the film, Hearst often retired to his private suite of rooms on the third floor.

His library, called the Gothic Study, contains 3,700 books behind wrought-iron decorative screens. The room's lofty ceiling is supported by a series of painted Gothic arches. An avid

Elaborate twin bell towers provide an ecclesiastical air and house a custom-made 36-bell carillon brought to San Simeon from Belgium. In ordering the bells, architect Julia Morgan said William Randolph Hearst had specified bells "sweet in tone, wide in range, operated by organ bench at will."

collector of books, letters, and documents, Hearst maintained a distinctive collection of signed works by U.S. Presidents and his favorite author, Charles Dickens. In a library on the second floor, you will find another 4,000 texts and a collection of more than 150 ancient Greek and Etruscan vases, some placed on the shelf encircling the room. For all its treasures, the space is cozy, with a low ceiling of coffered wood panels resembling an enormous carved honeycomb.

Hearst Castle is outfitted with two spectacular swimming pools. The glorious blue-and-gold indoor pool, modeled on Italian precedents and known as the Roman Pool, cost nearly one million dollars to complete. All wall and floor surfaces in the room, including the pool basin, are covered in lavish mosaics of one-inch-square tiles, created by fusing a layer of 22-carat hammered gold between two layers of glass. On the grounds outside lies the breathtaking Neptune Pool, one of the most popular areas at the estate. When you come to the

pool you will be standing on a promontory 1,600 feet above sea level, commanding wide vistas across the landscape, visible through curved marble colonnades at either end. A Greek-style temple facade at the center is reflected in the 345,000-gallon, marble-lined water basin. Sculptural figures preside over this picturesque assemblage of classical architecture.

Integral to the estate, the landscape surrounding the home was also designed by Morgan. Five greenhouses provided the 700,000 annuals propagated each year on the estate. Native trees were preserved during construction of the estate and in several cases oak trees were moved to allow work to proceed as planned without destroying the trees. Although some distance from the estate and its formal gardens, the pergola is worth a visit. Here stand 1,500 columns—each with its own grape vine—with 950 espaliered fruit trees spaced between them. The grape vines were allowed to grow over the cross beams of the pergola, to shade the pathway underneath. A significant collection of nine Roman sarcophagi of marble and limestone, embellished with high-relief mythological figures, are scattered among the gardens. One of the oldest collections of outdoor statuary at the castle is the set of four figures of Sekhmet, a lion-faced Egyptian goddess. The statues, placed around a fountain and patio designed by Morgan, date from 1650 to 1200 B.C. Close by the main house are three guest "cottages"—picturesque Renaissance-style mansions, the largest with 18 rooms. Named for their views, Casa del Sol faces the sunset, Casa del Monte overlooks the neighboring mountain range, and Casa del Mar, the largest and most elaborate of the three, opens out toward the wide Pacific Ocean.

In 1947, near the end of his long and eventful life, Hearst was forced by ill health to move away from his beloved mansion. After his death in 1951, the Hearst Corporation donated the house and a portion of the grounds to the state of California, which maintains the regal mansion as Hearst left it.

26 *Hearst Castle* 750 HEARST CASTLE ROAD, SAN SIMEON, CALIF. 93452. (805) 927-2020 OR (800) 444-4445. OPEN DAILY. FOUR SEPARATE TOURS ARE OFFERED, EACH LASTING SLIGHTLY UNDER TWO HOURS. TOUR ONE IS RECOMMENDED FOR VISITORS WITH LIMITED TIME. YOU ARE STRONGLY ADVISED TO CALL AND RESERVE WELL IN ADVANCE OF A VISIT. WWW.HEARSTCASTLE.ORG

William Randolph Hearst's lavish entertaining called for a grand dining room. Opposite, a butler stands guard over luncheon guests in the Refectory in the mid-1930s. Hearst kept an extensive wine collection.

*G*amble House

PASADENA, CALIFORNIA

A California
Masterpiece
in American
Craftsman
Style

The international fame of Greene and Greene, noted California architects, hinges largely on their work at the Gamble House—a premier example of American Craftsman bungalow architecture. Brothers Charles S. and Henry M. Greene designed the house, interior, and outdoor landscape in 1908 for clients David Berry Gamble and his wife, Mary, heirs to the Procter & Gamble fortune. The Greene brothers made their own fortune with the development of this unique building style, blending motifs from Japanese design and the American Arts and Crafts movement, which emphasized a return to handmade goods and fine workmanship. The resulting California bungalow gained instant fame, fostering countless imitations in Los Angeles and throughout the country. Many of the features of this movement are exemplified in this sophisticated residence made almost entirely of Pacific Northwest woods crafted with unparalleled skill and finesse.

The Gamble House rises from a hilltop lot surrounded by gardens and terraces. The horizontal emphasis of the low-pitched double gable roof and wide overhanging eaves, supported by enormous Oregon pine timbers, connects house to landscape. The link to the land is further accentuated by projecting sleeping porches and bands of stained and split redwood

The Gamble House was built as a vacation retreat for David Gamble in 1908. An art-glass doorway opens to impeccably detailed interior spaces (pages 298-299), which remain furnished as conceived by the Greene brothers.

shingles on the exterior walls. The facade is precisely detailed, a signature feature of Greene and Greene's architecture, featuring exposed metal strapping securing structural beams, custom-designed art-glass windows, and rustic metal light fixtures supported by hand-shaped wood posts.

The Greenes' reputation for perfectionism is evident in the house's interior, a beautifully simple composition of warm-colored woods, handwoven rugs, and comfortable furniture. A triple doorway decorated with the "Tree of Life," a spectacular design by Charles Greene rendered in art glass by Emil Lange, bathes the wide entry hall with warm yellow and green light. The hall leads you to the living room near the back of the house, both spaces paneled in highly polished, Burma teak wood. Be sure to notice the carved redwood frieze encircling the living room, depicting natural scenes in low relief. Here, too, is a craftsman inglenook—a cozy, partially enclosed area with benches and bookshelves for conversation and reading near the fireplace. The Greene brothers designed all of the rugs, furniture, and light fixtures in this room including the piano, fireplace accessories, and light switch plates. The central focus of the dining room, across the entry hall, is the expandable, cantilevered wood table, capable of seating up to 14 people, supported by a single central pedestal. The nearby kitchen, separated from the dining room by the butler's pantry, is largely original, with white tile walls, bird's-eye maple door and window surrounds, and sugar pine countertops.

A noted feature of the house is the handcrafted stairway to the second-floor rooms, connected with metal straps and secured by exposed wood pegs. The teak wood balustrade marches up the stair, each riser marked by a separate panel and step-shaped railing. There are four major bedrooms upstairs, three with outdoor sleeping porches overlooking the quiet gardens and shallow fish pond. For the master bedroom, the Greenes designed a pair of black walnut beds decorated with inlaid ebony and semiprecious stones. The architects allowed the bathrooms to be painted rather than stained, the natural tones of the wood covered with white for cleanliness. The Gamble family enjoyed the home for almost 60 years until 1966, when heirs presented the residence to the city of Pasadena and the University of Southern California School of Architecture, now caretakers of this original American architectural masterpiece.

27 *Gamble House* 4 WESTMORELAND PLACE, PASADENA, CALIF. 91103. (626) 793-3334. OPEN THURS.-SUN. WWW.BCF.USC.EDU/~BOSLEY/GAMBLE.HTML

NEARBY: **Fenyes Mansion** *(part of the Pasadena Historical Museum, 470 West Walnut Street, Pasadena, Calif. 626-577-1660)* Built in 1905 on Pasadena's Millionaire's Row for Dr. Adelbert Fenyes and his wife, Eva, this neoclassic mansion displays the Fenyes' extensive collection of artwork and European antiques. **Tournament House** *(391 South Orange Boulevard, Pasadena, Calif. 626-449-4100)* Now headquarters of the Tournament of Roses Association, this Italian Renaissance mansion was built between 1908 and 1914 for William Wrigley, Jr., head of the chewing-gum family. **Hollyhock House** *(4800 Hollywood Boulevard, Los Angeles, Calif. 213-913-4157)* This Frank Lloyd Wright house, commissioned by oil heiress Aline Barnsdall, has been restored and furnished to reflect Wright's original design. **VDL Research House** *(2300 Silverlake Boulevard, Los Angeles, Calif. 323-953-0224)* Considered radically modern when built by and for architect Richard Neutra in the 1930s, this house was recently renovated with the help of Neutra's son, Dion. **Rancho Los Alamitos** *(6400 Bixby Hill Road, Long Beach, Calif. 562-431-3541)* This adobe structure, first built by the Spanish in about 1806, saw many owners and renovations over the years; its furnishings come from California's Bixby family, who occupied the house until the 1950s.

Its many windows and doors helped Kimberly Crest evolve from fortress to a peaceful country home where the family transformed an orange grove into a garden with curved stairways.

Kimberly Crest
REDLANDS, CALIFORNIA

*A Widow's
Gift to the
Public*

Built in 1897 for Cornelia Hill, this stately mansion was acquired by John Alfred and Helen Kimberly in 1905 and renamed Kimberly Crest. Alfred had been one of the founders of Kimberly, Clark and Company in Neenah, Wisconsin. He and Helen came to Redlands seeking a warm climate for the winter months, and were charmed by the estate Mrs. Hill had built. Located on some 6 acres of grounds, which include orange groves, the house enjoys beautiful views of the San Gabriel and San Bernardino Mountains. Not as large as George Vanderbilt's Biltmore (see p. 138), Kimberly Crest nonetheless partook of the late 19th-century vogue for châteauesque country houses. Situated on an elevation, the house features a pair of round towers where, in an earlier century, archers would have kept watch over the approaches to the estate. Helen Kimberly quickly made some changes to the house, enclosing a second-floor porch to create a conservatory, and redecorating the parlor in a French mode, with damask wall panels, a gilded chandelier, and gilded furniture. She asked her son-in-law, the architect George Edwin Bergstrom (later one of the chief architects in the construction of the Pentagon), to design an Italian garden for the estate.

The Kimberly's youngest child, Mary, married Elbert Shirk, son of a wealthy Indiana manufacturing family. While serving in the Navy during World War I, Elbert suffered ear damage diving from the deck of his ship to rescue a drowning Belgian soldier and died of infection following an ear operation in 1919. The young widow moved in with her parents in 1920 and remained at Kimberly Crest for the remainder of her life, becoming involved in religious and educational philanthropies, and serving as acting president of Scripps College in the 1940s. When a local citizens group was attempting to raise funds to acquire nearby private land for a park, Mary Kimberly Shirk announced a challenge grant: If the group could raise the money to acquire the parkland, she would bequeath her house and 6-acre estate to the people of Redlands. The goal was duly met, and after Mary's death in 1979 Kimberly Crest came into the ownership of an association charged with preserving the house "for the education and enjoyment of the public."

 **28** *Kimberly Crest House & Gardens* 1325 PROSPECT DRIVE, REDLANDS, CALIF. 92373. (909) 792-2111. OPEN THURS.-SUN. HTTP://E2.EMPIRENET.COM/~KIMCREST/ 🅢 🚶 ♿ 🅿 🏛

Scotty's Castle
DEATH VALLEY, CALIFORNIA

*A Millionaire's
Estate Fit for
a Con Man*

Scotty's Castle rises like a mirage out of the Death Valley desert—a fanciful Mediterranean-style villa that shimmers with the aura of gold. According to Walter Scott, a self-promoting, ex-Wild West performer and consummate frontier con artist, the sprawling mansion built between 1922 and 1931 was created from the fortune he had made in his secret Death Valley gold mine. "Scotty's" Castle—and his larger-than-life personality—captivated the region, though the

true story was quite different from Scotty's tale. Albert Johnson, a self-effacing Chicago millionaire hampered by a bad back and asthma, had grubstaked Scott for years beginning in the early 1900s. Johnson probably realized that Scott was a charlatan—but he was such an entertaining one that the straight-laced Johnson did not mind parting with some cash to keep him around.

Johnson fell in love with Death Valley and decided to build a retreat in an oasislike canyon some 3,000 feet above sea level. Working with the interior designer Charles Alexander MacNeilledge, Johnson created his dream house—and stood by quietly while the irrepressible Scotty took credit for it. Local Shoshone and Paiute helped construct the

"Death Valley Scotty" liked to tell visitors that he paid for the sprawling castle with profits from his gold mine. He is buried on a hill overlooking the home that bears his name.

massive stucco-covered structure, which has three soaring storybook towers—one round, one square, and one octagonal. A relaxed atmosphere prevails throughout the interior, with overstuffed leather armchairs, Native American handicrafts, redwood ceiling beams, and wrought-iron door latches, grills, and wall ornaments. The rustic, western atmosphere is so pervasive that the visitor might overlook some of the most charming details—be sure to take note of the window shutters and wall sconces, formed of metal cutouts depicting desert plants and animals. The dramatic music room on the second floor includes a stage with artichoke-shaped carvings on the cornice and a pipe organ embellished with an iron grill from a cathedral.

At Johnson's behest, "Death Valley Scotty" lived at the castle during its construction. Afterwards, Johnson built him a house nearby, but Scott remained a colorful presence at Scotty's Castle, drawing attention to himself—just as Johnson wanted.

㉙ Scotty's Castle DEATH VALLEY NATIONAL PARK, P.O. BOX 579 (FROM NEV. 95 TAKE NEV. 267 W 26 MILES), DEATH VALLEY, CALIF. 92328. (760) 786-2392. OPEN DAILY. WWW.NPS.GOV/DEVA/SCOTTYSI.HTM $ ⚐ ♿ 🍴 🅿 🏛

*I*olani Palace

HONOLULU, HAWAII

The United States' Only Royal Palace

Regal abundance and royal splendor characterize the formal Iolani Palace, official residence of the last Hawaiian monarchs, King Kalakaua and his successor Queen Liliuokalani. The name Iolani is derived from the Hawaiian *io* or hawk and *lani,* meaning heaven or royalty. When you visit, you will be entering the only royal palace on United States soil.

The grand, Second Empire-style mansion stands near the Hawaii State Capitol, the Coronation Pavilion, the State Archives, and Washington Place, the former private residence of Queen Liliuokalani which is currently used as the Governor's Mansion. At one time an 8-foot-high coral block wall surrounded the palace's spacious grounds. Shortened to a little more than 3 feet in 1891, the wall connects four gates once designated for statesmen, royalty, or retainers. Each gate bears the Hawaiian royal coat of arms with the motto, "The life of the land is preserved in righteousness."

Work on the palace began in 1879 with the laying of the cornerstone, a copper box filled with contemporary memorabilia within a hollow concrete block. (An extensive search of the building foundations conducted during renovations failed to reveal the box, and its location remains a mystery.) After construction on the mansion began, King Kalakaua, an adventurous man, began a worldwide tour, traveling through Japan, China, Siam, India, Italy, France, Germany, and England. Welcomed warmly around the globe, the king visited Asian and European castles as well as other stately residences, buildings that may have influenced the design of his own palace. Laborers finished the enormous building after more than four years of construction, the result measuring 42,000 square feet at a cost of $350,000.

The palace exterior, an eclectic mix of French and Italian motifs, was designed by Thomas Rowe, an architect from Australia, with substantial later revisions by Thomas Baker, Isaac Moore, and Charles J. Wall. Many of the materials used in the building were imported from the mainland, with cast-iron Corinthian columns from San Francisco forming the verandas and a silvery slate roof quarried in Pennsylvania. Each corner of the building has a three-story, square pavilion outlined with corner quoins and capped by a short French mansard roof. The central entrance pavilions, one each for the front and rear, carry a similar motif of quoins framing paired columns, leading to lofty, matching, full-height mansard roof dormers.

Enormous double doors at the front and rear of the building, shaded by the deep verandas, lead visitors into the ornate home. Each door is custom-made, decorated with etched sheet crystal panels depicting dancing figures and floral motifs. These grand ceremonial doors are crowned by curved transoms emblazoned with the family coat of arms between outstretched taro leaves, a native tropical plant. You will step into a wide hall running the entire width of the building, where portraits of previous Hawaiian kings and queens look down from the walls. The hall and adjacent formal rooms are accented with decorative woodwork carved from such native Hawaiian woods as koa, kou, and kamani. At the far end of the long hall, an exquisite polished-wood stairway made of native woods by Hawaiian carpenters leads to the second floor. At its base, a pair of bronze figurines on each newel-post hold electric lights high above their heads.

The rooms on the main floor are elaborately furnished, restored to their appearance

Hawaii's last ruling monarch, Queen Liliuokalani (inset), lived in Iolani Palace until 1893, when she was arrested, brought to trial in the palace's throne room, and imprisoned in an upstairs bedroom.

during the king's reign more than a hundred years ago. Named for its blue satin draperies trimmed with velvet, the Blue Room hosted small receptions, musical recitals, and other informal events. Here you will find an enormous portrait of Louis Philippe of France, a gift to King Kamehameha III in 1848, as well as matching portraits of King Kalakaua and Queen Liliuokalani, painted by the American artist William Cogswell. To reach the adjacent State Dining Room you will pass through a pair of elaborately carved sliding doors of koa wood with inset kamani wood panels. The tables in the dining room are set generously, with French china, crystal glasses, and silver utensils. Up to 40 guests could be served here at one time, with the monarch seated at the main table in the largest chair. A.H. Davenport & Co., a Boston firm, built the Gothic-detailed furnishings for this and other rooms in the palace.

Perhaps the most impressive space remains the dazzling Throne Room, a gathering area for receiving royal guests and completing official business. Decorated with heavy maroon satin draperies and crystal chandeliers hanging from the plasterwork ceilings, its tall windows are topped by crossed spears supported by gilded cornice moldings. The royal thrones stand at the end of the room, elevated on a dais beneath a red velvet canopy with a carved pediment and gold tassels.

The monarch and the royal family lived on the second floor, where the king and queen kept separate suites, one blue and one red, each including three rooms with attached dressing and bathrooms. All the bedrooms, including the yellow and blue guest rooms, hold Gothic Revival canopied bedsteads, dressers, armchairs, and writing tables. Look carefully as you enter the king's bedroom and be sure to notice one of the palace's treasures—a rare sky-blue-and-green Minton vase, decorated with acanthus leaves, snakes, and mythical figurines. This English porcelain piece, completed in 1867, is one of only six left in existence from this pattern. Next, leave the king's bedroom and enter his library, the focus of official business in the palace. Here you will see where he met with his advisers, sitting at a large table, almost 10 feet long, in high-back, Elizabethan-style leather and wood chairs surrounded by book-cases, pictures, and statuary.

The palace was wired for electric lights—the first residence on the Hawaiian Islands to have electricity installed—less than ten years after the invention of the incandescent bulb. The palace also featured the latest in plumbing technology, with four full bathrooms on the second floor outfitted with Italian marble wash basins. In the king's bathroom you will find a copper-lined tub, 7 feet long. Pipes on the main floor and in the basement provided running water at a time when few homes had the luxury of indoor plumbing. The basement housed 40 to 60 servants, their rooms scattered among storerooms for silver and wine. The chamberlain's offices, center of household operations, occupied additional space downstairs.

The king lived in the palace from 1882 until his death in 1891, hosting a variety of luminaries and a number of lavish parties. His sister, Queen Liliuokalani, succeeded him until forced to move at the overthrow of the Hawaiian monarchy in 1893. American militia, at the instigation of Anglo planters, occupied the palace while the planters established a republic. During this period, Queen Liliuokalani was arrested, put on trial in the throne room of her own palace, and confined to her bedroom. The republic lasted only until 1898, when the United States annexed Hawaii (it became a state in 1959). The palace served as the capitol until 1968, and in the next year a new state capitol building was completed. The state also began extensive restorations of Iolani Palace to the period of the last monarchy; restorers are still seeking furnishings removed from the palace at the time of the overthrow.

30 *Iolani Palace* CORNER OF RICHARDS AND KING STREETS, HONOLULU, HAWAII 96813. (808) 522-0832. OPEN TUES.-SAT. 🔵 🚶 ♿ 🅿️ 🏛️

NEARBY: **Queen Emma Summer Palace** *(2913 Pali Highway, Honolulu, Hawaii. 808-595-3167)* This Greek Revival house, used as a summer home by Queen Emma of Hawaii in the mid-1800s, was assembled in Hawaii after being designed and cut in Boston. **Hulihee Palace** *(75-5718 Alii Drive, Kona, Hawaii. 808-329-1877)* This elegant stone house, a favorite retreat of the Kamehameha royal family, is furnished with period pieces created from native woods and displays royal artifacts.

Russian Bishop's House

SITKA, ALASKA

The Wilderness
Home of a
Saint

A marvel of frontier construction, this 64-foot-long by 43-foot-wide residence, built in the 1840s with full-length Sitka spruce logs, is one of only four buildings in the Western Hemisphere that date from the colonial Russian era—and the only one restored to its original condition. The Russian tsar allowed the Russian-American Company to hunt the abundant local seals and sea otters; in turn, the company agreed to aid the Russian Orthodox missionaries at work in the wilderness that later became part of the state of Alaska. As part of that agreement the Russian-American Company hired Finnish shipbuilders in 1841 to construct a massive two-story house for the area's newly appointed Russian bishop. The building, now part of the Sitka National Historical Park, contained his personal residence, as well as a chapel, administrative offices, a seminary, and eventually a parish school.

The house has proven to be a historical treasure trove. When restoration workers peeled back the layers of wallpaper, paint, and canvas that covered the log walls and ceilings, they found strips of Cyrillic manuscripts, glued onto seams during construction in an attempt to keep out the bitter Arctic winds. Paper was so scarce in this remote capital of Russian America, then known as New Archangel, that the builders used whatever they could put their hands on—pages from 19th-century ledgers, journals, letters, and diaries concerning the

The chapel in the Russian Bishop's House still contains most of the furnishings present at its dedication in 1843. At that time, Bishop Innocent wrote of his joy at having "a temple of God within my house."

Rising over the waters of Sitka's Crescent Harbor, the Russian Bishop's House was constructed in 1843 for 25,000 rubles. The house served as a bishop's residence for nearly 130 years.

operations of the Russian-American Company and the Russian Orthodox Church. Today the documents reveal rich details about what life was like in the colony. Among the insulating strips were found an early map of Cook Inlet, and a week's menu that included a heavy dose of fish soup and Russian pie.

A consecrated chapel with original Russian icons remains on the second floor of the residence. The first occupant, Bishop Innocent—now canonized as a saint in the Russian Orthodox Church—was a larger-than-life figure. Described as "Paul Bunyan in a cassock," he traveled thousands of miles by dogsled, kayak, and on foot to visit his vast diocese, while finding time to translate Scripture into the native Alaskan languages. A skilled craftsman, he made barrel organs and clocks, as well as two pieces of furniture that remain in the house—the desk in his study and a cabinet in the chapel. The rest of the ornate wooden furniture, specially designed so that it could be easily disassembled and shipped in parts across Siberia to Sitka, came from St. Petersburg. Its high quality and its gold velvet upholstery reflect the bishop's status as an equal of the Russian nobility. The Russian Bishop's House, center of Russian Orthodox authority for nearly 130 years, remains an important artifact of the days when Russia controlled this vast region.

31 *Russian Bishop's House* CORNER OF LINCOLN STREET AND MONASTERY, SITKA, ALAS. 99835. (907) 747-6281. OPEN DAILY MID-MAY THROUGH SEPT. AND BY APPOINTMENT. WWW.NPS.GOV/SITK/

Architectural Styles

Gamble House, p. 296

Arts and Crafts

Arts and Crafts houses emphasize natural materials, primarily wood and stone, and exposed structural components, such as rafter rails projecting from low, overhanging eaves and visible interior roof beams. Some examples of this style feature wooden elements bound together by metal strapping and pegs rather than nails. American Arts and Crafts architecture first appeared in California in the early 1900s, defined by the landmark designs of the architects Charles Sumner Greene and Henry Matthew Greene. The brothers were inspired by the English Arts and Crafts movement (championed by John Ruskin and William Morris), which encouraged a return to handmade items for a simpler and healthier lifestyle.

The Breakers, p. 46

Beaux Arts

Formal design principles and exuberant decor are prominent features of beaux arts residences. The style arose from the École des Beaux-Arts in Paris, an exclusive school where many of America's finest architects studied Roman, Italian Renaissance, and French classical art and architecture in the late 19th and early 20th centuries. Beaux arts planning emphasizes a symmetrical elevation. Neoclassic architectural motifs abound, with enormous columns distinguishing facades topped by detailed cornices and artistic friezes. Round-arched arcades, applied medallions, corner quoins, and paired side wings frequently appear in this style.

Biltmore, p. 138

Châteauesque

Only a few houses in the United States are considered châteauesque. This elaborately detailed and costly style was popularized in the late 1800s by Richard Morris Hunt, who took inspiration from the 16th-century châteaus of France. Houses of this type display Gothic and Italian Renaissance motifs as well, resulting in a picturesque combination of high turrets, ornate dormers, and shaped chimneys projecting from steeply pitched roofs. Châteauesque buildings feature stone facades with classical details including carved swags, porch arcades, and colonnettes.

McFaddin-Ward House, p. 247

Colonial Revival

The colonial revival style first arose after the 1876 Centennial Exposition in Philadelphia, but gained popularity in the 20th century, after restorations of colonial houses and towns such as Williamsburg, Virginia, were widely publicized. Post-Victorian designers appreciated the simplicity of colonial buildings and furnishings, copying the restrained facades, ornamented front entryways, and painted wood interior detailing. Colonial revival architecture draws on a variety of sources, resulting in Georgian, federal/Adamesque, Dutch, and Spanish interpretations.

Harrison Gray Otis House, p. 30

Federal/Adamesque

Following the American Revolution, architects and builders designed houses in the new federal style. The symmetrical facades of federal houses are characterized by keystone lintels over the windows, decorative fanlights above the entry door, and Palladian windows centered over small pediments. A simple rectangular exterior and low-pitched roof frequently encloses an elegant Adam-style interior. Based on the work of Robert Adam in late 18th-century England and inspired by archaeological discoveries in Pompeii, Adamesque interiors feature graceful carved ornaments. Swags, garlands, and stylized floral motifs are common, created from carved wood or molded plaster and applied to mantels and ceilings.

Stratford Hall, p. 114

Georgian

Noted for their formal symmetry and dignified facades, Georgian houses follow the architectural designs of Inigo Jones and Christopher Wren, renowned designers in early 17th-century England. Many of the grand mansions along Virginia's James River were built in this style. Georgian houses are frequently brick with stone or wood detailing. Typically, the front door is framed with pilasters or half-columns supporting a small pediment, while windows are capped with keystone lintels.

Lyndhurst, p. 57

Gothic Revival

Designers introduced the picturesque Gothic Revival to the United States in the 1830s as a romantic interpretation of the medieval manors of England and France. The masonry buildings feature steeply pitched roofs, finials, and pointed-arch windows filled with small-pane leaded glass. Many of the castlelike structures are also decorated by towers with battlements, oriel windows, heavy beamed ceilings, and medieval tracery patterns in wood or stone.

Stanton Hall, p. 166

Greek Revival

Though its name summons images of temples surrounded by columns, the Greek Revival style (1820-1850) often manifested itself in houses and public buildings of beautiful simplicity. Not as severe as Georgian buildings, Greek Revival structures often emphasize spare, rectilinear proportions. Low-pitched roofs sometimes support shallow, decorative domes. The houses of Natchez, Mississippi popularized the portico of gigantic two-story columns, which became the signature architectural style of the antebellum plantation South.

Gropius House, p. 33

International Style

The international style, developed in the early 20th century by European designers seeking a new architectural expression, is named for the groundbreaking exhibit produced by the Museum of Modern Art in New York in 1932. Pioneers in the field, such as Walter Gropius, explored the use of modern materials and technology, using concrete, steel, and glass to design elegant houses characterized by their strongly expressed structure and functionalist aesthetic. The modernist buildings are noted for their open floor plans, white walls, ribbon windows, absence of applied ornament, and flat roofs.

Ace of Clubs House, p. 262

Italianate

The Italianate style reached its zenith between the mid- and late 19th century. It was one of the most popular designs for American houses during that period. Italianate buildings follow the style of Italian country villa architecture, characterized by bracketed cornices below overhanging eaves, tall windows marked by applied hoods, and airy single-story porches. Many of the largest examples feature a three-story "watch tower" or a central cupola soaring high above the low-pitched hip roof.

Monticello, p. 126

Neoclassic

Greek Revival and Roman Revival styles of architecture gained popularity immediately following the American Revolution, as architects sought non-English precedents, and resurfaced in the 19th century for high-style monumental estates and large-scale civic structures. Roman architectural influences are distinguished by the use of round arches, not evident in Greek Revival buildings.

Pettigrew Home, p. 239

Glessner House, p. 198

Vaile Mansion, p. 227

Queen Anne

Queen Anne is one of the most beloved styles in the United States, combining a range of decorative details applied to projecting gables, window bays, and dormers. Most of these Victorian-era buildings are characterized by a cross-gable form accented by a round tower and full-width porch supported by spindlework columns and brackets. Multiple building materials are common, including brick, stone, carved wood, tile, terra-cotta, and shingle laid to create patterns in gable ends, on walls, and even on chimneys high above the steep roofs—patterns often painted in contrasting colors to create a spectacular appearance. The interiors are frequently paneled in polished woods, a different type for each of the main rooms, and are noted for large, colorful stained-glass windows depicting naturalistic themes.

Richardsonian Romanesque

Richardsonian Romanesque houses are easily recognizable by their rough-faced solid masonry walls, round arches supported by squat piers, and tall corner towers. The style is named for Henry Hobson Richardson, a master American architect with a bold personality. His interest in Romanesque architecture translated well to house design, which he refined to create a distinct residential style in the latter part of the 19th century. The facades are typically embellished with finely carved sandstone, seen in column capitals, arch surrounds, or decorative plaque insets. Often two or more types of stone in varying tones of color appear on facades for a polychromatic effect.

Second Empire

The dual-pitched slope of the mansard roof is the distinguishing feature of this style. The form takes its name from French architect François Mansart, a 17th-century designer. Mansart's ideas were revived by Baron Haussman in 19th-century Paris, when Haussman was commissioned by Napoleon III to redevelop the city during France's Second Empire. The unusual roof shape is frequently topped by iron cresting and, in high-style forms, a central cupola. Most Second Empire buildings feature multiple dormer windows decorated by elaborate surrounds. Heavy cornices under eaves are emphasized with carved brackets, often paired, along an undecorated frieze. Italianate precedents inspired bold exterior ornaments visible in the corner quoins, belt coursing, and hooded windows.

Naumkeag, p. 38

Shingle Style

Though architecturally complex, with turrets, verandas, and irregular rooflines, shingle-style houses feature a smooth skin of wooden shingles that softens and unifies the structure. Such houses paradoxically appear simple and complex at the same time. Stanford White was a master of the style, popular at the turn of the century.

Villa Philmonte, p. 264

Spanish Colonial

Spanish Colonial-style houses, popular from 1492 to the 1820s throughout what are now the southwestern states and east to Florida, have flat earthen roofs drained through projecting rainspouts, or low-pitched roofs covered with concave red tiles. Interior and exterior walls are hand-laid adobe brick or stone rubble coated with white stucco. A few windows and heavy carved doors decorate the otherwise flat facades. Protected interior courtyards are an important feature of these early houses, sited in the middle of a series of rooms or at the rear of the residence.

Stan Hywet Hall, p. 187

Tudor Revival

Designers of Tudor Revival-style houses were inspired by stately English medieval manors and emulated their steeply pitched roofs, decorative half-timbered gables, and narrow diamond-pane casement windows. Brick or stone, laid in patterns, forms the walls and emphasizes door and window openings. The roofline is characterized by enormous chimney stacks capped by sets of chimney pots and multiple dormers. Particularly popular in the 1920s, large examples of the style include castellated towers, oriel windows, and projecting porches. A number of Tudor Revival houses also feature Italian Renaissance motifs, evident in elaborate entries framed by classical columns and keystone arches.

About the Authors

HENRY WIENCEK is author of *The Hairstons—An American Family in Black and White,* the history of an African-American family and the white family who owned them. Published by St. Martin's Press in 1999, the book explores slavery and its legacy from the Revolution to today. Wiencek was Series Editor of the *Smithsonian Guide to Historic America,* a 12-volume, descriptive guide to the country's historic sites, praised by *Library Journal* as "unparalleled in quality." He is also the author of *Old Houses,* a book of essays on the histories of 18 American houses and the families who built them, published with the National Trust for Historic Preservation; two books on southern architecture, *Mansions of the Virginia Gentry* and *Plantations of the Old South;* and several books for Time-Life. In addition, he has contributed articles to *American Heritage, American Legacy, Smithsonian,* and *Connoisseur.* He and his wife, Donna M. Lucey, live in Charlottesville, Virginia, with their son, Henry.

DONNA M. LUCEY is the author of *Photographing Montana 1894-1928: The Life and Work of Evelyn Cameron,* a biography based on the diaries, letters, and photographs of a woman pioneer in the badlands of Montana. Lucey was awarded two grants from the National Endowment for the Humanities to complete the book, which won the Mountains & Plains Booksellers Association award for the best work of non-fiction in 1991. A freelance writer and photo editor, Lucey has worked for Time-Life Books, Reader's Digest Books, Rolling Stone Press, *The New York Times Magazine, Money, People, GEO,* and *American Heritage.*

Index

Composition for this book by
David Skolkin Design, Santa Fe,
New Mexico. Printed and bound
by R.R. Donnelley & Sons,
Willard, Ohio. Color separations
by North American Color, Inc.,
Portage, Michigan. Cover printed
by Miken Companies, Inc.,
Cheektowaga, New York.

 *Credits*

Text copyright © 1999 Henry Wiencek and Donna M. Lucey

Copyright © 1999 National Geographic Society. All rights reserved. Reproduction of the whole or any part of the contents without written permission is prohibited. Printed in USA.

Published by
THE NATIONAL GEOGRAPHIC SOCIETY

John M. Fahey, Jr.
President and Chief Executive Officer

Gilbert M. Grosvenor
Chairman of the Board

Nina D. Hoffman
Senior Vice President

William R. Gray
Vice President and Director, Book Division

David Griffin
Design Director

Elizabeth L. Newhouse
Director of Travel Publishing

Barbara A. Noe
Assistant Editor

Caroline Hickey
Senior Researcher

Carl Mehler
Director of Maps

Lise S. Sajewski
Editorial Consultant

Lewis R. Bassford
Production Project Manager

A LUDERS CREATIVE BOOK

Mary Luders
Project Editor

David Skolkin
Designer

Mary Z. Jenkins
Photo Editor

Equator Graphics, Inc.
Cartography

Kristin M. Edmonds
Copy Editor

Mark A. Wentling
Indexer

Anna Gallegos, Deavours Hall, Karen Ivory
Editorial Assistants

Dale Allen Gyure, Karen Ivory, Christine Madrid, Barbara Noe, Victoria M. Young, Catherine W. Zipf
Contributing Writers

Library of Congress Cataloging-in-Publication Data
Wiencek, Henry.
National Geographic guide to America's great houses: more than 150 outstanding mansions open to the public/by Henry Wiencek.
p. cm.
Includes index.
ISBN 0-7922-7424-5
1. Mansions—United States—Guidebooks. 2. United States—Guidebooks.
I. Title: Guide to America's great houses. II. Title: America's great houses.
NA7205.W485 1999
728.8'0973—dc21   98-53013

Illustrations Credits
Abbeville Press, Alex McLean 33; Adams, Ian 187,192, 195; Amranand, Ping 60, 61, 85, 86, 94 , 96, 99, 111; Bean, Tom 267; Biltmore Estate, Asheville NC 139, 140-141, 308 bot.; Bishop Museum 304 bot.; Brink, Brian Vanden 8, 16, 19, 160, 162, 170, 172/173, 236; Brown Mansion, Billy Durham 234; Cantigny Foundation 204/205; Cheek, Richard 2-3, 44, 45, 116, 123; Choroszewski, Walter 72-73, 75 top; Colorado Historical Society 269; Country Folk Art Magazine, Kevin Kerin 191; David Davis Mansion 206; Degnan, Michael 274-275; Doody, David M. 119; Dorrance, Scott 77; Edison National Historic Site 75 bot; Edsel & Eleanor Ford House 184, 185; Elk, John 216-217, 229, 258, 268, 272, 278, 281, 282, 284, 286, 291, 292, 295; Esto, Peter Aaron 4, 12-13, 67, 68, 296, 298-299, 308 top; Evergreen House 90, 91; Evergreen House, Ron Solomon 92-93; Filoli 290; Flagler Museum 153; Folio/Walter Bibikow 302; Frick Art & Historical Center 80; Greg Ryan/Sally Beyer 215; Gunston Hall 108; Hales, Mick 7, 151, 242-243; Hall, John 171; Hearst San Simeon State Historical Monument 294; Hedrich Blessing Photographers 196, 199, 200; Homewood House, James T. Van Rensselaer 88-89; John and Mable Ringling Museum of Art, the State Art Museum of Florida 152; Johnson's Photography 20, 23, 26-27; Kalish, Martin 24; Kimberly Crest House 300; Korab, Balthazar 182, 186, 201, 213, 214; Lautman, Robert, Thomas Jefferson Memorial Foundation 127; Leis, Dianne Dietrich 5, 100-101, 310 top; Lyndhurst, Jim Frank 58, 310 top; Martin, Van Jones 148, 149, 163, 164/165, 168 top, and back cover; Maymount Foundation, Richard Cheek 124; McFaddin-Ward House 246, 248, 309 top; Memphis Pink Palace Museum, Cupo & Petersen 137; Monticello/Thomas Jefferson Memorial Foundation, Inc., L. Phillips 128-129, 311 center; Moody Mansion & Museum 255, 256; Moss Mansion, John Reddy 276; Museum of Fine Arts/Bayou Bend Collections and Gardens, Rick Gardner 250, 251; Pabst Mansion, Ricki Thompson 209, 210-211; Philmont Scout Ranch 265; Philmont Scout Ranch, Bob Hawks 264; Photo Resource Hawaii 304; Piumatti, Sergio 260, 261; Place, Chuck 271; Preservation Society of Newport County 41, 46, 47, 308; Richardson, Terry 1, 143, 144; Riggs, Bryan 147; Rocheleau, Paul 28, 29, 39, 50, 51, 52, 79, 104, 107, 113, 120, 155, 157, 158-159, 168 bot., 175, 202, and back cover; Rosemount Museum, John Wark 270; Russian Bishop's House, National Park Service 307; Salisbury House, Scott Little 222; Shadows-on-the-Teche Archives 176; Shadows-on-the-Teche Archives, Darlene Tighe 177 ; SPNEA, David Bohl 31, 35, 36, 309 center, 311 bot.; Stan Hywet Hall 188; State Historical Society of North Dakota 240, 241; State Historical Society of Wisconsin, Dale Hall 207; Stratford Hall Plantation, Richard Cheek 114, 115, 309 bot.; Swanson, Bob 289; Texas Highways Magazine, J. Griffis Smith 263, 311 top; Thompson, Tim 6, 178/179, 218, 220, 230, 231, 238, 239, 254, 306, 311 bot.; Thousand Islands International Tourism Council, Nancie Battaglia 70/71; Vaile Mansion, Bruce Mathews 226; Wallen, Jonathan, Cover, 38, 42/43, 49, 55, 56, 63, 64, 135, 224, 232; Whye, P. Michael 235; Winterthur Museum 81, 82; Wright, David 133.

Visit the Society's website at
www.nationalgeographic.com